Guidance of Young Children

Fourth Edition

Marian Marion

University of Wisconsin–Stout

1995

Merrill,
an imprint of Prentice Hall
Education, Career & Technology

Englewood Cliffs, New Jersey   Columbus, Ohio

Library of Congress Cataloging-in-Publication Data

Marion, Marian.
    Guidance of young children / Marian Marion.—4th ed.
      p.   cm.
    Includes bibliographical references and index.
    ISBN 0-02-376061-3
    1. Child psychology. 2. Child rearing. I. Title.
HQ772.M255   1995
649'.1—dc20
                                                  93-47484
                                                       CIP

Cover photo: Lawrence Migdale/Tony Stone Images
Editor: Ann Davis
Production Editor: Jonathan Lawrence
Photo Editor: Anne Vega
Text Designer: Julia E. Zonneveld Van Hook
Cover Designer: Julia E. Zonneveld Van Hook
Production Manager: Patricia A. Tonneman
Electronic Text Management: Marilyn Wilson Phelps, Matthew Williams, Jane Lopez, Karen L. Bretz
Illustrations: Steve Botts

This book was set in New Baskerville and Futura by Prentice Hall and was printed and bound by R.R. Donnelley & Sons Company. The cover was printed by Phoenix Color Corp.

Photo credits: pp. 50, 73, 165, 178, 193, and 247 by Barbara Schwartz/Macmillan; pp. 52, 189, and 209 by Strix Pix; p. 60 by Todd Yarrington/Macmillan; pp. 75, 130 by The Child and Family Study Center, University of Wisconsin–Stout; p. 132 courtesy of Children's Hospital, Columbus, OH; p. 256 by Bruce Johnson/Macmillan; all other photos by Anne Vega/Macmillan.

Printed in the United States of America
10 9 8 7 6 5 4 3 2 1
ISBN: 0-02-376061-3

Prentice-Hall International (UK) Limited, *London*
Prentice-Hall of Australia Pty. Limited, *Sydney*
Prentice-Hall Canada Inc., *Toronto*
Prentice-Hall Hispanoamericana, S. A., *Mexico*
Prentice-Hall of India Private Limited, *New Delhi*
Prentice-Hall of Japan, Inc., *Tokyo*
Simon & Schuster Asia Pte. Ltd., *Singapore*
Editora Prentice-Hall do Brasil, Ltda., *Rio de Janeiro*

For Bill

*For my revered friends and future
storytellers: Lady, Harvey, Casey,
Catherine Marie, Cami, Katie, Roxie, and Bekka*

Preface

The first edition of *Guidance of Young Children* was published in 1981, the second edition in 1987, and the third in 1991. My purpose in writing the fourth edition is exactly the same as it was with earlier editions—to give you a book grounded in solid theory and research, a book that will help you understand the process of child guidance. I have built this textbook around my beliefs about children and child guidance.

I believe we have a choice about how we think about and behave with children. John Steinbeck said in *East of Eden* that the beauty of being human is our ability to make choices. What we choose to think about children, how we act with them, and the discipline strategies we use *do* matter. The strategies we use affect children on a daily basis; they also have a long-term impact on children—helping them become self-responsible, competent, independent, cooperative people who like themselves and who have a strong core of values.

I believe that our style of guiding children has an effect on several parts of their personality and on their approach to life—for example, their moral compass and their level of self-esteem, how they manage anger and aggression, how they manage stress, their willingness to cooperate with others, whether they can take another person's perspective, and their social skills.

I believe that all effective child guidance is based on solid knowledge of child and family development. Without this knowledge, we might have unrealistic expectations of children. Having this knowledge gives us a firm foundation on which to build child guidance skills.

I believe that a child's behavior is influenced by the several systems in which the child exists—family, peer group, school, community, and culture. Different children have quite different histories, and we should not expect all children to think or behave in exactly the same way. Some children in your classes, for example, will have had very good models of anger management, but others will have had irresponsible models and will themselves have poor anger management skills.

I believe that there is no one right way to deal with any issue, but that there are many good ways. This is not a cookbook where you will find nice, neat answers. I will not give you a set of *tricks* to use with children. You will, however, find numerous exercises and questions that should help you understand the basic concepts of child guidance. My hope is that you will enjoy using these concepts to make decisions about child guidance.

I believe we should each develop a personal approach to guiding children and that this approach is best built on theoretical eclecticism. In this text, you will study the decision-making model of child guidance, a model that evolves from understanding various theoretical approaches to child guidance. It is wise to understand the positive strategies that come to us from each theory and not to discount any theory, because you may well use strategies from any of these approaches to help children. I believe that all the theories deserve our respect, and I have tried to treat each fairly in this book.

I believe that some things hurt children and should never be used, such as shaking, hitting, and other forms of physically hurtful interaction, hostile humor, embarrassment, ridicule, sarcasm, judging, manipulation, mind games, hurtful punishment, ignoring, terrorizing, isolating, and boundary violations. These personality-numbing horrors are abusive and have no place in our lives with children. We do our job of teaching and protecting children most effectively when we make active, conscious decisions about positive strategies and when we refuse to use strategies that are degrading or hurtful.

Special Features of *Guidance of Young Children*

I am, first of all, a teacher, and it was my goal to write a *student-friendly* book that encourages you to be actively involved in your learning. Therefore, I've retained certain features from other editions that have worked, and I have added specific features designed to help you learn this material even more effectively. Here are some of these features:

▼ *Objectives* for each chapter.

▼ A *chapter overview* that outlines the chapter.

▼ A *chapter summary* for you to read both before studying the chapter and after you have finished the material. The objectives, chapter overview, and chapter summary are learning devices called *advance organizers* that should help you get an overall picture of the chapter content before you begin studying it.

▼ *Case studies* at the beginning of every chapter. New for this edition, each case study was designed to illustrate the major points in each chapter.

▼ *Case study analysis* and *Case study problem-solving* features in every chapter. Also new to this edition, these require your active participation in immediately applying newly acquired knowledge to the chapter's case study.

▼ *Special focus* features on topics of interest and concern to early childhood educators.

▼ Expanded use of *Examples* throughout the text describing children from birth through age 8.

▼ An *observation* at the end of every chapter to help you see child guidance in action.

▼ An *appendix* that summarizes the major positive discipline strategies in outline form.

▼ Liberal use of *italics* to highlight definitions and other important terms.

▼ A *writing style* that is conversational yet informative.

Structure of the Fourth Edition

This edition is organized by chapters within three parts. The first part is called *Building Blocks of Developmentally Appropriate Child Guidance*. In response to reviewers' comments, I moved the chapter on child development to the beginning of the book. The three other building blocks are knowledge of adult styles of caregiving, *direct* guidance through positive discipline strategies, and *indirect* guidance through good management of the physical environment.

The second part, *Special Topics in Child Guidance*, targets five topics of current interest to early childhood educators. A new chapter on anger management, for example, will give you information on how anger develops and offer suggestions that may help you teach children (and yourself) how to manage this strong emotion responsibly. A new chapter on stress management focuses on how to help children effectively cope with stresses in their lives.

The third part, *Developing a Personal/Eclectic Approach to Child Guidance*, presents specific information on various child guidance theories and on the positive strategies that come from each one. You will have lots of opportunities to solve specific problems using these strategies and to discover how useful theory is in real-life situations with real children. In the final chapter you will also learn about and practice using the decision-making model of child guidance as a way to bring closure to this book—but certainly not to your study of child guidance.

Acknowledgments

Many thanks to my colleagues in Early Childhood Education, Human Development, Family Studies, and Home Economics Education within my very large department at the University of Wisconsin–Stout, whose *systems/ecological* framework keeps me centered in this approach. The dean of my school, Esther G. Fahm, believes in applied work and supports faculty efforts in activities such as grant and book writing that ultimately make the quality of life better for children and families. Our chancellor, Charles Sorenson, has strongly supported scholarly activities through an expanded sabbatical appointment program.

The students in my child guidance classes have asked questions that have made me think and then think some more. For example, time-out has been a subject of debate in my classes for a couple of years now, and I credit my students with asking the questions that helped me deal with some of the issues swirling around this most overused of discipline strategies.

A special note of thanks to the double-section classes of fall and spring semesters 1990, 1991, and 1992 for field testing much of the material that has found its way into the case studies, case study analyses, and case study problem-solving features sprinkled throughout this edition. My students do an excellent job with the decision-making model of child guidance, and I believe their developing skill will carry over into their teaching.

Several colleagues from around the country who have used the other editions reviewed material for the fourth edition: Richard Ambrose (Kent State University), Nancy Benz (South Plains College, Lubbock, Texas), Elaine Goldsmith (Texas Woman's University), Kathy Hamblin (Aims Community College, Greeley, Colorado), Karen Peterson (Washington State University), and M. Francine Stuckey (Eastern New Mexico University). Their comments were especially helpful as I refined the book's content and structure, and I am grateful for their suggestions about reorganizing the text, incorporating additional research, and using the term *personal* when speaking about the eclectic approach.

My ideas about child guidance have evolved as I have taught this material in my university classes, parenting classes, and in workshops in various states. It is a real pleasure to attend state, regional, and national conferences and to see and hear about how other instructors present the material in this book in class or how teachers of young children apply the material in classrooms for young children. Another great time for sharing information is at the NAEYC conference each year, and it is there that I've gained insights from both old and new friends.

Marian Marion

Brief Contents

Contents

→ Day 9 Kunz Ch 1

Chapter 2   Adult Styles of Caregiving   36

wed
Ch 1
an 2 (part)

Chapter 3 Positive Discipline Strategies: Direct Guidance 60

Chapter 4 Effective Design and Management of Physical Environments for Children: Indirect Guidance 96

Was) Ch. 9

New

Chapter 8   Understanding and Coping With Aggression in Children   178

was Ch. 10

PART THREE   DEVELOPING A PERSONAL/ECLECTIC APPROACH TO CHILD GUIDANCE   232

Chapter 10   Theories and Their Strategies: Roadmaps to a Personal Approach to Child Guidance   234

Day & Kunz Ch. 3

Was Ch 12

Part One

Building Blocks of Developmentally Appropriate Child Guidance

Chapter 1. Understanding Child Development: Our Foundation for Developmentally Appropriate Child Guidance. Building developmentally appropriate child guidance skills requires that you understand how children develop. This knowledge base allows you to have realistic expectations of children and enables you to make informed decisions about child guidance issues. Chapter 1 describes different areas of child development, such as memory and perception, and lists implications for child guidance.

Chapter 2. Adult Styles of Caregiving. In this chapter you will study the authoritarian, authori*tative* (positive, responsible), permissive-by-choice, and permissive-by-default styles, each of which has a different combination of demandingness and responsiveness. You will notice that each style operates with a different set of "system rules," and that adults in each have a specific style of communication. You will analyze case studies to identify the adults' caregiving styles.

Chapter 3. Positive Discipline Strategies: Direct Guidance. An important building block in developmentally appropriate child guidance is skill in matching a positive discipline strategy with a specific child's problem. This chapter describes many positive, specific, and practical discipline strategies. You will practice using each strategy to solve problems and analyze case studies.

Chapter 4. Effective Design and Management of Physical Environments for Children: Indirect Guidance. This chapter discusses how to use *indirect guidance* by designing and managing the physical environment effectively. You can minimize or even prevent problems by setting up your room well, by developing appropriate activities, and by managing materials well. You will have an opportunity to analyze case studies of classroom activity areas and activities.

Some things to remember as you read this unit:

▼ *Children develop in a number of systems that are nested within each other* (Bronfenbrenner, 1977; Maccoby & Martin, 1983). This means that there are many forces that contribute to how a child develops. Consider how children become aggressive because they exist in systems that teach and encourage aggression. Families are embedded in the community, the community is embedded in a culture, and both give messages about violence and aggression through a variety of media.

▼ *Adults and children are partners in the "dance of interaction," but adults have a greater responsibility.* This is the heart and soul of child guidance. Yes, children influence us—for example, babies smile or cry in an attempt to draw us in to interaction; 3-year-olds try to "help" us in lots of ways; a 4-year-old might embarrass us by cursing; and a 6-year-old might scare us and make us sad when he hits his baby brother—but our adult role is to recognize the signals, pay attention to them, and make active, conscious decisions about how to act. The point? As adults we are responsible for knowing the "steps" in the dance of interaction.

1

Understanding Child Development: Our Foundation for Developmentally Appropriate Child Guidance

Chapter Overview

After reading and studying this chapter, you will be able to

▼ *Explain* the meaning of "developmentally appropriate child guidance."

▼ *Summarize* the positive cognitive accomplishments of the first three Piagetian stages and *explain* how your guidance strategies may be affected by a child's level of cognitive development.

▼ *Trace* the development of social perspective-taking and *explain* why perspective-taking skills are important.

▼ *Describe* a young child's memory capacity, memory skills, and perceptual problems, and *list and describe* specific guidance strategies for helping children remember things and for dealing with preschool perceptual limitations.

▼ *Define* "temperament" and *describe* different temperament styles. *Explain* how temperament style may affect a child's development and interactions.

▼ *Describe* how young children view the behavior of others, friendship, and conflict relations.

▼ *Trace* the development of self-control and give examples of self-control in children.

▼ *Analyze* case studies on developmentally appropriate child guidance.

"Authentic teaching is a passionate profession which . . .
can make a difference in the lives of others."
(Smith, 1982, p. 3)

CASE STUDY: Mr. Moore's Classroom—Selected Observations

Monday: "I'm making *apples*," said Sylvia, smoothing bright red fingerpaint onto her paper and swirling circles into the paint with her knuckles. "So are we," called Tim and Janet as they rolled chunks of red dough into applelike shapes. Mr. Moore's group of 3- to 5-year-olds dictated a story about their trip to the apple orchard.

Tuesday: Tim, Janet, and Sylvia bent red pipe cleaners into apple shapes and placed them on a big branch stuck in a bucket—their version of an apple tree.

Wednesday: Throughout the morning, several children at the water table engaged in a familiar activity, pouring water from one unbreakable container into others.

Thursday: Tim ran into the classroom and zoomed right into the crowded block area. Mr. Moore called Tim aside and said, "Tim, please look at the sign. It says '5.' Now, count the children. There are five children here already. Let's find something else for you to do until you can play with the blocks."

Friday: Kathy and Jane scooped out tunnels in sand. When the tunnels met they argued about which direction the tunnel should take. Mr. Moore said, "You each have an idea about which way the tunnel should go. How can the two of you dig one tunnel to the bridge?" "Let's dig it *this* way," said Kathy. "OK, but let's use both of our spoons," replied Jane.

CASE STUDY: Mrs. Vang's Infant Room

Mrs. Vang planned some "memory" games for 6-month-old Kevin: He smiled when his teacher showed him his favorite stuffed bear, which had been lost for about two weeks. Then Mrs. Vang turned Kevin away so he couldn't see it.

When Kevin turned his head to look for the bear, she praised his effort and helped him retrieve the toy. On another day, Mrs. Vang showed Kevin a plastic block and then slowly covered it with a cloth. He grabbed the cover and pulled it off. She said, "Oh, Kevin, you found the toy!"

Seventeen-month-old Ben waddled out the door as the aide opened it, and then he started down the corridor. Mrs. Vang called, "Ben, stop." Ben turned and looked at his teacher, who had stooped and held out her arms. "Come on, Ben." Ben walked toward Mrs. Vang and she scooped him up, "You came when I called you, Ben."

THE CONCEPT OF DEVELOPMENTALLY APPROPRIATE CHILD GUIDANCE

Teachers like Mr. Moore and Mrs. Vang use developmentally appropriate child guidance. This means that several factors have come together for these two adults.

1. *They understand child development, the most basic building block in developmentally appropriate child guidance.* Each has realistic expectations of children of different ages in terms of motor, physical, cognitive, social, and emotional development. They understand family development and the impact that a child's family may have on a young child's development.

2. *Their guidance is developmentally appropriate because it is both age appropriate and individually appropriate.* Both teachers use age-appropriate guidance in that their strategies are appropriate for the general age group that they teach. And both use individually appropriate strategies when they choose a strategy appropriate for a specific child, regardless of the child's age, as Mr. Moore did with Tim.

3. *They understand that adults and children are engaged in a "dance of interaction," that each influences the other in any interaction* (Bell, 1968; Bell & Harper, 1977).

4. *They understand their role in the "dance," or in the guidance system.* They realize that children have an important part in any interaction, but they know that adults always have a greater responsibility (Maccoby & Martin, 1983). Mrs. Vang realizes, for example, that a very young infant will gaze or smile at her, but that it is her responsibility to tune in appropriately to the infant's efforts. Mr. Moore knows that his 3- to 5-year-olds will offer to help with cleanup, but it is his responsibility to recognize and encourage their effort and cooperation.

PIAGET: COGNITIVE DEVELOPMENT

Adults who use developmentally appropriate guidance understand the link between a child's cognitive and social development. They know that they are most effective with children when they keep in mind how a specific child thinks, whether she can understand what an adult says, whether she can take somebody else's perspective, and whether she can even remember what is said. This section focuses on cognitive development during very early childhood (infancy and toddlerhood) and early childhood in Piaget's framework (Piaget, 1952, 1965, 1968, 1976a, 1976b, 1983).

The Sensorimotor Stage

Piaget called the first stage of cognitive development (birth to approximately 24 months) the sensorimotor stage because infants are equipped with sensory actions (looking, listening, touching) and motor actions (grasping, head turning, hitting, etc.). They use sensorimotor actions or schemes to acquire information about and impose order on their world. Infants do not think or reflect on problems as older children or adults do.

Piaget divided the sensorimotor stage into six substages to describe an infant's blossoming cognitive skills. An infant spends most of her first few months of life practicing those sensory and motor (sensorimotor) schemes, but by 24 months she will be starting to use symbols. Progress through the six substages occurs partly because of an infant's ability to imitate, which is evident quite early in life and improves as the infant gets older. Infants also acquire knowledge about object permanence as they progress through the sensorimotor stage.

Human infants are competent, active, information-processing creatures. A baby's perceptual skills are good enough, even at birth, to allow her to explore and discover her world, but perceptual skills change in several ways as infants grow older (Gibson & Spelke, 1983). Young infants seem to prefer some patterns over others and are able to perceive depth and color in their surroundings. The visual and nervous systems undergo continual development during a child's first year, making more sophisticated perception possible.

How well babies are able to learn and remember things is affected by sensorimotor and perceptual skills. Infants do not process information as well in their first few months because their motor skills and their neurological systems are somewhat immature. Sensory, perceptual, and attentional skills develop rapidly from birth to 12 months. From about 6 months to a year, infants use all of their skills to acquire and retain a knowledge base.

Profound cognitive changes occur between 12 and 24 months. We see the result of all of these changes when they converge in the development of *symbolic thought*. By age 2, a child does several things to show us that she is able to use symbols: she pictures things in her mind, imitates things she saw earlier (such *deferred imitation* is actually seen by 9 or 10 months), and understands and uses language.

The Preoperational Stage

Two- to five-year-old children are usually in the second of Piaget's stages of cognitive development, the preoperational stage. The early childhood years are a time of positive intellectual accomplishment, but preoperational thinkers also have some major limitations on their ability to think. This section focuses on the positive features and describes some of the cognitive limitations of preoperational thinking. These cognitive abilities and limitations influence the child's interactions with adults and the child's capacity for self-control.

How 2- to 5-Year-Old Children Represent Their Experiences

Two- to five-year-old children can use symbols to represent (stand for) their experiences (Flavell, 1977; Piaget, 1952, 1976, 1983). In early childhood classrooms there are many examples of how 2- to 5-year-olds are able to represent their experience.

Deferred imitation.   Young children learn from models. They observe an event, form and hold a visual image of the event, and then may "defer" or put off imitating the action until some later date.

Examples   Maura slapped her doll on the face and said, "There. That'll teach you not to sass me!"

Joseph smeared shaving cream on his face and then scraped it off with his finger.

Sarah softly sang "Hush, little baby," as she cradled her doll in her arms.

Language.   One of the major ways that children have to tell us about their experience is to talk about it (Flavell, 1977).

Examples   Maura's teacher noticed blue bruises that circled Maura's upper arms (a physical indicator of child abuse) and reported it to Child Protective Services. Maura used language to tell a social worker about how her father grabbed her arm.

Jackie told the whole group that his cat had been stranded on the roof of their house during the flood.

Use of art media.   Children record their experiences through art media such as painting, drawing, or play dough.

Example   John came to school the day after watching fireworks, took a sheet of black paper, glue, and glitter, and created a fireworks collage to represent his experience.

Implications for guidance.   Expect children to represent—to tell you about—their experiences. Realize that children will tell you about their experiences in a variety of ways. You will see evidence of a child's past experience in her behavior; for example, one child might hit another person and another will help others. In either case you will have seen *deferred imitation*. Responsible adults believe that they influence children by modeling positive behavior, no matter what that child's other models have been. Even children who experience negative discipline at home can observe and learn a different, more positive way of behaving from us.

Yoko has observed someone rocking a baby and has **deferred** *imitation until now.*

Limitations of Preoperational Thinking

A 4-year-old's cognitive skills seem so much more advanced than the skills of an 18-month-old because the older child can represent experiences. But our 4-year-old preoperational thinker still has a limited ability to think logically. These limitations have implications for how we guide children during this phase. Preoperational thinkers tend to be egocentric, to judge things by how they look, to focus on the before-and-after, to ignore *how* things change (transformations), and to have trouble reversing a process.

Preoperational thinkers tend to be somewhat egocentric.   Listen to a preschool child for a short time and you will smile at some of the funny things she says and the charm with which she says them. You may also be slightly puzzled, as I was in the following conversation with my 5½-year-old niece.

> Marian (adult):   "Lisa, tell me how to get to the ice cream store."
>
> Lisa: "You go to the corner and then turn."

Marian: "Which corner?"

Lisa: "You know, the one with the trees."

At the time of our conversation, Lisa was somewhat egocentric and not very good at perspective-taking. She did not give me all the necessary information, largely because she did not understand exactly what I needed to know. She probably also thought I had the same information she did.

Egocentric thinkers center on themselves and what they want, but this is *not* the same thing as being selfish. A selfish person understands somebody else's perspective and chooses to ignore it, but an egocentric thinker cannot take the other person's perspective; there is a blurring of their own viewpoint with the perspective of the other person (Piaget, 1968). A preoperational thinker like Lisa believes that everyone thinks the same way she does (Jackson, Robinson, & Dale, 1977).

Some researchers have noted that, under certain conditions, children may be somewhat less egocentric than originally thought (Black, 1981; Flavell, Flavell, Green, & Wilcox, 1981; Gelman & Baillargeon, 1983; Newcombe & Huttenlocher, 1992). Nevertheless, children are not yet very skillful in dealing with different viewpoints or confrontations and need adult guidance to learn and practice these skills.

Implications for guidance.   Social interaction is one of the best ways to decrease egocentricity and increase understanding of another person's point of view (Piaget, 1968, 1976). Manage your classroom so that children have plenty of chances to play with other children—for example, blocks, dramatic play, water or sensory table, playground—in order to expose them to challenging ideas from others. Rely on positive discipline strategies to help children acknowledge and deal with different ideas.

Preoperational thinkers have difficulty with perspective-taking.   Perspective-taking is a cognitive developmental skill that takes several years to develop and which is first evident at the end of early childhood from age 6 or 7 on (Dixon & Moore, 1990; Newman, 1986). Selman (1976) describes an orderly series of "levels" in perspective-taking (ages are approximate):

▼ *Level 0: Egocentric Perspective* (3 to 6 years old). Major characteristic: the child usually does not distinguish between her own and someone else's perspective.

▼ *Level 1: Social-Informational Role-Taking* (6 to 8 years old). Major characteristic: the child still believes that another person shares her perspective, but for a different reason. The child's guiding rule is "same situation equals same viewpoint"; that is, because the other person is in the same situation as the child herself, she believes that the other person will respond to the situation just as she would. (*Note:* this book is about children up to 8 years of age. We can expect children we teach to be inexperienced in the art of perspective-taking.)

▼ *Level 2: Self-Reflective Role-Taking* (8 to 10 years old). Major characteristic: the child is now able to see herself as another person might and is aware that two persons can have different perspectives.

SPECIAL FOCUS: Q & A: Why Are Social Perspective-Taking Skills Important?

Question: What is social perspective-taking?
Answer: It is the ability to control one's viewpoint when making judgments of others (Higgins, 1981).

Question: Why is social perspective-taking an important skill for all people?
Answer: These skills form the foundation of effective social interaction (Chalmers & Townsend, 1990; Chandler, 1973; Looft, 1972; Selman, 1980). Good perspective-taking skills enable us to anticipate what others might be thinking, and this makes our interactions more predictable (Dixon & Moore, 1990). We can actually see ourselves as others see us if we can take their perspective. If, for example, one of the reactions that you arouse in others is that they seem to like you, then you will begin to use this information as you *define* your self. You can use this information in deciding that the self you see is well-liked.

Question: Do people with poor perspective-taking skills have any specific problems?
Answer: Yes. They systematically misread societal expectations. They misinterpret the actions and intentions of others. They act in ways judged to be callous and disrespectful of the rights of others (Chalmers & Townsend, 1990; Chandler, 1973). Parents with these tendencies use harsh discipline (Marion, 1991), and adults who cannot take a child's perspective are "at risk" for child abuse (Milner, Robertson, & Rogers, 1990).

Question: What does the research tell us about children who have good social perspective-taking skills?
Answer: Children who are good at perspective-taking are better at persuading others and are better able to regulate aggressive impulses (Jones, 1985). Older children with good perspective-taking skills tend to be more generous, helpful, and cooperative.

▼ *Level 3: Mutual Role-Taking* (10 to 12 years old). Major characteristic: children are now aware of the recursive nature of different perspectives (e.g., "Mom thinks that I think that she wants me to . . .").

▼ *Level 4: Society or In-Depth Perspective* (adolescence and adulthood). Major characteristics: a person at this level of perspective-taking believes that perspectives among individuals form a network, and has conceptualized society's viewpoints on legal or moral matters.

Preoperational thinkers tend to judge things by how they look.   When presented with two containers, one short and one tall, which contain the same amount of water, preoperational thinkers say that the tall container has more

Social interaction helps children understand that others have a perspective or point of view.

water in it "because it looks like it has more." They are often deceived by appearances because they tend to judge something by how it appears on the surface.

Implications for guidance.   Remember that children focus on appearances and that their ability to take the perspective of others is very limited. Rely on this knowledge when you make guidance decisions—for example, when you have to deal with a child's own hurtful behavior. Avoid using negative, hurtful (and ineffective) discipline that simply mirrors the young child's behavior.

Example   When 27-month-old Jack pinched another child, his babysitter grabbed and pinched him, hissing, "Now you know how it feels when you pinch other people." (Do not use this negative strategy.) To a child Jack's age, deceived by appearances, it looks like this adult wants to hurt him. His attention will be on the intense stimulus—the painful squeezing of his skin, and he will not understand what she says. The babysitter's hurtful strategy grew out of her misunderstanding of a toddler's ability to take someone else's perspective.

Jack's dad took a different approach. He said, "Oh, no, Jack! Ouch! Pinching hurts Sara. Use words to tell her to move. No pinching." Dad's discipline was positive. He was firm but kind in making it clear that pinching was not allowed. He understands his egocentric son's need for information along with limit setting: "Use words to tell her to move."

Preoperational thinkers focus on the "before and after." Preoperational thinkers ignore the process through which something changes, the transformation. As shown in Figure 1.1, a preoperational thinker focuses first on water in the two short glasses (the "before" state). Then she focuses on water in one short glass and one tall glass (the "after" state). She tends to ignore the pouring of the water from the short glass to the tall glass (the transformation) (see Figure 1.2). An older child, adolescent, or adult, aware of the pouring, would explain things by saying, "All you did was pour water from one container to another."

How does this cognitive limitation affect how young children operate in their social world?

Example   Three-year-old Jeff watched as his older brother, Erik, transformed himself into a Halloween monster. Jeff cried and ran to Dad when he saw the finished product, and Dad made the mistake of trying to explain the transformation: "Oh, Jeff, that's just Erik." Jeff was *not* convinced, having focused on plain old Erik (the "before" state) and then on the monster (the "after" state). In

Figure 1.1
Step 1: Child agrees that each container holds an equivalent volume of water. *Step 2:* Child watches adult pour liquid from container B into container C. A preoperational thinker will say that container C contains more than container A. Her reason: She will say that it simply looks like more.

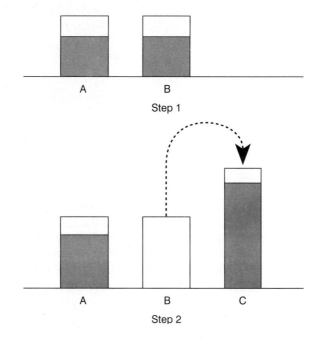

Figure 1.2
The *pouring* of the liquid is the *transformation*.

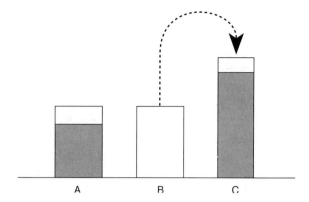

spite of having intently observed the whole makeup and costume process, Jeff seems to have ignored it completely.

Implications for guidance.   Do not waste your time trying to explain a transformation to a child. A child tends to pay attention to the "before and after" and simply does not attend to transformations, even though she observes a transformation (such as the pouring of the water or putting on of makeup). Instead, give children lots of chances to do "transformations."

Provide lots of opportunities for children to perform **transformations** *like pouring water from one container to another.*

Examples   Jeff's dad encouraged Jeff to put on some of the makeup to create his own disguise, thus having Jeff actually perform a transformation.

Mr. Moore's curriculum includes daily opportunities to transform things, such as pouring things from one container to another (water table, sand table, outdoor sandpit) or changing the shape of things (squishing play dough from a large ball to a flat pancake, rolling the pancake into a sausagelike shape).

Preoperational thinkers have difficulty reversing a process.   You realize that you could quickly show that the amount of liquid in the tall glass is equivalent to that in the short glass by simply pouring the contents of the tall glass back into the short glass (Figure 1.3), but young children would not think so logically.

Implications for guidance.   Do not expect young children to know how to reverse or undo a process. Alex's mom makes this mistake.

Example   Alex was supposed to share the french fries with his sister, but he dumped all of them onto his tray. Noticing this, his mom said, "I'm going to get more napkins, and you'd better be sharing when I get back."

His mom is justified in expecting him to share, but Alex needs some help in figuring out what Mom means. She would have been more helpful had she clearly stated what she meant by ". . . you'd better be sharing." For example, "Alex, your sister needs some french fries, too. I want you to share with her. Here are two napkins. Put about half the fries on each."

The Concrete Operational Stage

Children in this stage of cognitive development are usually between the ages of about 6 and 11 and in elementary school. The cognitive skills of the concrete operational child are qualitatively different from those of the preoperational thinker.

An elementary school child is even better able than the preoperational thinker to distinguish reality from appearances. Concrete operational thinkers are not deceived by the appearance of apparent changes as easily as preoperational thinkers are.

Figure 1.3
Preoperational thinkers have difficulty reversing their thought. They will *not* say that you could prove that the two containers hold an equivalent volume by simply pouring the contents of container C back into container B.

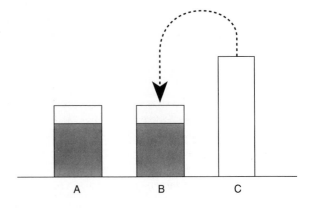

Concrete operational thinkers are better able than preschool children to attend consistently to both relevant dimensions (height and width) in the standard conservation task. A concrete operational thinker uses this information about dimensions to arrive at an understanding of conservation.

One of the changes in cognition during this period is that the concrete operational child can now attend to transformations, even in standard conservation tasks. Thus, they show evidence of the further development of skills that emerged during the preschool years. Concrete operational thinkers still have some cognitive milestones to accomplish, however, and these milestones are reached in the next stage of cognitive development.

Implications for guidance.   Rely on positive discipline as you guide these children. They are fairly sophisticated in their ability to comprehend your modeling, direct instruction, and coaching; your statements of what you expect from them; and your attempts to help them understand why they should or should not do things.

MEMORY
Definitions

Memory is the process by which we retain information and then retrieve it for use some time later.

Recognition memory is the realization that we have seen or experienced some information that we now encounter (Perlmutter & Myers, 1979). For example, you see a stuffed animal version of Garfield the cat in a store and say, "That's Garfield." Recognition tasks are easier than the next type, recall.

Recall memory is used when you are required to actually retrieve or call up some information. The game show Jeopardy, based on this concept, would use a statement such as "This cartoon animal loves to eat lasagna and to sleep." Students usually find test questions based on recall memory (fill-in-the-blank) more difficult that multiple-choice questions, in which the answer is listed.

Long-term memory is used to store a permanent record of events (Jackson, Robinson, & Dale, 1977). We tend to store strong sensory images of places and events from years ago, such as the odor of disinfectant in a hospital; the aroma of chocolate as the family car rolled into Hershey, Pennsylvania; the sirens of fire engines and the flames following an explosion; or the clickety-click of a teacher's metal signal used to line children up.

Short-term memory is "working" memory, and we use it to temporarily store new information or well-known information to which we need access. Researchers believe that a child's space for short-term memory increases with age, allowing her to work with more information and for longer periods of time (Case, 1984).

Example   Four-year-old Peter observed the procedure for finger painting: Put on apron; write name on paper; wet paper; blob paint on paper; paint; hang up painting; wash table, apron, hands; take off and hang apron. He forgot three of the steps when it was his turn, but 5½-year-old Janet remembered all but one of the steps.

Example   A small group in Mr. Moore's class was preparing to make cup-cakes, and the teacher encouraged them to call up information from long-term memory and put it in short-term (working) memory by reminding them of a similar baking activity 6 weeks earlier. "We made a heart-shaped cake for Valentine's Day. Tell me what things we used: a bowl, a mixer, and what else? What sorts of things went into the cake? Flour, sugar, butter, and . . . ? What went into the bowl first? Second? When everything was in the bowl, what did each of you do? Well, today we're going to use exactly the same things, but we'll pour the batter into small cupcake pans instead of one large cakepan."

This is only one of several strategies that Mr. Moore has used to "set the stage for memory development" (Jackson, Robinson, & Dale, 1977). He knows that his early childhood classroom is filled with opportunities during various learning activities to focus on memory development. Please see the *Special Focus: Setting the Stage for Memory Development* for other things that he has done that you can also try.

Developmental Trends

At birth humans are equipped to recognize familiar objects. Infants become bored with—habituated to—a stimulus, for example, a toy that is put in front of them several times, and this boredom indicates that they recognize the object. But, between 5 and 12 months of age, babies are able to recognize an object after seeing it only a few times, meaning that their recognition memory has improved. They also seem to be able to remember the object for several weeks (Fagan, 1984).

Recall memory is also evident in infants, but it also improves during a baby's first year. Researchers taught 2- to 3-month-old infants to kick a mobile and reminded the babies 18 days later about the mobile by moving it while the babies looked on. The infants recalled having kicked the mobile (Rovee-Collier, 1984, 1987). Note, however, that the researchers had to remind the babies, so the recall was actually passive. Infants actively recall things from memory during the last several months of their first year.

Older infants and toddlers, approximately 12 months to 36 months, show improved memory (Perlmutter, 1986). Recall memory improves most dramatically from 3 to 12 years; however, preschool children are still much better able to recognize objects and experiences than to recall them.

PERCEPTION

Infancy is a time of remarkable perceptual development, and 2- to 5-year-old children have a large repertoire of perceptual skills. But young children still have problems with directing their attention. These problems fall into four areas (Jackson, Robinson, & Dale, 1977).

SPECIAL FOCUS: Setting the Stage for Memory Development

1. *Use familiar pictures, sounds, and objects.* Mr Moore used slides of their trip to the apple orchard to help the children retrieve information from their long-term memory. Similarly, after a visit to the zoo he played a tape of sounds made by the animals that the children had seen.

2. *Plan activities and lessons with fewer steps.* He arranged an obstacle course with only four parts so that the children could easily remember it: over the rope, through the tire, up the ladder, and down the slide.

3. *Present only a few bits of new information.* Mr. Moore introduced the names of six birds in one lesson and discovered that the children could not handle this much new information. But they easily remembered the names of the birds when he focused on only three.

4. *Encourage children to use memory strategies.* Preschool children remember better when they use memory strategies, but they tend to use them only when prompted by adults. Verbal rehearsal (e.g., repeating the names of the bones in the leg until you memorize them) is one memory strategy. Mr. Moore encouraged the children to use verbal rehearsal when they sang a "name song" at the beginning of the year to learn each child's name.

5. *Think of different and creative ways to repeat things.* Mr. Moore showed the pictures of the three birds at several group times and repeated their names with the children. Remembering that a square is a rectangle with four equal sides was easier when he repeated the information in creative ways over several days using transparencies, styrofoam models, a construction paper mural, and square cookie cutters.

6. *Actively involve children with things to be remembered.* Active involvement enhances memory. Learning and remembering the route to the emergency fire escape was easier when the class practiced walking it a number of times and talked about it with the firefighter who visited the class. The children learned about squares by forming one themselves at group time with four children on each side of the square.

7. *Name things and experiences.* Labeling things helps children remember them. Before the trip to the zoo, Mr. Moore showed pictures of animals he thought might be unfamiliar and named them for the children. At the zoo he repeated the names. Later, when making a pizza crust, he labeled the process of dough rising, and many of the children remembered the name of the process when they made yeast bread two weeks later.

Perceptual Problems During Early Childhood

Young Children Have Poor Searching and Scanning Skills

Young children can search for something they have lost, but they are not systematic in their search. Their search is not as accurate or efficient as an older child's, and they do not seem to realize that they should stop searching at some point.

Example   Marty watched her teacher write her name and birth date on a tagboard birthday cake. Marty easily recognized hers when the teacher showed Marty her cake and three others. The next day, however, Marty's cake was on the wall with 22 others. Marty looked for a long time, but got frustrated when she could not recognize hers.

Young Children Have Difficulty "Tuning Out" Irrelevant Information

Another perceptual problem is caused by a preschooler's inability to completely control her attention. Young children have difficulty tuning out (ignoring) meaningless information or stimulation. Their attention is more likely to be captured by stimuli that are intense or novel.

Example   A new student teacher was frustrated when she read a story to her 3-year-olds. A squealing sound from the parking lot and the squeaking from wheels on the lunch cart easily distracted them. Older children might also have noticed the noise, but would have been better able to "get back" to listening to the story (provided the story was developmentally appropriate and interesting).

Young Children Have Difficulty Focusing on More Than One Aspect of a Problem

Example   Mr. Moore said to 4-year-old Julia, "Now, we have to look for a special puzzle piece. It will have two straight sides so that it can go in this corner. And it should be curved in on the third side." Julia excitedly handed over a piece with one straight side, seeming to ignore the other sides. Julia focused on only one aspect of the problem and therefore picked out the wrong puzzle piece. Older children are much better able to simultaneously attend to several aspects of a problem.

A Young Child's Degree of Impulsivity May Affect Perception

Children who are reflective work slowly enough to be accurate. Impulsive children tend to work too quickly, thereby missing important information and making unnecessary mistakes. Tim, in the case study at the beginning of this chapter, is an example. Younger children tend to be more impulsive, and this creates an additional perceptual problem for them.

How Perception Changes as Children Get Older

More mature reasoning skills, more efficient memory, more mature language abilities, abstract concepts, and more experiences to draw on are some of the things that go along with changing perceptual abilities as children get older (Jackson, Robinson, & Dale, 1977).

Selective Attention Becomes Refined

Even infants select—and seem to prefer—certain patterns (Fantz, 1966). A 2-year-old has the ability to attend selectively to stimuli, but this ability improves during childhood as she eventually learns to ignore distracting stimuli.

Children Spend More Time "On Task" as They Get Older

Older children tend to stay with a task for a longer period of time than younger children do. The length of time a child spends on an activity, whatever a child's age, depends in part on how attractive the activity is to the child.

Example   There were two books on Vinnie's grandmother's coffee table. Vinnie hardly glanced at the one about flowers, but spent nearly 1½ hours with the family album. He seemed to be fascinated by pictures of his father as a child.

Children Are Better Able to Redirect Their Attention as They Get Older

Older children can more easily redirect their attention than can younger children. When a task has a number of parts, the older child has an advantage because she is able to shift her focus from one aspect to another quickly. A child who can shift focus quickly and accurately is better able to pick out relationships between two parts of a task.

Implications for guidance

1. *Screen for sensory impairments*. Children who are challenged with a sensory impairment are limited in how they function in their environments. This can pose problems for the adult-child relationship (Levitt & Cohen, 1977).

Example   "Kathy is driving me crazy. She just keeps on playing when I call the group together or when I announce cleanup." Kathy's teacher was unaware that Kathy had a mild hearing problem until a screening identified the problem.

2. *Manage the environment well by minimizing intense intruding stimuli*. The idea that children have a short attention span seems to be taken as a given when adults talk about young children. A young child is distracted by sudden or intense stimuli, but adults can help children concentrate on activities and learn self-control by minimizing intruding intense stimuli.

3. *Teach children to scan systematically*. Mr. Moore noticed Marty's frustration and inability to pick out her name and birth date when all the "birthday cakes" were hanging on the wall. She scanned quite unsystematically. Mr. Moore decided to teach some scanning skills.

Example   "Marty, look at this row. Touch each cake as you look at it. Your name begins with M. Look for the first letter. Look for M." He encouraged Marty to ignore names beginning with other letters.

4. *Encourage impulsive children to slow their reaction time*. Impulsive children work very quickly and are frequently less accurate in their responses. They search even less efficiently than age mates (Hartley, 1976). They get themselves in trouble because they are so impulsive.

TEMPERAMENT

The term *temperament* refers to relatively stable individual differences in how children (and adults) express emotion, their behavioral "style" or characteristic way of responding to events (Campos, Caplovitz Barrett, Lamb, Goldsmith, & Stenberg, 1983; Kagan, 1989; Kagan, Reznick, Snidman, Gibbons, & Johnson, 1988; Thomas, Chess, & Birch, 1970). Components of temperament include one's *activity level, irritability level, soothability*, and *levels of fearfulness and sociability* (Buss & Plomin, 1984; Rothbart, 1981; Goldsmith et al., 1987).

Every child has a behavioral style, or temperament, that has an impact on the effectiveness of your guidance. All humans, of whatever age, express emotions such as fear, anger, or joy, but they differ in how they express these emotions—that is, they differ in temperament.

The Thomas research group carried out longitudinal research to investigate how 3-month-old infants differed in emotional expression and then followed the same children until they were 14 years old (Thomas et al., 1970; Thomas & Chess, 1977, 1986). Their results are presented in the following section.

Three Basic Temperament Styles

The Thomas research group found three basic temperament styles:

▼ *Easy babies*. Mood predominantly positive, highly adaptable, regular in bodily functions (eating, eliminating), positive approach to new situations, mild expression of emotions.

▼ *Slow-to-warm-up babies*. Cautious, moody, slow to adapt to change, withdrew from or were passively resistant to new objects and people, very mild expressions of emotion. Like the easy babies, their responses of happiness or anger were of low intensity.

▼ *Difficult babies*. Irregular bodily functions, withdrew from new stimuli, slow to adapt to change, predominantly negative in disposition, highly intense expression of emotion.

There is some evidence that an infant's basic temperament remains stable (Rothbart, 1981), but that does not mean that we cannot help children learn to understand and deal effectively with their temperament style (Thomas & Chess, 1986).

Effect of Temperament on Children

Data on the effect of temperament on children was gathered by Buss and Plomin (1975); Hutt, Lenard, and Prechtl (1969); and Sostek and Anders (1977).

▼ *Easy babies*. Spend little time crying. Spend time watching, listening to, and playing with things and people. Have more time to take in and assimilate perceptual information. Have more time to accommodate to that information, to learn. Smiley babies who vocalize more to unfamiliar observers have higher sensorimotor scores (Peter-Martin & Wachs, 1981; Uzgiris & Hunt, 1975).

▼ *Slow-to-warm-up babies*. Their reluctance to try new things might well result in their being ignored by others.

▼ *Difficult babies*. Spend a lot of time crying. Tense up. Highly distractible. Unable to pay attention to important stimuli. All of this interferes with habituation and problem solving. Older children with difficult temperaments are more irritable, aggressive, and more likely to have trouble adjusting to school (Brody, Stoneman, & Burke, 1987).

Temperament and the Dance of Interaction

An infant's temperament is very likely to affect how responsive her caregiver is, which in turn affects how securely attached the baby becomes (Waters & Deane, 1982). This is especially true if an adult's style of caregiving clashes with the baby's temperament.

▼ *Easy babies*. Their predictability and responsiveness draw parents into effective cycles of interaction by making the parents feel competent in the caregiving role.

▼ *Difficult babies*. Extremely fussy and irritable, cry a lot, resist being held or rocked, difficult to soothe or comfort. Need caregivers to be calm, sensitive, to resist the urge to hold and try to comfort this baby if baby does *not* want to be held, and to let the infant take things "at her own pace." This approach helps children effectively deal with their temperament.

Trouble brews, however, when parents do not understand their baby's temperament, think she is crying or resisting parental contact on purpose, become irritable, or punish the baby. When caregiving style and infant temperament clash, adults can easily feel incompetent.

Implications for guidance.   Think about your own temperament "style." Then, tune in to the temperamental differences of children in your care. Acknowledge that you may well be puzzled or even irritated by the behavioral styles of some children when they differ from your own, and occasionally even if a child's style matches your own. Finally, learn and consciously use the positive guidance strategies described in this text. Along with your sense of humor, patience, sensitivity, and goodwill, they will help you deal with different temperaments so that you can help children to thrive (Brazelton, Tronick, Adamson, Als, & Wise, 1975; Thomas et al., 1970).

SOCIAL COGNITION

The term *social cognition* refers to how children think about the behavior, motives, feelings, or intentions of others (Shaffer, 1993). Piaget showed us that children construct more complex ideas about their physical world as they grow older. At the same time, children construct increasingly more complex ideas about their social world (Shantz, 1983). For instance, how will the children you teach describe how other people behave? Will they understand the difference between another person's accidental behavior and intentional behavior? How will they view friendship? How will they think about resolving conflict? Your knowledge about these developmental issues will enable you to make developmentally appropriate child guidance decisions.

This section focuses on social cognition through the early childhood period. All of a child's developments in perception, attention, memory, and verbal expression seem to converge, enabling her to more accurately describe how others behave and feel, to tell the difference between accidental and intentional behavior, to make and maintain friendships, and to resolve conflicts.

How Children Describe Other People and Their Behavior

Children's behavior is very often affected by how they understand the behavior of other people. What do children of different ages pay attention to? What do they remember, and how do they describe other people and their behavior?

Younger Than 7 or 8 Years

During early childhood, children tend to use concrete terms to describe another person, such as "My teacher is pretty. She smells good." They do not often describe more abstract qualities, such as trustworthiness or honesty. Occasionally, a young child will describe someone by using what seems to be a more abstract term, such as "He's *mean!*" Here, though, the child usually is describing something the other has recently done, such as yelling at the child for running onto the lawn, rather than identifying a major psychological characteristic (Rholes, Jones, & Wade, 1988).

Show a video to young children and ask them to describe what they saw. Again, they will concentrate on describing concrete, observable actions: "She opened the gate and the kitten got out." They might describe obvious emotional reactions, ". . . and the girl cried." But, young children will not try to interpret feelings (Flapan, 1968).

After Age 8

Children at this age use fewer concrete terms and begin using broader terms to describe other people (Barenboim, 1981).

Example   When Tom was 6 years old, he described his friend Carl as "the fastest runner," but at 8 years Tom says, "Carl is the most athletic person in our class."

Eight- to ten-year-olds are also much better able to describe another person's behavior. Show a video to this group and you will hear interpretations of some of the feelings and intentions of other people, but only in familiar situations.

Example   "She cried when the kitten got out of the yard. She's probably feeling sad and afraid that her kitten will get hurt."

Implications for guidance.   Expect young children *not* to understand how somebody else feels. Be helpful. Use age-appropriate child guidance and give this age group information about how other people usually feel in different situations. Expect older children to understand feelings and to begin to interpret feelings. Remember, though, that some children have poor models and might not be very good at recognizing feelings. Use individually appropriate child guidance with these children by teaching them about emotions or by reminding older children about how somebody might be feeling.

Examples   Teacher to 3-year-old: "Oh, Sarah! The gerbil is hiding. I think you scared him when you banged on his house."

Teacher to kindergarten class: "The cook seemed irritated when she had a hot meal all ready for us and we weren't ready to eat."

Teacher to 8-year-old: "Terry is crying. She's upset because you called her that name. People in this class do not hurt others by name calling."

How Children Understand Intentional/Accidental Behavior

Children are better able to control themselves when then can look at another's behavior and decide whether the person intended to act that way or whether the behavior was accidental. Children can distinguish between accidental and intentional behavior as their cognitive skills develop. Four-year-olds tend not to differentiate between intentional and accidental behavior, but by 5½ years many children can make the distinction, and at 9 they are even more accurate (King, 1971).

Implications for guidance.   Do not expect the youngest children to know the difference between accidental and intentional behavior. Use age-appropriate guidance strategies with this group by explaining what an accident is. Expect older children to understand the difference if they have learned the difference. If they do understand the difference, use age-appropriate strategies and *remind* them of the difference between accidental and intentional behavior. If an older child has not learned the difference, use an individually appropriate strategy to teach her what it is.

Examples   "Mary didn't mean to run into you, Chuck. It was an 'accident'" (Chuck was 4 years old).

Teacher to a 7-year-old: "Sometimes, Tom, people aren't very careful, and I think Sammi ran into you by accident. He really wasn't looking at where he was going. He didn't mean to hurt you."

Having Friends and Resolving Conflict

With his arm around Pat's shoulder, Frank proudly said to his dad: "This is Pat. He's my friend!"

Having Friends

Friends play an important part in Frank's social development now, at the age of 7, and will continue to do so throughout his life. Peer relations become important during early childhood years for three reasons (Damon, 1983). First, children have a blossoming sense of moral obligation, a willingness to share or to take turns. Even though the roots of sharing or turn-taking were evident earlier, they now occur with regularity. Second, children now begin to view peers as friends as well as momentary playmates. Social interactions are seen for the first time as part of a system of relationships that go beyond the present moment. Third, a wide range of social interactional possibilities opens because of a young child's developing symbolic awareness (Youniss & Volpe, 1978).

Social Skills Needed for Effective Interaction

Asher, Renshaw, and Hymel (1982) reviewed the research on the competencies, or social skills, needed for effective interaction with peers. They focused on a child's ability to initiate interaction with peers, the ability to maintain a relationship, and the ability to deal with conflict.

Popular and unpopular children initiate contact with peers differently. When asked how a new child could get acquainted with others in the class, unpopular kindergarten children suggested that an adult help the child get to know the others. The popular children, however, demonstrated superior social skills when they volunteered to play with the new child themselves (Asher & Renshaw, 1981; Asher et al., 1982). Corsaro (1979) observed how preschool children attempt to become a part of a group activity with peers whom they know. Children who approached the group, watched the ongoing activity, and then engaged in the same behavior without disrupting the group were likely to be admitted to the group.

Implications for guidance.   Teach specific social skills to children who are aggressive or unpopular and who are therefore rejected by their peers (Bullock, 1991). Renee, for example, had been having a lot of trouble with the other children because she barged in on play groups and tried to take over the play. She did not seem to know a better way to join a group. Mr. Moore decided to teach her this social skill. He followed the practical, step-by-step strategies of modeling, direct instruction and coaching, and feedback and reinforcement recommended by Asher et al. (1982).

Example   *Modeling.* Mr. Moore showed a short video about a child who successfully joined a group playing in the housekeeping corner by asking if she could play and then by sitting at the table while "dinner" was served. This was an excellent example of modeling and was likely to be successful with Renee because the model was similar to Renee and because the teacher focused attention on what the model was doing and why she joined the group in that specific way.

Example   *Direct instruction and coaching.* After watching the video, Mr. Moore gave specific direct instructions to Renee on how to join a group. "OK, Renee. You want to play at the water table, and there are two children there already. Go over to the table and pick a spot where you won't be in somebody's way, and then use a toy that nobody else seems to be using. Remember our water table rules? That's right. No splashing and no grabbing!" Renee then practiced by joining the group at the water table.

The teacher modeled a behavior and then gave direct instruction, or coaching, which involves telling a child how to perform a social skill. Direct instruction, or coaching, is an effective tool for helping children gain acceptance by peers (Bullock, 1991; Oden & Asher, 1977; Zahavi & Asher, 1978).

Example   *Encouragement/Positive reinforcement.* Mr. Moore nodded encouragingly at Renee when she took her place at an unoccupied side of the water table and played with an unclaimed toy. After observing for about 3 minutes, he walked over to the table and said to the entire group, "Each one of you is playing at her own spot and only with her own water toys, and the water is staying in the table."

Renee will probably continue to use her new and positive social skill because her teacher encouraged her by nodding and through verbal reinforcement.

A child who has initiated contact with peers must be able to maintain the relationship. Children who are cooperative and friendly when interacting with peers are generally successful in maintaining relationships. Children who are unfriendly, make fun of, or interfere with other children have great difficulty maintaining relationships and are often rejected by other children (Asher et al. 1982).

Resolving Conflict

The ability to resolve conflict peaceably is an important social skill. By the age of 5, children realize that they can defend their rights (e.g., not allow somebody to take a toy with which they are playing), but their skill in resolving conflict varies considerably.

Example   A researcher asked Jon and Jim, both 5-year-olds, "How can you get back a toy that another child has taken from you?" Jim's only response was an aggressive one: "You could hit him, or you could grab the truck." Jon, however, generated several nonaggressive solutions, "Well, you could tell him, 'I was playing with that and want the truck back' and then take it [a direct assertive action], or say, 'You're supposed to ask first!' [an appeal to social convention]." Jon suggested two other strategies: turn-taking (a compromise) or appealing to an authority figure.

Successful conflict resolution requires that a child be able to think of alternative ways of solving problems (Jon was able to do this; Jim was not); to know how another person is likely to respond to different solutions; and to use means-and-ends problem solving (Shure & Spivack, 1978; Spivack & Shure, 1974).

HELPING CHILDREN ACHIEVE SELF-CONTROL
What Is Self-Control?

Self-control is voluntary, internal regulation of behavior. First, children actually construct their concept of self as their cognitive system develops. Second, they observe and then evaluate the self, deciding whether they like the self that they see (these two facets are described more fully in chapter six). Third, the self must learn to regulate its own behavior (Harter, 1983). Self-control is a major issue in *metacognition*, one's knowledge and control of the cognitive domain (Brown, Bransford, Ferrara, & Campione, 1983).

Self-control, or self-regulation, may well be one of the most significant changes during a child's preschool years (Flavell, 1977). Self-regulatory functions are an integral part of the learning process, are important mechanisms in a child's growth and development, and are an essential part of preserving social and moral order (Brown et al., 1983; Harter, 1983).

Demonstration of Self-Control

Children demonstrate self-control when they . . .

▼ *control impulses, wait, and suspend action.* Children show self-control when they step back, examine a situation, and then decide how to act. They resist reacting impulsively.

Example   Things went smoothly in the block corner until Kyle joined the group and took a block from Joel's structure. Joel's usual reaction has been an aggressive one, such as slugging or screaming at the other child. But Mr. Moore has been teaching him to be self-controlled and verbally assertive. So he "used words" like his teacher suggested: "Kyle, I was using that block. Give it back!"

▼ *tolerate frustration.* A child demonstrates self-control when she can refrain from doing something that is either forbidden or inappropriate to the situation.

Example   While on a Christmas shopping trip, Joel was attracted to a huge tree with hundreds of glass ornaments. He stood and looked, raised his hand to touch one, and then withdrew his hand, showing self-control.

▼ *postpone immediate gratification*. Adults demonstrate self-control when they carry through with some important task and only then engage in some gratifying (pleasurable) activity, for example, studying before meeting a friend for coffee. Please try to remember how difficult it is for you, an adult, to delay gratification, when dealing with people far younger than you.

Encourage children to delay gratification by using modeling, direct instruction, and all the other methods of influence to teach delay of gratification. Even older children need our guidance to figure out when it is important to put off until later something that they want right now.

Example   Michael, 6 years old, popped several chocolate chips into his mouth as he and his brother helped Dad make chocolate chip cookies. Dad said, "Hey, Mike. Remember the ad on TV where that man sings 'Please don't eat all the morsels—or your cookies will look like this' [a chipless chocolate chip cookie]? Put the chips into the mix, not your mouth." Mike said, "O-OK!" and sang the jingle a few times as he added chips to the batter.

▼ *initiate a plan and carry it out over a period of time*.

Example   Suzanne decided to build a structure in the sand when she went to the beach with her family. She lugged water to the sand, mixed dry sand and water, and patiently patted and pushed the sand into place. Dad took pictures of her afternoon-long project.

How Does Self-Control Evolve?

Self-control evolves "from the outside to the inside," slowly and haltingly.

Self-Control Evolves "From the Outside to the Inside"

Responsible adults actually perform most of an infant's or toddler's ego functions (e.g., remembering things for the infant, reminding a toddler to hold the kitten gently), thereby regulating the young child's behavior for her. In this case, the very young child's actions are heavily controlled by an external agent, the adult. But responsible adults also understand child development and realize that a child can and should take on more responsibility for controlling herself as she grows older and acquires different cognitive skills. They expect children to begin to internalize control taught by the adult. Responsible adults communicate this expectation when they gradually transfer executive control to children (Brown et al., 1983; Flavell, 1977). The adult might, for example, expect a child to try solving a problem with the adult observing and offering advice or help only when necessary.

Pulkkinen (1982) noted that child-rearing practices affect a child's level of self-control. She found that parents of adolescents with strong self-control used positive guidance strategies. These parents used strategies that helped adolescents understand why control was necessary and did it in such a way that the parents did not seem to be on a "power trip." Parents of adolescents with weak self-control used selfish, negative guidance strategies. They tried to use raw power and thought it unnecessary to explain their adult actions.

Self-Control Develops Slowly

Children are not born with self-control, but begin to develop it around the age of 2. It takes several more years before this emerging ability develops fully. Children are better able to control themselves as they get older, for a number of reasons. First, their cognitive, perceptual, and linguistic systems have developed, allowing them to understand things from a different perspective and giving them access to better skills for dealing with impulses. Control of the self also implies that a child realizes that a self exists; this knowledge develops during late infancy and early childhood.

Self-Control Evolves Haltingly

Preschool children often astonish adults with remarkable self-control, but they also demonstrate considerable lack of control at other times. Joel controlled himself in the block corner, but on the same day he shoved someone out of the way in his rush to the sliding board. Young children have to practice self-control, just as musicians and athletes have to practice their skills. It is reasonable to expect some measure of self-control in young children, but it is usually a mistake to expect perfect control.

Stages in the Development of Self-Control

Birth to Approximately 12 Months

Kopp (1981) believes that young infants are not capable of self-control. The reflex movements of the first several months of life give way to voluntary motor acts such as reaching and grasping, but, she notes, infants do not consciously control the movements.

Twelve Months to About 24 Months

At this age children begin to be able to start, stop, change, or maintain motor acts or emotional signals. They also demonstrate an emerging awareness of the demands made on them by caregivers. Communication skills become more sophisticated, enabling a child to understand another person's instructions and modeling. Caregivers usually discover that children this age are ready to follow an adult's lead.

At Approximately 24 Months: Emerging Self-Control

Children are now able to recall what someone has said or done, and they are also able to engage in representational thinking. These new abilities help them make the transition to beginning self-control. At this stage, however, children have a very limited ability to control themselves, that is, to wait for their turn or to delay gratification.

Advanced Self-Control Emerges at About 36 Months

Children are now able to use certain strategies that help them delay gratification, and this sets the stage for better self-control. Kopp (1981) did research with groups of 18-, 24-, and 36-month-old children to find out how they differ in their use of strategies to better tolerate delay. Raisins were hidden under a cup, and the child being tested was told not to eat them. The older children did things spontaneously to distract themselves, such as singing, talking, sitting on their hands, or looking away. Younger children could be instructed to use delaying strategies, but they did not use them automatically (Meichenbaum & Goodman, 1971).

Childhood to Late Adolescence

Pulkkinen (1982) carried out a longitudinal study of 8-year-olds in which individual differences in behavior were again examined when the children were 14 and 20 years old. The individual tendencies noted in the children at age 8 in how they coped with impulses seemed to endure through adolescence.

CASE STUDY ANALYSIS: Mr. Moore's Classroom

Explain how Mr. Moore demonstrated his understanding of child development.

1. *Monday/Tuesday:* Mr. Moore planned *age-appropriate* follow-up activities to the apple orchard trip—dictation of a story, red play dough and finger-paint, and "pipe cleaner apples." I agree with this statement because children in Piaget's preoperational stage represent (recall and tell about) their experiences by:

2. *Wednesday:* Mr. Moore planned another *age-appropriate* activity when he set up the water table with cups for pouring water from container to container. I also agree with this statement because children in Piaget's preoperational stage have the following cognitive limitation:

3. *Thursday:* Mr. Moore also seems to understand that developmentally appropriate guidance is *individually appropriate*. Explain how he responded appropriately to individual differences by helping Tim deal with an impulsive way of selecting activities.

4. *Friday:* Mr. Moore believes that young children like Kathy and Jane become less egocentric through social interaction. Explain how the arguing, acknowledging other viewpoints, and negotiating about the tunnel was actually a developmentally appropriate strategy for these 4½-year-old children.

CASE STUDY ANALYSIS: Mrs. Vang's Classroom

1. Kevin showed that he has "recognition memory" when he . . .

2. Kevin also showed that he has "recall memory" when he . . . (two specific actions)

3. Mrs. Vang gave Kevin a "reminder" about bear and block, thus helping him with recall memory, when she . . .

4. Explain why her reminders are a developmentally appropriate strategy for a 6-month-old.

5. Mrs. Vang also encouraged Kevin's willingness to try to recall things by saying . . .

6. Review Kopp's stages in the development of self-control. Ben (case study) is in the _____ stage.

7. During this stage infants begin to be able to start, stop, or change motor acts. I think that Ben demonstrated this ability by . . .

8. Ben showed that he is becoming aware of demands placed on him by adults when he . . .

9. Mrs. Vang helped Ben do as she requested when she . . .

SUMMARY OF KEY CONCEPTS

1. Adults who guide children effectively use *developmentally appropriate* guidance, meaning that it is both age-appropriate and individually appropriate. Adults who use developmentally appropriate child guidance have a knowledge base in child and family development and understand each person's part in an interaction, but they acknowledge an adult's greater responsibility in an interaction with a young child.

2. Developmentally appropriate child guidance grows out of understanding children's cognitive development. Children from birth to approximately 24 months are in the first of Piaget's stages of cognitive development, during which perceptual skills become refined, language is acquired, motor skills improve, and cognitive skills evolve. Two- to five-year-old children are usually in the second, and 6- to 8-year-olds in the third, of Piaget's stages of cognitive development. Our guidance strategies are most effective when they are based on the cognitive accomplishments of a child's current level of development and when they also take into account the cognitive limitations of a particular stage or level of development.

3. Developmentally appropriate guidance strategies are based on the somewhat limited *memory* capacity and skills of young children. There are several things that adults can do to set the stage for memory development.

4. Young children have some difficulty with directing their attention, which is a problem with *perception*. They have poor searching and scanning skills, have difficulty tuning out irrelevant information, and have difficulty focusing on more than one aspect of a problem. A child's degree of impulsivity may also affect perception.

5. Each child has her own behavioral style, or *temperament*—individual differences in how she expresses emotion. A child's temperament influences how

she interacts with adults and plays a part in determining how effective an adult's guidance will be.

6. *Social cognition* refers to a child's ability to conceptualize and reason about the social world, a skill directly affected by and similar to her level of cognitive development. A child's conceptualizations of how other people behave, the differences between intentional and accidental behavior, and the social areas of friendship and conflict change as cognitive development changes.

7. Control is a lifelong issue for every human being. Responsible adults regulate the behavior of very young children but understand that a child can and should be expected to take on increased responsibility for controlling herself as she grows older and acquires cognitive skills. Adults who use developmentally appropriate child guidance teach children how to control themselves and gradually transfer executive control to the child.

OBSERVE CHILD GUIDANCE IN ACTION
Helping Young Children Develop Self-Control

Infants. Observe an adult-infant interaction. Look for evidence that the adult actually performs the infant's ego functions for her—that is, that the adult does not expect the infant to control herself. Record your observations by using the following format.

Date: _____

Setting: _____

Approximate age of child (infant): _____

Describe specific things an adult does for the infant (rocks her to sleep, calms her down, burps her, wipes her mouth, changes her diaper):

Older children. Observe an adult interacting with a child who is between 2 and 8 years old. Record samples that indicate that this adult is indeed transferring control to the child and that the adult expects a child of this age to begin to control herself.

Date: _____

Setting: _____

Approximate age of child: _____

Specific example showing that this adult expected the child to control herself to some degree:

REFERENCES

Asher, S. R., & Renshaw, P. D. (1981). Children without friends: Social knowledge and social skill training. In S. R. Asher & J. M. Cottman (Eds.), *The development of children's friendships*. New York: Cambridge University Press.

Asher, S. R., Renshaw, P., & Hymel, S. (1982). Peer relations and the development of social skills. In S. Moore and C. Cooper (Eds.), *The young child: Reviews of research* (Vol. 3). Washington, DC: NAEYC.

Barenboim, C. (1981). The development of person perception in childhood and adolescence: From behavioral comparisons to psychological constructs to psychological comparisons. *Child Development, 52,* 129–144.

Bell, R. Q. (1968). A reinterpretation of the direction of effect in studies of socialization. *Psychological Review, 75,* 81–95.

Bell, R. Q., Harper, L. V. (Eds.) (1977). *Child effects on adults.* Hillsdale, NJ: Erlbaum.

Black, J. K. (1981). Are young children really egocentric? *Young Children, 36,* 51–55.

Brazelton, T. B., Tronick, E., Adamson, L., Als, H., & Wise, S. (1975). Early mother-infant reciprocity. In M. Hofer (Ed.), *Parent-infant interaction.* Amsterdam: Excerpta Medica.

Brody, G. H., Stoneman, Z., & Burke, M. (1987). Child temperaments, maternal differential behavior, and sibling relationships. *Developmental Psychology, 23,* 354–362.

Bronfenbrenner, U. (1977). Toward an experimental ecology of human development. *American Psychologist, 32,* 513–531.

Brown, A. L., Bransford, J. D., Ferrara, R. A., & Campione, J. C. (1983). Learning, remembering and understanding. In P. Mussen (Ed.), *Handbook of child psychology* (Vol. 3). New York: Wiley.

Bullock, J. (1991). Supporting the development of socially rejected children. *Early Child Development and Care, 66,* 15–23.

Buss, A. H., & Plomin, R. A. (1975). *A temperament theory of personality development.* New York: Wiley.

Buss, A. H., & Plomin, R. A. (1984). *Temperament: Early developing personality traits.* Hillsdale, NJ: Erlbaum.

Campos, J. J., Caplovitz Barrett, K., Lamb, M. E., Goldsmith, H. H., & Stenberg, C. (1983). Socioemotional development. In P. Mussen (Ed.), *Handbook of child psychology* (Vol. 2). New York: Wiley.

Case, R. (1984). The process of stage transition: A neo-Piagetian view. In R. J. Sternberg (Ed.), *Mechanisms of cognitive development.* New York: W. H. Freeman.

Chalmers, J. B., & Townsend, M. A. (1990). The effects of training in social perspective-taking on socially maladjusted girls. *Child Development, 61,* 178–190.

Chandler, M. J. (1973). Egocentrism and antisocial behavior: The assessment and training of social perspective-taking skills. *Developmental Psychology, 9*(3), 326–332.

Corsaro, W. A. (1979). "We're friends, right?" Children's use of access rituals in a nursery school. *Language in Society, 8,* 315–336.

Damon, W. (1983). *Social and personality development.* New York: W. W. Norton.

Dixon, J. A., & Moore, C. F. (1990). The development of perspective-taking: Understanding differences in information and weighting. *Child Development, 61,* 1502–1513.

Fagan, J. F. (1984). Infant memory: History, current trends, and relations to cognitive psychology. In M. Moscovitch (Ed.), *Infant memory: Its relation to normal and pathological memory in humans and other animals.* New York: Plenum.

Fantz, R. L. (1966). Pattern discrimination and selective attention as determinants of perceptual development from birth. In A. H. Kidd & J. L. Rivoire (Eds.), *Perceptual development in children.* New York: International Universities Press.

Flapan, D. (1968). *Children's understanding of social interaction*. New York: Teacher's College Press.

Flavell, J. H. (1977). *Cognitive development*. Englewood Cliffs, NJ: Prentice-Hall.

Flavell, J. H., Flavell, E. R., Green, F. L., & Wilcox, S. A. (1981). The development of three spatial perspective-taking rules. *Child Development, 52*, 356–358.

Gelman, R., & Baillargeon, R. (1983). A review of some Piagetian concepts. In P. Mussen (Ed.), *Handbook of child psychology* (Vol. 3). New York: Wiley.

Gibson, E. J., & Spelke, E. S. (1983). The development of perception. In P. Mussen (Ed.), *Handbook of child psychology* (Vol. 3). New York: Wiley.

Goldsmith, H., Buss, A., Plomin, R., Rothbart, M., Thomas, A., Chess, S., Hinde, R., & McCall, R. (1987). Roundtable: What is temperament? Four approaches. *Child Development, 58*, 505–529.

Harter, S. (1983). Developmental perspectives on the self-system. In P. Mussen (Ed.), *Handbook of child psychology* (Vol. 4). New York: Wiley.

Hartley, D. G. (1976). The effect of perceptual salience on reflective-impulsive performance differences. *Developmental Psychology, 12*, 218–225.

Higgins, E. T. (1981). Role taking and social judgement: Alternative developmental perspectives and processes. In J. H. Flavell & L. Ross (Eds.), *Social cognitive development*. Cambridge, MA: Harvard University Press.

Hutt, S., Lenard, H., & Prechtl, H. (1969). Psychophysiological studies in newborn infants. In L. P. Lipsitt & H. W. Reese (Eds.), *Advances in child development and behavior* (Vol. 4). New York: Academic Press.

Jackson, N. E., Robinson, H. B., & Dale, P. S. (1977). *Cognitive development in young children*. Monterey, CA: Brooks/Cole.

Jones, D. C. (1985). Persuasive appeals and responses to appeals among friends and acquaintances. *Child Development, 56*, 757–763.

Kagan, J. (1989). Temperamental contributions to social behavior. *American Psychologist, 44*, 668–674.

Kagan, J., Reznick, J., Snidman, N., Gibbons, J., & Johnson, M. D. (1988). Childhood derivatives of inhibition and lack of inhibition to the familiar. *Child Development, 59*, 1580–1589.

King, M. (1971). The development of some intention concepts in young children. *Child Development, 42*, 1145–1152.

Kopp, C. B. (1981). The antecedents of self-regulation: A developmental perspective. Unpublished manuscript, University of California, Los Angeles.

Levitt, E., & Cohen, S. (1977). Parents as teachers: A rationale for involving parents in the education of their young handicapped children. In L. G. Katz (Ed.), *Current topics in early childhood education* (Vol. 1). Norwood, NJ: Ablex.

Looft, W. R. (1972). Egocentrism and social interaction across the life-span. *Psychological Bulletin, 78*, 73–92.

Maccoby, E. E., & Martin, J. A. (1983). Socialization in the context of the family: Parent-child interaction. In P. Mussen (Ed.), *Handbook of child psychology* (Vol.4). New York: Wiley.

Mussen (Ed.), *Handbook of child psychology* (Vol. 4). New York: Wiley.

Marion, M. (1991). *Guidance of young children* (3rd ed.). New York: Merrill/Macmillan.

Meichenbaum, G., & Goodman, J. (1971). Training impulsive children to talk to themselves: A means of developing self-control. *Journal of Abnormal Psychology, 77*, 115–126.

Milner, J. S., Robertson, K. R., & Rogers, D. L. (1990). Childhood history of abuse and adult child abuse potential. *Journal of Family Violence, 5*(1), 15–34.

Newcombe, N, & Huttenlocher, J. (1992). Children's early ability to solve perspective-taking problems. *Developmental Psychology, 28*(4), 635–643.

Newman, D. (1986). The role of mutual knowledge in the development of perspective-taking. *Developmental Review, 6*, 122–145.

Oden, S., & Asher, S. R. (1977). Coaching children in social skills for friendship making. *Child Development, 48*, 495–506.

Perlmutter, M. (1986). A life-span view of memory. In P. B. Baltes, D. L. Featherman, & R. M. Lerner (Eds.), *Life-span development and behavior* (Vol. 7). Hillsdale, NJ: Erlbaum.

Perlmutter, M., & Myers, N. A. (1979). Development of recall in 2- to 4-year-old children. *Developmental Psychology, 15*, 73–83.

Peters-Martin, P., & Wachs, T. D. (1981, April). *A longitudinal study of temperament and its correlates in the first year of life.* Paper presented at the meeting of the Society for Research in Child Development, Boston.

Piaget, J. (1952). *The origins of intelligence in children.* New York: W. W. Norton.

Piaget, J. (1965). *The moral judgment of the child* (M. Gabain, translator). New York: Free Press.

Piaget, J. (1968). *Six psychological studies.* New York: Random House.

Piaget, J. (1976a). *The grasp of consciousness: Action and concept in the young child.* Cambridge: Harvard University Press.

Piaget, J. (1976b). The stages of intellectual development of the child. In N. Endler, L. Boulter, & H. Osser (Eds.), *Contemporary issues in developmental psychology* (2nd ed.). New York: Holt, Rinehart, & Winston.

Piaget, J. (1983). Piaget's theory. In P. Mussen (Ed.), *Handbook of child psychology* (Vol. 1). New York: Wiley.

Pulkkinen, L. (1982). Self-control and continuity from childhood to late adolescence. In P. Bates and O. Brim (Eds.), *Life-span development and behavior* (Vol. 4). New York: Academic Press.

Rholes, W. S., Jones, M., & Wade, C. (1988). Children's understanding of personal disposition and its relationship to behavior. *Journal of Experimental Child Psychology, 45*, 1–17.

Rothbart, M. K. (1981). Measurement of temperament in infancy. *Child Development, 52*, 569–578.

Rovee-Collier, C. K. (1984). The ontogeny of learning and memory in human infancy. In R. Kail & N. E. Spear (Eds.)., *Comparative perspectives on the development of memory.* Hillsdale, NJ: Erlbaum.

Rovee-Collier, C. K. (1987). Learning and memory. In J. D. Osofsky (Ed.), *Handbook of infant development* (2nd ed.). New York: Wiley.

Selman, R. L. (1976). Social-cognitive understanding. In T. Lickona (Ed.), *Moral development and behavior.* New York: Holt, Rinehart, & Winston.

Selman, R. L. (1980). *The growth of interpersonal understanding: Developmental and clinical analysis.* New York: Academic Press.

Shaffer, D. R. (1993). *Developmental psychology* (3rd ed.). Pacific Grove, CA: Brooks/Cole.

Shantz, C. U. (1983). Social cognition. In P. Mussen (Ed.), *Handbook of child psychology* (Vol. 3). New York: Wiley.

Shure, M. B., & Spivack, G. (1978). *Problem-solving techniques in childrearing*. San Francisco: Jossey-Bass.

Smith, C. A. (1982). *Promoting the social development of young children*. Palo Alto, CA: Mayfield.

Sostek, A., & Anders, T. (1977). Relationships among the Brazelton neonatal scale, Bayley infant scales, and early temperament. *Child Development, 48*, 320–323.

Spivack, B., & Shure, M. B. (1974). *Social adjustment of young children: A cognitive approach to solving real-life problems*. San Francisco: Jossey-Bass.

Thomas, A., & Chess, S. (1977). *Temperament and development*. New York: Brunner/Mazel.

Thomas, A., & Chess, S. (1986). The New York longitudinal study: From infancy to early adult life. In R. Plomin & J. Dunn (Eds.), *The study of temperament: Changes, continuities, and challenges*. Hillsdale, NJ: Erlbaum.

Thomas, A., Chess, S., & Birch, H. (1970). The origin of personality. *Scientific American, 223*, 102–109.

Uzgiris, I., & Hunt, J. (1975). *Assessment in infancy: Ordinal scales of psychological development*. Urbana: University of Illinois Press.

Waters, E., & Deane, D. (1982). Infant-mother attachment: Theories, models, recent data, and some tasks for comparative developmental analysis. In L. W. Hoffman, R. A. Gandelman, & H. R. Schiffman (Eds.), *Parenting: Its causes and consequences*. Hillsdale, NJ: Erlbaum.

Youniss, J., & Volpe, J. (1978). A relational analysis of children's friendships. In W. Damon (Ed.), *New directions for child development: Social cognition*. San Francisco: Jossey-Bass.

Zahavi, S., & Asher, S. R. (1978). The effect of verbal instructions on preschool children's aggressive behavior. *Journal of School Psychology, 16*, 146–153.

2

Adult Styles of Caregiving

Chapter Overview

After reading and studying this chapter, you will be able to

▼ *Name* and *describe* three styles of caregiving.

▼ *Explain* the major similarities and differences between the two types of permissiveness.

▼ *Explain* and *give examples* of developmentally appropriate child guidance.

▼ *Explain* how an adult's choice of discipline strategies reflects the system rules and communication patterns that the adult has experienced.

▼ *Describe* the negative discipline strategies used by authoritarian caregivers.

▼ *Explain* how each style may affect a child's development.

▼ *Analyze* case studies and *determine* how each case illustrates a specific caregiving style.

▼ *List* six processes through which adults influence children.

▼ *Give examples* of how an adult from each caregiving style would use specific processes.

"Above all, we shall not harm children. We shall not participate in practices that are disrespectful, degrading, dangerous, exploitative, intimidating, psychologically damaging, or physically harmful to children. This principle has precedence over all others in this code."

(Code of Ethical Conduct, 1990, NAEYC)

CASE STUDIES: Styles of Caregiving

Matthew

Matthew parked his bike in the driveway. His mother called out to him, "Put the bike away, Matt." Matthew heard but ignored her as he walked away. "Matthew, did you hear me? Put that bike away this instant. I mean it. No Dairy Queen for you tonight if you don't put that bike away." Matthew shuffled on and Mom continued, "Matthew, get back here. I want that bike put away." Finally, Mom just turned back to the house. "That boy never listens to me." Matt pays little attention to his mother's limits. He also knows that she hardly ever follows up on her threats. That night, for example, Mom took Matthew to the Dairy Queen, seeming to have forgotten the bike incident.

Joel

At 18 months, Joel, when visiting a friend with his mother, banged on the friend's television screen and pushed at the door screen. His mom said nothing until the friend expressed concern for her property. Then she said, "Joel, do you think you should be doing that?" To the friend she said, "You know, I want Joel to know that the 'world is his oyster,' and I don't think I should order him around." At 4 years Joel stayed up until 11:30 when company was over. To the friend who inquired about his bedtime Mom replied, "Oh, I let Joel make decisions on his own." Joel fell asleep in the book corner at his child care center the next day. At 6 years Joel smacked another child on the face at school, and Mom said to the teacher, "Boys will be boys!" He pushed his way ahead of others at a zoo exhibition and Mom ignored others when she said, "Go ahead. Can you see? Move up closer."

Jim

Dad barks orders and expects his children to obey immediately despite anything else they might be doing. Jim has watched as Dad used a belt on an older brother. To a neighbor who looked disapprovingly on a slapping incident Dad said, "Got a problem? Butt out. These are my kids. They're not hurt."

During toilet training, 2½-year-old Jim was spanked when he had an accident. When Jim was 4 years old Dad grabbed one of Jim's arms and yanked him to make Jim move along at the store, saying, "I'm sick of you holding us up all the time." At preschool Jim had trouble with other children because he hit them when he was angry. The children started to leave him out of activities. Now that he is 8, he has a dog who he wants to train. When she does not sit on command, Jim tightens Ginger's choke chain until she howls in pain. Jim and his brothers avoid Dad as much as they can. And Ginger avoids Jim, too.

Krista

Krista's mother is a home care provider for Krista, 18 months old, and her friend's two children, Robert, 24 months, and Steven, 9 months. Steven's mother asked Krista's mom what to do when Steven bites her during feeding. "Quickly tell him NO and pull his mouth off your breast. Don't make a joke of it, either, or he'll think you're playing a game." Krista wanted a toy that Robert had but didn't seem to have the words for asking. She grew more agitated and then, even to her own surprise, she bit him! Krista's mother, also surprised, immediately took care of the bite on Robert's arm. Then, to her daughter, she said, "No, Krista. Biting is a no-no. Biting hurts Robert. If Krista needs help, come to Mommy and I will help you get a toy."

STYLES OF CAREGIVING

Each of us has a *style of caregiving,* and it is through our style that we set the tone for our homes and classrooms. Researchers have long been interested in the characteristics that differentiate parents and other adult caregivers, as well as in how these differences affect children. Forty years ago Becker (1954) analyzed several studies and classified a parent's style by looking at whether the parent was (a) hostile or warm and (b) restrictive or permissive. Diana Baumrind believes that a parent's degree of *responsiveness and demandingness* forms the basis of his caregiving "style" (Baumrind, 1967, 1971, 1977, 1979; Baumrind & Black,1967).

Baumrind identified and labeled several styles of parenting or caregiving. The most prominent caregiving styles are described in the following sections. For the authori*tarian* and authori*tative* styles, you will read about the *system rules* that govern choices made by adults, the *communication style* used in the system, the adults' level of *demandingness and responsiveness,* the *discipline strategies* used by the adults in that system, and the *impact of that style on children.* In this chapter I discuss in detail the authori*tarian* and permissive styles and the negative discipline strategies used by authoritarian and permissive adults. I devote chapter 3 to a discussion of positive, responsible, authori*tative* caregiving.

The Authoritarian Style
System Rules

Adults and children face a variety of normal issues as they interact. How an adult deals with the issues or problems is largely determined by his *system rules.* Parents or teachers, confronted with what they think is misbehavior by a 4-year-old, will use one of their system rules in deciding how to deal with the misbehavior. If their rules are adequate, they will likely be able to deal appropriately with the challenging child behavior. But if the caregivers do *not* have a sufficient variety of rules, they might react to the misbehavior with an old, and often inappropriate, response (Broderick & Smith, 1979). Authoritarian parents often fall into this second group.

The following system rules guide the decisions of authoritarian adults in dealing with children: control all behavior, be perfect, blame others when wrong, deny feelings, and do not talk openly or directly (Bredehoft, 1991).

Style of Communication

The communication style of authoritarian, or *troubled,* systems is phoney, hidden, harmful, and destructive. Here are the major patterns they use (Bredehoft, 1991; Satir, 1976):

1. **Blaming.**   These adults are faultfinders, directors, and guilt inducers. They negate others. Blaming creates distance and prevents others from getting too close ("I hope you're satisfied now. We missed the beginning of the movie because of you.").

2. **Intellectualizing.**   These adults take pride in being reasonable. They are like computers in that they show few feelings and use big words to avoid dealing with the real issue or with feelings (Dad to 3-year-old Pete, "Well now. I think you'll understand why we can't get a kitten right now if you just stop and listen carefully.").

3. **Distracting.**   These adults avoid issues and make completely irrelevant statements.

    Example   Four-year-old Jamel was irritated when Sammy grabbed a gelatin wiggler from his plate and told the teacher about the incident. Teacher, "Let's go look at the new tulips that just came up yesterday. Won't that be fun?"

4. **Criticizing.**   These adults focus on the negative and criticize even when a child does something he has been asked to do or when they *think* they are encouraging a child.

    Example   David sat quietly through the entire group time, something his teacher has been requesting for quite a while. Teacher, "David, you finally made it through the group time. It took you long enough, don't you think?"

5. **Ordering.**   These adults deal ineffectively with issues because they order someone to feel a certain way or to do something.

    Example   When Danielle noted how cold the classroom was, her teacher said, "Stop thinking about how cold it is and find something to do!"

Level of Demandingness and Responsiveness

Authoritarian adults are high in demandingness, but their limits are arbitrary and poorly stated. These adults are low in responsiveness, regardless of the child's age. For example, they would very likely ignore their baby's signals or cries, and when they do respond their irritation is evident when they abruptly pick up the baby and perhaps hold the baby too briefly.

Authoritarian caregivers usually view toddlerhood as the time of an inevitable clash of wills as the toddler tries to achieve independence and the parent tries desperately to exert absolute control (which is impossible). With 3- to 8-year-olds these parents also ignore their child's needs and signals, concentrating on what they themselves want, regardless of whether it hurts or is in the best interests of their child.

Authoritarian adults use the rules and communication style of their system to attempt to shape, control, and evaluate the attitudes and behavior of their children according to an absolute set of standards. They place great value on obedience, preservation of order, work, and tradition; discourage verbal give-and-take between parent and child; and suppress individuality and independence or autonomy in their children.

Authoritarian adults view their role as caregiver as more difficult and less enjoyable. They have a rigid interactional style with children and also report negative perceptions of children (Aragona, 1983; Trickett & Susman, 1988).

Authoritarian Adults Use Negative Discipline

Adults in authoritarian systems use a combination of the following *negative discipline strategies,* which reflect their need to control and blame and their inability to deal openly with issues. They tend to focus on short-term control, possess fewer actual discipline skills than more positive adults, and are more critical and less praising of children's behavior (Aragona, 1983). Our concern about the discipline style of authoritarian parents is justified in view of evidence showing that adult ineffective and failed discipline attempts frequently precede child abuse (Gil, 1970; Herrenkohl, Herrenkohl, & Egolf, 1983).

Authoritarian adults rely on punishment.   They equate discipline with punishment, and their system rules seem to foster a tendency to react to challenges from children with old, often hurtful, strategies. Many authoritarian adults rely on coercion to try to make children behave in certain ways, and they use punishment as their main type of discipline regardless of the type of child behavior (Trickett & Kuczynski, 1986).

Example   Six-year-old Bernie left the gate to the backyard fence open, and his puppy escaped. Bernie found the puppy next door, but when Bernie's mother heard about the incident she exploded with anger. "That does it! You can't be trusted to do anything right. That dog is going back to the Humane Society!"

Adults control material goods, and they are in charge of rewards (Hoffman, 1960). Bernie's mother, like many authoritarian adults, used this control over resources unfairly. Bernie's mother punished her son quite harshly by depriving him of his puppy.

Example   At breakfast, Bobby said he wanted to stay home from kindergarten. His mother tried to find out what was wrong and discovered that he was afraid of getting "the chair" at school. Puzzled by this, she went to his school and discovered that children who misbehaved were forced to sit in a chair in the corner for 30 minutes and their names were placed on the "bad children" list on the blackboard.

Bobby's teacher, like Bernie's mother, is relying on punishment to try to get what she thinks would be more appropriate behavior. She punishes but does not teach a better way to act, and makes the punishment even worse by humiliating the children (displaying their names on a list).

See article

Authoritarian adults use corporal punishment.   There are many ways to hurt a child in the name of discipline, and, sadly, we have all seen examples of this hurtful strategy: slapping, hitting with hands or some other instrument, punching, biting, pinching, pushing, yanking. The common thread that ties all of these together is the use of physical force (*coercion*) to try to change behavior.

Why would an adult do something this hurtful to a child? And, once they see the effect, how can they continue to hurt a child? These are good questions that are asked by responsible adults. Researchers have identified possible explanations, all of which may help us as we work to help authoritarian adults change their style. Adults who inflict physical pain either refuse to or cannot take the perspective of the child they have hurt, and they even try to defend what they think is their right to use harsh physical punishment (Bavolek, 1980; Bavolek, Kline, McLaughlin, & Publicover, 1978).

Because they have trouble with perspective-taking, adults who inflict physical pain also tend to minimize the real harm that they do by saying something like "It's for her own good, you know. She's not hurt; I only slapped her face." "Kids bounce back!"

Examples   Two-year-old Judy bit her playmate on the arm. Judy's babysitter, frustrated and angry about Judy's biting, grabbed and bit Judy and said, "How does *that* feel?" Later, the babysitter told a friend that she taught Judy not to bite other children when she showed her how much it hurt to be bitten. Judy did not stop biting.

Two-year-old Sam ran out into the street. His father ran out after him, grabbed him by both arms and started shaking him. Sam's neck and head were whipped back and forth. (Shaking causes serious damage such as hematomas, retinal detachment, and hemorrhages to children of all ages and should *never* be used [Faller, Bowden, Jones, & Hildebrandt, 1981]).

Three-year-old Caitlin, sitting in the grocery cart, tried to reach a box of her favorite cereal and knocked several boxes off the shelf in the process. Her mother slapped her on the face and said, "Cut it out, Caitlin!"

Authoritarian adults use threats.   Garbarino, Guttman, and Seeley (1986) and Tower (1993) cite terrorism as a form of psychological abuse, a form whose goal is to create a climate of fear and anxiety. Threats create fear and anxiety and are negative and hurtful because a child knows that the threat may actually be carried out.

Examples   At the garden store, 5-year-old Tom was fascinated by the flowers and dawdled and poked his nose in different pots. Dad wanted to leave the garden store and said, "You come with me right now or I'll leave you here."

The teacher's aide to Lorna, "Whine at me one more time and just see what happens."

Some authoritarian adults lie to children.   Adults with an authoritarian style do not talk openly and honestly about issues. So, instead of identifying and stating their needs or legitimate limits, some use lies, a form of manipulation, to change or control a child's behavior. However, this ends up eroding whatever trust has been established between them and their children. They also teach children to lie to others and that lying is the lazy person's way of getting out of the hard work of interacting honestly with others. Philosopher Sissela Bok (1978) notes that lying is almost never an acceptable way to interact with others, even with other liars.

Example   Four-year-old Jeannie's parents did not want her to go down to the basement by herself, so they told her that a monster lived there.

Authoritarian adults often use <u>shaming</u>, <u>ridicule</u>, and <u>sarcasm</u>.   Authoritarian adults are also *shame-bound* adults and use shaming strategies to try to change children's behavior. These adults shame or ridicule their children, or allow a sibling to shame a younger child. When a child feels shamed, he thinks that he is fundamentally bad or unworthy. Constant shaming may prevent adapting appropriately to life and may interfere with the development of self-discipline (Bradshaw, 1988; Bredehoft, 1991; Greenberg, 1991). Authoritarian adults, who deny their own feelings, have great difficulty allowing children to acknowledge feelings, especially unpleasant feelings such as anger. As a result, they shame a child's anger (Marion, 1993; Marion, 1994).

Examples   Joe, 6 years old, forgot to take his lunch to school, and his father had to make a trip to drop it off. As he handed the lunch to Joe he slowly shook his head and said, "I just don't know about you, Joe. You can't even remember a simple thing like taking your lunch."

Jon, 3 years old, has three older siblings, all in school. Two are brothers who tease Jon mercilessly. "What a baby, riding a tricycle." "Can you read this, baby?" "Playing with a doll? Your name must be Jane and not Jon." "Look at the weightlifter, Jon. You'll never be able to do that."

Authoritarian adults often use <u>hostile</u> <u>humor</u>.   A sense of humor is a gift we have been given, a gift that helps us put things in perspective and relate to others in a funny, loving way. But there are several ways in which humor can be misused, and one of these misuses is when humor is employed as a weapon, to express hostility. Adults who cloak their anger and hostility as humor demean children. Teasing children in a mean-spirited way or humiliating them is not humor but aggression, and it has no place in a relationship in which both adult and child have a right to respectful treatment.

Example   Joe, who had forgotten his lunch that morning, was going to an after-school baseball game with his dad and his two older brothers when Dad decided to teach Joe a lesson by telling a "funny story." "That's our Joe! You should have seen him standing there with his hand out for his lunch. Think you can remember your lunch tomorrow?"

Some authoritarian adults withdraw love.   Some adults, thinking that a child has misbehaved, show disapproval, not for the child's behavior but for the child. Adults can withdraw love in a variety of ways: refusing to talk or listen to the child, threatening to leave or abandon the child, or glaring at the child (Hoffman, 1970). Adults tend to withdraw love when they have trouble dealing with their own feelings and when they can't figure out how to deal with problems. They rely on an old, ineffective system rule to decide how to deal with the child's annoying behavior.

Withdrawing love has some of the same negative effects as hitting or being sarcastic. The adult does not tell the child why he is angry, and therefore does not help the child understand how the child's behavior caused a problem for others. Withdrawing love does not help a child develop empathy, and it diminishes interaction between adult and child.

Example   Michael was late coming home for dinner, and his family had already started eating. As he ate, Michael sensed that his father was angry because he was silent. Every once in a while Dad glared at Michael and shook his head, but he said nothing.

Authoritarian adults forget or refuse to teach and encourage a different way to behave.   These adults tend to focus on misbehavior, putting lots of energy into telling children what *not* to do. But they forget to teach children what *to* do, and they also tend to ignore children's efforts at doing things right. These adults follow their system's rules, and the rules do not allow the adults to think about new and more appropriate ways to deal with issues.

Example   When 5-year-old Seth cursed, Dad would say, "Knock it off now, Seth!" Seth's dad never told Seth why cursing might not be acceptable and never gave him any other ways to express his emotions.

Impact of Negative Discipline on Children

Authoritarian caregivers deny the effect of their actions on children's development. Responsible adults refuse to use negative discipline, both because it is unethical and because negative discipline has disastrous effects on children.

Negative discipline does not foster self-control.   Self-control evolves slowly as adults transfer control from adult to child as children get older. One of the major system rules followed by authoritarian adults is to control others, so they disagree with the idea that adults should help children make the gradual transition from external control (control by adults) to internal control (control exercised by the child).

Children achieve internal control when adults teach them about how their behavior affects others and when they learn more acceptable behaviors. Authoritarian adults fail to give these important lessons, and their children do not learn or practice self-control. Children whose control is external tend to have lower scores when conscience is measured (Hoffman, 1970). They show little guilt or remorse when they have hurt someone, and they are not very willing to confess a misdeed if they think they can get away with it.

Negative discipline does not suppress unacceptable behavior.   Many adults are convinced that harsh forms of discipline are the best way to suppress what they perceive as misbehavior. The problem is that high levels of punishment can suppress behavior for only for a short time and, surprisingly, can make the undesired behavior even worse (Church, 1963; Rollins & Thomas, 1979).

Undesired behavior seems to occur at a more intense level than it did before the punishment, a phenomenon called *response recovery*. After the punishment is meted out the behavior appears to stop, but after the punishment is withdrawn the behavior often *recovers* and is often more intense.

Adults are negatively reinforced for using harsh discipline.   Authoritarian adults believe that hurtful discipline works because they have actually been *negatively reinforced* for using physical punishment. For example, when Jim was a toddler and kicked his highchair, Dad slapped Jim's legs and Jim stopped kicking. Dad was negatively reinforced for using slapping. The sequence goes like this:

Jim kicked his highchair.

Dad slapped Jim's legs.

Jim was surprised and stopped kicking—for the moment.

Dad thought, "Hmm, that worked." (Dad was *negatively* reinforced because hitting seemed to work to stop an annoying behavior.)

The next day, Jim kicked his highchair again. (When his father hit him the day before, he did not explain why Jim should not kick the chair. Response recovery is operating.)

Dad slapped Jim again. (Remember, slapping *seemed* to work yesterday.)

The real problem here is that hitting Jim became firmly entrenched in his father's repertoire of disciplinary strategies because he soon mistakenly believed that hitting was effective (Patterson, 1982; Patterson & Cobb, 1971). It becomes easy for adults to rely on an ineffective technique, especially when they do not know or do not practice more effective strategies and when they rationalize their harsh behavior.

Negative discipline can and often does become child abuse.   It is a short journey from negative discipline to child abuse. There are several reasons for this. First, we live in a society in which violence is an accepted method of conflict resolution. Many parents reflect the societal acceptance of violence by using violence to solve family problems. Thus the use of physical force for the discipline of children is closely tied to this acceptance and use of violent conflict resolution (Marion, 1983; Steinmetz, 1977).

Second, while negative discipline *seems* to work, adults who use it do not realize just how ineffective negative discipline strategies really are (Sheppard & Willoughby, 1975). Third, as noted above, adults are negatively reinforced for using negative discipline (Patterson & Cobb, 1971) and will tend to use the same method again. Finally, an adult who uses negative discipline soon discovers that he must increase the intensity of the punishment in order for it to be "effective" (Parke & Collmer, 1975).

Example   An abusive mother told the following story in an interview in a film on child abuse:

"Tommy really got to me when he tapped his fork on the table, so I slapped his hand." (Tommy stopped tapping and Mom thought that slapping his hand stopped the obnoxious behavior.)

"You know, he started tapping that fork at the very next meal! So, I slapped his hand again." (Mom used the method that seemed to be so effective. This time, though, he did not stop tapping [response recovery].)

Surprised, Mom hit his hand with greater force. "When I say to stop, you stop!" (Mother and son were now engaged in a "dance of abuse" because Mom discovered that she had to slap her son a little harder to get his attention.)

Tommy, angry about how Mom was treating him, continued to tap the fork, and Mom, infuriated, grabbed her fork and jabbed his hand. (This was the abuse that she herself reported because she was frightened about what she had done.)

It is this gradual intensification of negative discipline that becomes abuse. The mother, given the right circumstances, seriously injured her son. The same sort of progression occurs with psychological punishment as well, as the following example illustrates.

Example   Some families, like Claire's, are tension-ridden. Claire's parents expected Claire to do well in *everything*, but 7-year-old Claire could not meet their unrealistic expectations. Her parents lacked the parenting *skills* to cope effectively and started making *rejecting* statements to Claire when she did not meet their expectations. Claire has developed an explosive temper. Her parents do not know how to deal with Claire's angry outbursts and have begun to make increasingly harsh rejecting comments to her.

Negative discipline fosters aggression in children.   Children who live in authoritarian systems tend to be more aggressive than children who live in more positive systems. They either aim their aggression toward the adult who hurt them (Eron, Walder, & Lefkowitz, 1971; Parke, 1977; Patterson, 1982) or they recycle their anger and use the same degrading behavior with people or animals who had nothing to do with hurting the child.

Example   Mom, angry with 5-year-old Gail about her whining, yelled "Shut up, Gail. I'm sick of your whining!" Gail walked away. Once outside, Gail pushed her 4-year-old brother off his trike and said, "Get off the bike. I want it!"

Negative discipline socializes children into child abuse.   The family is a powerful vehicle for transmitting child-rearing information, and parents who use harsh physical discipline provide a training ground for child abuse. There is a growing body of evidence indicating that children imitate the discipline style of their parents. A possible long-term effect of harsh discipline, then, is the duplication of these aggressive tactics by that child when he becomes a parent (Egeland, Breitenbucher, & Rosenberg, 1980; Egeland, Jacobvitz, & Papatola, 1987; Egeland & Sroufe, 1981; Lefkowitz, 1977; Mead, 1976; Steinmetz, 1977; Walters & Stinnet, 1971).

Children avoid adults who discipline harshly.   Most of us tend to avoid people with whom we are uncomfortable and who ridicule us. Children who are disciplined harshly try to avoid adults who punish them. This avoidance behavior results in *social disruption*, a breaking off of contact between adult and child, which is considered one of the most serious side effects of negative discipline (Azrin & Holz, 1966; Parke, 1977). Adults must build a relationship with a child based on trust if they hope to have a positive influence on the child, and that positive influence is diminished when the child avoids adults.

Negative discipline damages self-esteem.   Children of authoritarian parents tend to have negative self-esteem (Apolonio, 1975; Coopersmith, 1967; Loeb, Horst, & Horton, 1980; Tower, 1993). Children mirror the parental lack of trust that is communicated through negative discipline. Tower (1993) believes that children are in great conflict when parents use negative discipline. The child feels threatened by his parents' aloofness and nonnurturance and tends to blame himself. These children, lacking confidence, also have poor social skills (Baumrind, 1967; Baumrind & Black, 1967).

CASE STUDY ANALYSIS: Jim

Apply information in the section on the *authoritarian* style to Jim's case study at the beginning of the chapter.

1. Jim's father's level of demandingness is high/low. Give reasons for your choice.
2. Dad's level of responsiveness is high/low. Give reasons for your choice.
3. Cite instances when Dad used corporal punishment.
4. One system rule in an authoritarian system is to blame others, and blaming is also a specific pattern of communication. Jim's father used blaming when he . . .
5. Cite examples of how Jim's authoritarian family system is affecting his level of aggression.

The Permissive Style

Baumrind (1967, 1971) labeled parents as permissive if

1. They allow the child to regulate his own behavior and make his own decisions whenever possible.
2. They have very few rules about when the child eats, watches television, or goes to bed.
3. They make few demands for mature behavior, such as showing good manners or carrying out tasks.

4. They avoid imposing any controls or restrictions whenever possible, and they use little punishment.

5. They have a tolerant, accepting attitude toward the child's impulses, even aggressive ones.

Degree of Demandingness and Responsiveness

There are two types of permissiveness. All permissive parents are low in demandingness, setting very few limits on behavior. Permissive parents differ, though, in their degree of responsiveness, with some being very responsive to their children and others not very responsive.

The first type is called *permissive-by-choice*. These are low in demandingness but high in responsiveness, and are permissive because they choose to be permissive. They are convinced that children have rights that ought not to be interfered with by parents (Sears, Maccoby, & Levin, 1957). While these parents do not demand much from their children, they tend to be warm and responsive.

The second type of permissiveness is called *permissive-by-default*. These adults are low in both demandingness *and* responsiveness. This group does not want to be permissive but has drifted into being permissive. They are permissive not because of a strong philosophical belief in a child's rights but because their method of discipline has been so ineffective (Patterson, 1982). They would like to be able to set and maintain limits, but have been so ineffective in getting compliance from their child that they have given up trying and might even begin to see some behaviors, such as aggression, as normal (Olweus, 1980). Once on the slippery slope of permissiveness, these parents could not get off and have become unresponsive and indifferent toward their children—they have become permissive. In its extreme form, permissive-by-default is where child neglect can be found.

Permissive Adults Use Unhelpful Discipline Strategies

Permissive adults tend to use unhelpful discipline. They do not hurt children, but they are not very helpful, either.

Permissive adults often fail to set or maintain appropriate limits.

Examples   Sarah's mother was angry because Sarah, without permission, had invited a friend to play in the yard. However, Sarah's mother had never told her to ask for permission first.

Liz's teacher told the children that they were responsible for cleaning up after they were finished with an activity, and that this included cleaning their space at the art table. When Liz left the art table without cleaning her space, the teacher just shrugged her shoulders and walked away.

Part of the art of child guidance is to be helpful to children by giving them enough of the right type of information so that they will be able to act appropriately under various circumstances. Mom and teacher used nonhurtful, but also unhelpful, strategies. They failed to communicate what the limits were. Liz's teacher failed to follow up with a legitimate limit.

Permissive-by-default adults natter and nag.   These adults have tried to set limits but have been very ineffective. On occasion they still try to set limits, but they tend to talk so much that their child ignores their limits.

CASE STUDY ANALYSIS: Matthew and Joel

Determine the specific permissiveness style of parents in the case studies at the beginning of this chapter.

1. True or False: Matthew's mother sets limits effectively and is effective in getting Matt to comply with her limits. Justify your response.
2. Joel's Mom is high/low in responsiveness. Matt's mom is high/low in responsiveness. Give your reasoning for your choices.
3. Matthew's mother uses nattering and nagging, as shown by the following:
4. Joel's mom seems to have a strong view that her son has rights with which even she ought not to interfere. Give an example.

Summary: Based on my responses to these questions, I would classify Matt's mom's style of caregiving as permissive-by-_____. Joel's mother's style of caregiving is permissive-by-_____.

Permissive adults use erratic or inconsistent discipline.   Adults can be inconsistent in two ways. One type of inconsistent discipline, called *intra*agent inconsistency, refers to an adult's unwillingness or inability to deal with an issue in the same manner each time it occurs. Jerod's teacher, for example, believes that biting other children is not acceptable behavior and decides to tell Jerod "No, no, Jerod. Biting hurts." But she demonstrated intraagent inconsistency by alternately ignoring his biting and then using her stated strategy.

The other type of inconsistent discipline, called *inter*agent inconsistency, refers to disagreement between two or more adults regarding how they will deal with a given issue. Jerod's parents, for example, inconsistently deal with Jerod's biting, with Dad hitting him and Mom ignoring the biting (both techniques are *in*effective and negative [Greenberg, 1991]).

The Impact of Permissiveness on Children

Both children and adults pay a heavy price when adults refuse to make or give up making demands for maturity or to set clear, firm standards of behavior. Children from permissive systems tend to be low in impulse control and self-reliance, dependent, and not very competent either socially or cognitively. These results held when the children were 8 and 9 years old (Baumrind, 1967; 1971).

The Authoritative Style

System Rules

One rule is that there is mutual respect, and another is that rules are overt, negotiable (when possible), and flexible. Rules allow both individual and family needs to be met, and they allow for differences in system members (Bredehoft, 1991).

Communication Style

Communication in an authoritative system is open, honest, congruent, nurturing, validating, and direct.

Level of Demandingness and Responsiveness

Authoritative, responsible, positive parents are high in both demandingness and responsiveness. They set and maintain reasonable, fair limits, but they are also highly responsive to their child, whatever the child's age. They use what early childhood professionals call *developmentally appropriate* child guidance, which means that their guidance is *appropriate for this child at this specific time*.

Authoritative adults expect mature behavior from children and set clear, reasonable limits for them.

Authoritative Adults Use Positive, Developmentally Appropriate Discipline Strategies

An adult with this style uses what this book calls *positive discipline*, a group of strategies that are described in detail in chapter 3.

Impact of the Authoritative Style on Children

Baumrind (1967, 1971, 1977, 1979) and Baumrind and Black (1967) concluded that this pattern was more closely related to greater competence in children than either the authoritarian or the permissive pattern. Children of authoritative parents tended to be socially responsible and independent when first observed in nursery school. When they were 8 and 9 years old, both boys and girls were still quite competent in the cognitive and social spheres.

Several studies indicate that the authoritative pattern—making reasonable, firm demands accepted as legitimate by the child, making demands and giving directions in ways that give the child some degree of choice, and not imposing unreasonable demands—is the pattern most likely to encourage high self-esteem in children (Comstock, 1973; Coopersmith, 1967; McEachern, 1973; Greenberg, 1991).

CASE STUDY ANALYSIS: Krista

Krista's mother has a positive style, the authoritative style. Give evidence by answering these questions.

1. Mother is high in demandingness in that she sets and maintains reasonable fair limits. An example is . . .

2. Explain how Krista's mom demonstrated a high level of responsiveness to Krista when she dealt with Krista's biting.

3. Adults in authoritative systems use a direct, but nurturant, pattern of communication. Krista's mom did this when she . . .

BASIC PROCESSES USED BY ADULTS TO INFLUENCE CHILDREN

All adults, whether they are authoritarian, permissive, or authoritative, influence children both directly and indirectly. In this section you will read about six basic processes used by an adult, whatever his caregiving style, to influence children (Radin, 1982). For example, all adults use the basic process of modeling, but an authoritarian parent models behavior that is very different from the behavior modeled by an authoritative parent. The process is the same, but the content is different.

Modeling

Much human behavior is learned simply by watching someone else perform the behavior and then imitating that person. The other person is the model, and the basic process is *modeling*.

Perhaps the best-known researcher to give us information about this process is Albert Bandura. His research (1971) demonstrates how effectively children learn a behavior just by watching it. Even though children can learn from several types of models (e.g., cartoon characters, pictures in books, and movie or video characters), Bandura's group demonstrated just how powerful adult models are in demonstrating aggression. You will read more about Bandura's work in chapter 10, which discusses different models of child guidance.

Children learn undesirable behaviors—such as aggression or abusiveness—by observing models. An authoritarian parent or teacher who disciplines by hitting

George's grandfather models cooperation in everyday activities like dishwashing.

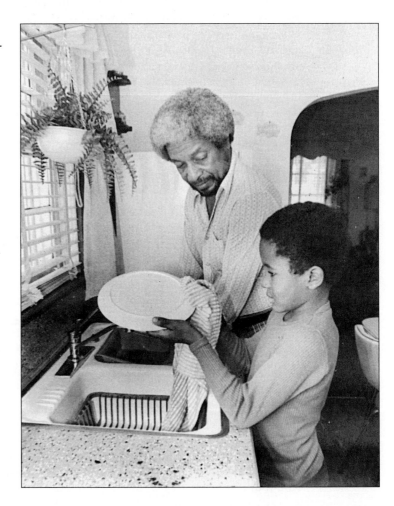

or with sarcasm actually models (demonstrates) aggressive behavior. You will also see evidence throughout this book that children just as effectively learn more desirable and positive behaviors—such as generosity, cooperation, kindness, and helpfulness—through the same basic process. An authoritative adult who uses positive discipline teaches quite a different lesson than does the authoritarian adult.

Direct Instruction and Coaching

Modeling involves showing a child how to do something. Direct instruction, or coaching, involves explicitly telling a child how to perform a skill. There are lots of examples of adults influencing children through direct instruction. Adults give instruction in academic subjects such as math, reading, and other cognitive skills. Adults also instruct children in matters of physical safety, such as traffic safety, safe use of toys, and how to recognize good and bad touches. And adults instruct children about the correct way to hold a baseball bat, build a campfire, or skate a figure eight.

We can also give children instruction in the social sphere: how to make and keep friends, how to take another person's perspective, how to work cooperatively with friends, and how to resolve conflicts (King & Kirschenbaum, 1992).

Using Reinforcement and Feedback

Feedback is critical to learning. Feedback gives a child information about how he is doing and allows for making changes. Maintaining a new skill is easier with a specific type of feedback called *reinforcement. Social reinforcement* refers to smiles, positive attention, praise, or positive physical contact. *Tangible reinforcement* refers to things like toys or food. Some adults use a *generalized reinforcement*, such as points, tokens, or smiley faces on a chart, and have the child acquire points or tokens for desired behavior and then trade them for an object or event that the child finds especially desirable.

Reinforcement, then, is the basic process that any adult may use. An important thing to remember, however, is that adults reinforce a wide variety of behaviors in children, and they do not always agree on what constitutes appropriate behavior. For example, some adults reinforce their children for fighting and hurting others, while others reinforce cooperation and generosity. What the adult reinforces is influenced by his value system and general caregiving style.

Managing the Child's Environment

Adults manage a child's environment by providing physical materials, the setting in which the child exists, and a time schedule. Researchers have examined the effects of a child's physical or temporal environment on several areas of development. For example, parents have a significant influence on their child's sex-typed behavior when they provide boys and girls with different toys and clothes (Rheingold & Cook, 1975).

Research has also focused on the effect of a child's physical environment on social behaviors such as cooperation and aggression (Hartup, 1983; Phyffe-Perkins, 1980). Throughout this book you will read about how the physical environment may affect a child's behavior. The chapters on aggression and prosocial behavior will show that adults can influence these behaviors by providing certain types of toys and materials.

Stating Expectations of Desired Behaviors

Example   Jane's dad said, "Hi, Mrs. Berg . . . How are you feeling now? . . . Let me open that door for you." To his daughter Jane he said, "Please push the other door open too, Jane."

Jane, in kindergarten, is very likely to be influenced by her father's ability and willingness to define behavior he considers appropriate. Authoritative adults like Jane's dad develop good rules or limits and then communicate them clearly to children. On the other hand, authoritarian adults tend to set too many arbitrary limits, and permissive adults may fail to communicate expectations at all.

Encouraging Children to Modify Attitudes and Understanding

Adults better influence children by remembering that infants, toddlers, and young children have a central nervous system that enables them to process information and make sense of the world. Children can modify their behavior when someone takes the time to present them with additional or different information in a way that is appropriate to the child's particular level of development. Focus on teaching children to understand why they should or should not do certain things. Be gently firm about the need for the children to act more appropriately, and make it clear that there is a *reason* for acting more appropriately.

An effective way to do this is to *help a child become more empathic*. The goal is to gradually help a child to understand how his actions affect others and to gradually be able to take somebody else's perspective. Like most learning, this takes place gradually over a period of years and begins in infancy. In the case study at the beginning of this chapter, Krista's mother did a good job of helping Krista, a toddler, understand that biting hurt Robert. The goal here is *not* to induce excessive guilt or to shame a child. A good way to arouse empathy is to describe another's situation in an open, direct way that still validates the other person and that does not accuse him.

Examples   After they opened the doors for Mrs. Berg, Dad said to Jane, "Mrs. Berg just got out of the hospital, Jane. She really needs help right now."

Teacher to 4-year-old Bill, "I see from the job chart that it's your day to feed the gerbils. I'll bet that they're hungry. So, get the gerbil food and I'll help you put it in their house."

"I think the rabbit's hungry! And I think she likes her snack as much as we like ours."

Same teacher to 3-year-old Matt, "No, Matt. Hitting hurts. Use words to tell him that you're mad."

Both adults avoided sarcasm, threats, and accusations while focusing on how things probably were for the other person or animal. Arousing a child's empathy—having him "walk a mile in somebody else's shoes"—is a powerful technique because it encourages the child to examine and begin to understand how his behavior may affect someone else.

A common thread linking different forms of antisocial behavior, including child abuse, is the perpetrator's inability to take another person's perspective (Chalmers & Townsend, 1990; Chandler, 1973). Preventing abuse involves helping abusive adults learn social perspective-taking. Helping children become empathic, to take the perspective of others, then, is an important task for caregivers during a child's first 8 years.

SUMMARY OF KEY CONCEPTS

1. Adults have a *style of caregiving* through which they set the emotional tone of homes and classrooms, and this style is much more than a set of discipline strategies. Your caregiving style is rooted in your personal history in your family system and your community. Your family's *system rules* and *style of communication* are major determinants of your style. You will notice that each

style has a specific combination of *level of demandingness and responsiveness*, and that each style adopts certain *discipline strategies*.

2. Diana Baumrind is a researcher who has identified different styles of caregiving, and other family scientists have described system rules and communication patterns in three different systems: *Authoritarian* caregivers share a set of characteristics based on the need to control, to blame, and to deny feelings. They use negative discipline strategies which have a harmful effect on a child's development. *Permissive* caregivers either cannot effectively set or refuse to set limits. They differ in level of responsiveness. *Authoritative* caregivers, skillful in *developmentally appropriate child guidance*, use positive discipline, which grows almost directly out of a variety of effective system rules and healthy communication patterns. Each style of caregiving tends to have a different effect on a child's development.

3. All adults, regardless of their style of caregiving, influence children through several specific processes. For example, most adult caregivers influence children when they model behavior, but what adults model depends on their general style. Authoritarian or even abusive caregivers demonstrate a model of aggression when they use harsh discipline, but responsible, authoritative caregivers present a much more positive model for children.

OBSERVE CHILD GUIDANCE IN ACTION
Recognizing Negative or Unhelpful Discipline

Observe adults and children together in several different settings. Use the following format to write brief descriptions of the interaction. Be specific and write only what you see or hear, e.g., what the adult and child said or did. Avoid writing your opinion.

Determine from your observations whether the adults used negative or unhelpful discipline.

Date: _____

Setting: _____

Approximate age of child: _____

Describe what the child did or said. (Include direct quotes.)

Describe what the adult did or said. (Include direct quotes.)

Describe the outcome.

The name of this negative or unhelpful strategy is:

REFERENCES

Apolonio, F. J. (1975). Preadolescents' self-esteem, sharing behavior, and perceptions of parental behavior. *Dissertation Abstracts International, 35*, 3406B.

Aragona, J. A. (1983). Physical child abuse: An interactional analysis (Doctoral dissertation, University of South Florida). *Dissertation Abstracts International, 44*, 125B.

Azrin, N. H., & Holz, W. C. (1966). Punishment. In W. K. Honig (Ed.), *Operant behavior: Areas of research and application*. New York: Appleton-Century-Crofts.

Bandura, A. (1971). Analysis of modeling processes. In A. Bandura (Ed.), *Psychological modeling*. Chicago: Aldine-Asherton.

Baumrind, D. (1967). Child care practices anteceding three patterns of preschool behavior. *Genetic Psychology Monographs, 75*, 43–88.

Baumrind, D. (1971). Current patterns of parental authority. *Developmental Psychology Monograph, 4*(1, Pt. 2).

Baumrind, D. (1977, March). *Socialization determinants of personal agency.* Paper presented at the meeting of the Society for Research in Child Development, New Orleans, LA.

Baumrind, D. (1979). *Sex-related socialization effects.* Paper presented at the meeting of the Society for Research in Child Development, San Francisco, CA.

Baumrind, D., & Black, A. E. (1967). Socialization practices associated with dimensions of competence in preschool boys and girls. *Child Development, 38*, 291–327.

Bavolek, S. (1980). Primary prevention of child abuse: The identification of high-risk parents. Unpublished manuscript, University of Wisconsin—Eau Claire.

Bavolek, S., Kline, D. F., McLaughlin, J. A., & Publicover, P. R. (1978). The development of the adolescent parenting inventory (API), identification of high risk adolescents prior to parenthood. Unpublished manuscript, Utah State University, Department of Special Education.

Becker, W. C. (1954). Consequences of different kinds of parental discipline. In M. L. Hoffman & L. S. Hoffman (Eds.), *Review of child development research* (Vol. 1). New York: Russell Sage Foundation.

Bok, S. (1978). *Lying: Moral choice public and private life*. New York: Partheon Books.

Bradshaw, J. (1988). *Healing the shame that binds you*. Deerfield Beach, FL: Health Communications.

Bredehoft, D. (1991). No more shame on you: Discipline without shame. *Family Forum, 6*–7. St. Paul, MN: Minnesota Council on Family Relations.

Broderick, C. & Smith, J. (1979). The general systems approach to the family. In W. Burr, R. Hill, F. I. Nye, & I. Reiss (Eds.), *Contemporary theories about the family* (Vol. 2). New York: Free Press.

Chalmers, J. B., & Townsend, M. A. R. (1990). The effects of training in social perspective-taking on socially maladjusted girls. *Child Development, 61*, 178–190.

Chandler, M. J. (1973). Egocentrism and antisocial behavior: The assessment and training of social perspective-taking skills. *Developmental Psychology, 9*(3), 326–332.

Church, R. M. (1963). The varied effects of punishment on behavior. *Psychological Review, 70*, 369–402.

Comstock, M. L. C. (1973). Effects of perceived parental behavior on self-esteem and adjustment. *Dissertation Abstracts International, 34*, 46513.

Coopersmith, S. (1967). *The antecedents of self-esteem*. San Francisco: W. H. Freeman.

Egeland, B., Breitenbucher, M., & Rosenberg, D. (1980). Prospective study of the significance of life stress in the etiology of child abuse. *Journal of Consulting and Classical Psychology, 48*(2), 194–205.

Egeland, B., Jacobvitz, D., & Papatola, K. (1987). Intergenerational continuity of abuse. In R. Gelles & H. Lancaster (Eds.), *Child abuse and neglect: Biosocial dimensions.* Hawthorne, NY: Aldine deGruyter.

Egeland, B., & Sroufe, L. (1981). Developmental sequelae of maltreatment in infancy. In R. Rizley & D. Cicchetti (Eds.), *New directions in child development: Developmental perspectives in child maltreatment.* San Francisco: Jossey Bass.

Eron, L. D., Walder, L. O., & Lefkowitz, M. M. (1971). *Learning of aggression in children.* Boston: Little, Brown.

Faller, K., Bowden, M. L., Jones, C. O., & Hildebrandt, M. Types of child abuse and neglect. In K. Faller (Ed.), *Social work with the abused child.* New York: Free Press.

Garbarino, J., Guttman, E., & Seeley, J. W. (1986). *The psychologically battered child.* San Francisco: Jossey-Bass.

Gil, D. G. (1970). *Violence against children: Physical child abuse in the United States.* Cambridge, MA: Harvard University Press.

Greenberg, P. (1991). *Character development: Encouraging self-esteem and self-discipline in infants, toddlers, & two-year-olds.* Washington, DC: NAEYC.

Hartup, W. W. (1983). Peer Relations. In P. Mussen (Ed.), *Handbook of child psychology* (Vol. 4). New York: Wiley.

Herrenkohl, R., Herrenkohl, E., & Egolf, B. P. (1983). Circumstances surrounding the occurrence of child maltreatment. *Journal of Consulting and Clinical Psychology, 51,* 424–431.

Hoffman, M. L. (1960). Power assertion by the parent and its impact on the child. *Child Development, 31,* 129–143.

Hoffman, M. L. (1970). Moral development. In P. Mussen (Ed.), *Carmichael's manual of child psychology* (Vol. 2). New York: Wiley.

King, C., & Kirschenbaum, D. (1992). *Helping young children develop social skills.* Pacific Grove, CA: Brooks/Cole Publishing Company.

Lefkowitz, M. M. (1977). *Growing up to be violent: A longitudinal study of the development of aggression.* New York: Pergamon.

Loeb, R. C., Horst, L., & Horton, P. J. (1980). Family interaction patterns associated with self-esteem in preadolescent girls and boys. *Merrill-Palmer Quarterly, 26,* 203–217.

Marion, M. (1983). Child compliance: A review of the literature with implications for family life education. *Family Relations, 32,* 545–555.

Marion, M. (1993, April). Responsible anger management: The long bumpy road. *Day Care and Early Education,* pp. 4–9.

Marion, M. (1994). Encouraging the development of responsible anger management in young children. *Early Child Development and Care, 97,* 155–163.

McEachern, L. V. H. (1973). An investigation of the relationships between self-esteem, the power motives and democratic, authoritarian, or laissez-faire home atmosphere. *Dissertation Abstracts International, 34,* 572A.

Mead, D. E. (1976). *Six approaches to childrearing*. Provo, UT: Brigham Young University Press.

Olweus, D. (1980). Familial and temperamental determinants of aggression behavior in adolescents—A causal analysis. *Developmental Psychology, 16*, 644–660.

Parke, R. D. (1977). Some effects of punishment on children's behavior—Revisited. In R. D. Parke & E. M. Hetherington (Eds.), *Contemporary readings in child psychology*. New York: McGraw-Hill.

Parke, R. D., & Collmer, C. W. (1975). *Child abuse: An interdisciplinary analysis*. Chicago: University of Chicago Press.

Patterson, G. R. (1982). *Coercive family process*. Eugene, OR: Castalia Press.

Patterson, G. R., & Cobb, J. A. (1971). A dyadic analysis of "aggressive" behavior. In J. P. Hill (Ed.), *Minnesota symposia on child psychology* (Vol. 5). Minneapolis: University of Minnesota Press.

Phyffe-Perkins, E. (1980). Children's behavior in preschool settings: The influence of the physical environment. In L. G. Katz (Ed.), *Current topics in early childhood education* (Vol. 3). Norwood, NJ: Ablex.

Radin, N. (1982). The unique contribution of parents to childrearing: The preschool years. In S. Moore & C. Cooper (Eds.), *The young child: Reviews of research* (Vol. 3). Washington, DC: NAEYC.

Rheingold, H. L., & Cook, K. V. (1975). The contents of boys' and girls' rooms as an index of parents' behavior. *Child Development, 46*, 459–463.

Rollins, B. C., & Thomas, D. L. (1979). Parental support, power, and control techniques in the socialization of children. In W. R. Burr, R. Hill, F. Nye, & I. Reiss (Eds.), *Contemporary theories about the family* (Vol. 1). New York: Free Press.

Satir, V. (1976). *Making contact*. Millbrae, CA: Celestial Arts.

Sears, R. R., Maccoby, E. E., & Levin, H. (1957). *Patterns of child rearing*. Evanston, IL: Row Peterson.

Sheppard, W. G., & Willoughby, R. H. (1975). *Child behavior*. Chicago: Rand-McNally.

Steinmetz, S. K. (1977). *The cycle of violence: Assertive, aggressive and abusive family interaction*. New York: Praeger.

Tower, C. (1993). *Understanding child abuse and neglect* (2nd ed.). Boston: Allyn and Bacon.

Trickett, P., & Kuczynski, L. (1986). Children's misbehaviors and parental discipline strategies in abusive and nonabusive families. *Developmental Psychology, 22*, 115–123.

Trickett, P., & Susman, E. (1988). Parental perceptions of child-rearing practices in physically abusive and nonabusive families. *Developmental Psychology, 24*(2), 270–276.

Walters, J., & Stinnett, N. (1971). Parent-child relationships: A decade of review of research. *Journal of Marriage and the Family, 33*, 70–111.

3

Positive Discipline Strategies:
Direct Guidance

Chapter Overview

After reading and studying this chapter, you will be able to

▼ *Define* discipline.

▼ *Defend* the position that discipline can be either positive or negative.

▼ *Define* positive discipline.

▼ *List* and *explain* how to use several positive discipline strategies, and *explain* why each is a positive strategy.

▼ *Describe* the effect of positive discipline on a child's development and on the adult-child relationship.

▼ *Demonstrate* how to use specific positive discipline strategies.

▼ *Analyze* case studies by *determining* how positive discipline strategies were or could be used.

Discipline: A word derived from the Latin disciplina,
teaching, learning, and discipulus, *a pupil.*

(Webster's Dictionary)

CASE STUDIES: Discipline

Jenny

Jenny, 4 years old, and Mom went to the store to buy a lunchbox for Jenny. It had to be purchased that day. They were in a hurry, and had just enough time to pick out the lunchbox and still get to the bank before it closed. Mom had just enough money for the lunchbox but not for anything else, but she forgot to tell Jenny about the hurried nature of the trip or the shortage of money. At the store Jenny started the "Look-Mommy-I-want-that-WHY-can't-I-have-it" game. "Mom, can I get the thermos?" "No, Jenny. No thermos." "But Mom, I want the thermos. It has Pebbles on it!" "Jenny, stop it. No thermos." "Why, Mom?"

At this point, Jenny increased her whining, and her mother responded with, "Shut up, Jenny!" Jenny then seemed to lose control and started crying. Mom grabbed her wrist, yanked her around and yelled, "Knock it off, Jenny, or you'll get what's coming to you!" (Jenny's mother typically uses corporal punishment.)

The Infants and Toddlers

In the infant/toddler room of the child care center, 7-month-old Yer grabbed the teacher's hair. The teacher removed Yer's hand and said, "O-o-o-h! Look at the birds, Yer," as she turned toward the window. Yer smiled broadly at the birds at the feeder. Seventeen-month-old Janie scooted across the room toward the kitchen area, and the teacher scooped her up and carried her back to a small table, singing, "Janie, Janie, bubbles, bubbles. Let's make some bubbles." "Bubbles, bubbles . . ." chanted Janie. When two 23-month-olds banged their paper cups on the table, the teacher placed her hands lightly on each small hand, saying "Listen carefully. Tell me whether you want grape juice or orange juice. John, tell me what kind of juice you want." John said, "I want grape!"

Mike

In the same child care center, in the room for older children, 4-year-old Mike stood next to the gerbil house and tapped rhythmically on the screen lid. The teacher's aide noted, "Good sound, Mike, but I can't let you disturb the gerbils. So I want you to come with me to the music corner to choose a drum for you to play." Later that day Mike drummed on the gerbil cage lid again, and the aide was gently persistent in her limit that he use drums and not the gerbil house. Mike got the drums and did not try to drum on the animal's house again.

Skillful teachers use a large number of different positive *strategies*, each strategy appropriate with a specific child at a specific time. They realize that they are most effective when they have a large repertoire of skills to meet the individual needs of the children.

Example   Mr. Cunningham repeated a limit to Meg, used an I-message with Juan, listened actively to Sean, who was upset that someone had run over his toys, ignored the why game two children played when it was time for cleanup, used a cue to remind Darnell to use his new behavior of washing hands, redirected behavior several times by using substitution, and taught Harry to withdraw from anger-arousing situations and then to responsibly manage angry feelings.

This teacher has achieved his high level of skill in the art and science of child guidance through learning, practicing, making mistakes, evaluating how *strategies* work, and learning and practicing some more. Now, when he is confronted with a specific situation, he automatically thinks about how to match a specific positive discipline strategy to a specific situation and child's needs. He has become increasingly more *skilled* in guiding children effectively.[1]

WHAT IS DISCIPLINE?

Discipline is any attempt by an adult to control or change a child's behavior (Brown, 1979; Rollins & Thomas, 1979). I repeat: *any* attempt. Adults use an amazingly large number of strategies when working with children. Their choices are based on their style of caregiving: authoritarian adults attempt to control children with hurtful strategies such as hitting or isolation, while more responsible caregivers use positive methods such as explaining rules, teaching new behaviors, and redirecting. This definition implies that discipline is merely a way to control children, but it is actually much more (Marion, 1992).

Discipline Is a Process

Like personality, positive, effective discipline is an evolving process, one that continues throughout the lifetime of a relationship between an adult and a child (Erikson, 1963). Discipline is a process acknowledging that all members of a system affect each other and that system members change over time. Adults in this type of system realize that both they and children have individual temperaments that affect how they deal with others (Grusec & Kuczynski, 1980). It is a process in which adults have a core set of beliefs about interaction with children, and it is a process that gives adults permission to search for new information about discipline as they and their children develop.

Discipline Tells Us How a Person Views the Use of Power

An adult's general style of discipline tells us how she views the use of power in relationships in general and how she views the use of power in child guidance in

---

[1]   The author thanks Stephanie Frantz of Cedar Rapids, Iowa, for differentiating between a skill and a strategy at a conference held by the Grant Wood Educational Agency in Cedar Rapids, March 1993.

particular. Just as some adults coerce or force other adults to do what they want them to do by exerting raw power, so do some adults use their superior physical size and control of resources to manipulate children. Adults who sexually abuse children use their more powerful status in a grossly unfair, reprehensible way to satisfy their adult needs at the expense of powerless children. Other adults, who have an authori*tarian* style, use their power unfairly when they use negative discipline.

Authoritative adults have a different perspective on power. They refuse to manipulate others by forcing them to do certain things. They do not even think about having power. Instead, they focus on their legitimate authority as an adult who has responsibilities to children but who also has rights as an adult. They realize that they have a responsibility to keep children safe and to act as socializing agents, and they realize that the differences between adults and children place children in a less powerful position. They accept their preschoolers' control needs, that is, the children's need to see themselves as competent, as having choices, and as being worthy of respect (Bishop & Rothbaum, 1992).

Authoritative adults believe that their responsibilities are balanced by legitimate rights, among them the right to expect certain types of mature behavior from children, depending on the child's developmental capabilities, and the right to establish and follow through with reasonable limits.

Discipline Is Learned

Caregiving style and specific discipline strategies are learned in childhood by observing other people: parents, teachers, television parents, adults in books, scout and church youth leaders, and others. Our learning continues as we observe, read about, and talk to others about child-rearing and discipline.

Discipline Is Powerful

An adult's caregiving style and discipline strategies have a powerful and long-lasting effect on a child's development. Children are influenced by a variety of factors, such as peers, church, and television, but they are also greatly influenced by their caregivers. Through their caregiving style and discipline strategies, adults affect how a child values herself and others, how she treats herself and others, how she solves interactional problems, how helpful or cooperative or generous she becomes, and her level of popularity (Dekovic & Janssens, 1992).

Discipline Can Be Positive or Negative

The word *discipline* is an umbrella term, and in itself it carries no positive or negative meaning. The word is derived from the Latin *discipulus,* a pupil of the teachings or example of another person.

The leader may set a good example to be followed (e.g., Jesus, Ghandi, and Martin Luther King). Responsible, authoritative adults who also fall into this category set a positive example that is imitated by their children. Other leaders, who set negative examples (e.g., Adolf Hitler, David Koresh, and terrorists), are also followed by large numbers of people. Adults who use discipline that hurts children set an example that is very likely to be imitated because children will observe, learn from, and follow the example of an adult, regardless of whether the adult uses positive or negative discipline.

There is a lot of confusion about whether discipline is positive or negative. Adults who use negative, hurtful discipline link discipline with punishment. Adults who use positive discipline link discipline with teaching or guidance, and believe in treating children with respect in the process of discipline.

Some professionals deny that discipline can be negative. However, our effectiveness in helping families caught in the web of hurtful negative discipline requires that, as professionals, we acknowledge that *all* forms of discipline exist. We best help these families change to a more positive approach when we understand what they do to children and why, and when we teach them a more positive approach that they can accept.

POSITIVE DISCIPLINE STRATEGIES

Positive discipline is any adult disciplinary practice that treats children with respect and dignity. It is a child-centered, unselfish approach focusing on what a child needs and not so much on what an adult wants or needs (Pulkkinen, 1982). It is based on the ability to take a child's perspective and to demonstrate empathy toward the child. It is rooted in the beliefs that adults do not have the right to use raw power over a child and that adults have a responsibility to set the stage for appropriate child behavior. Positive discipline is "self-responsible" adult behavior used by authoritative adults.

Positive discipline focuses on teaching rather than on punishment. It gives children enough of the right type of information that they need for learning and practicing appropriate behavior. It is always helpful to a child and teaches a positive lesson to children about relationships.

You will work with or have worked with lots of children in your career. Each child's unique genetic make-up, temperament, personality, family system, and other experiences have created an *individual*. Each child's needs call for individual solutions to the expression of those needs. Therefore, discipline strategies should reflect this approach.

This section describes a large number of specific positive discipline strategies (see Figure 3.1). The value in knowing about these strategies and how to use each one effectively is that you will have more tools—a larger repertoire of positive strategies—for helping individual children meet their needs. You will be able to choose the most effective strategy in a variety of situations and will not be locked into dealing with each situation in the same way.

I have intentionally arranged the strategies in the order presented. Positive discipline begins with adult behaviors: good limit setting, clearly communicating limits, teaching more appropriate behavior and giving cues for the new behavior,

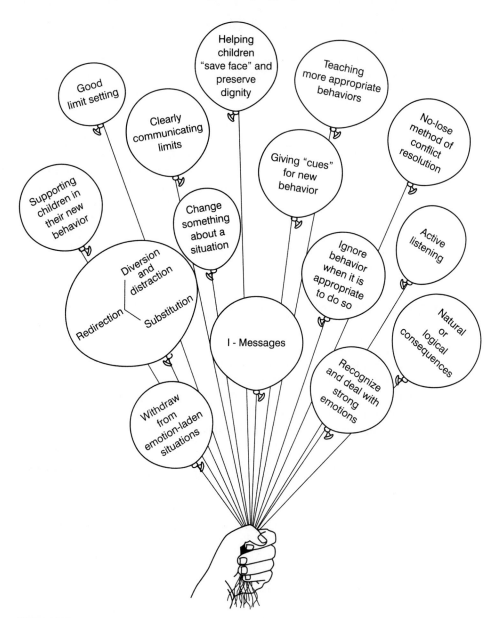

Figure 3.1
Positive discipline strategies

supporting children in their new behavior, changing something about a situation, and ignoring behavior when it is appropriate to do so.

Positive discipline continues when adults respond to typical interactional problems with positive, helpful strategies: redirection, active listening, I-messages, natural or logical consequences, conflict resolution, recognizing and dealing with strong emotions, and withdrawal from emotion-laden situations.

The core of positive discipline strategies, however, is the last one presented in this chapter: helping children save face and preserve their dignity in discipline situations. This is the sine qua non, the absolutely essential element, in positive discipline.

Develop Appropriate Limits

Adults influence children by stating their expectations for desired behavior and helping children understand that there are boundaries, or limits, on behavior. Authoritative caregivers understand the importance of proper boundaries in relationships in general and appropriate limits in an adult-child relationship in particular. They figure out and clearly communicate limits that will be most helpful in encouraging children to behave appropriately. They understand what a good limit is and what appropriate limits do for children (Marion, 1991, 1992; Minuchin, 1974).

Appropriate Limits Focus on Important Things and Are Never Arbitrary

Good limits focus on important, not on trivial, things. They protect children's health and safety, encourage the development of healthy self-control, and transmit our values of dignified, fair, humane treatment of people and animals to children.

Health and safety rules.   Disease spreads easily in group settings for children. Appropriate limits are designed to protect the health of both adults and children.

Examples   Thorough handwashing, proper handling of food, washing and sterilization of toys and other equipment, use of tissues when sneezing, handwashing after sneezing, wearing of appropriate bad-weather clothing, and proper diapering routines are all important in group settings for children.

Appropriate limits ensure safety. Think about safety on different levels. One level governs the use of toys and equipment. Typical rules might be "You can ride your trike, but crashing is not allowed," or "You can only play inside the playground fence."

Another level of safety rules deals with a child's inner feeling of safety and security. Children feel safe when they know that they will not be hurt; therefore, a safe place for children has rules that forbid hurting others.

Examples   "Yes, Joe. You *are* angry, and that's OK, but I won't let you hit Jim."

"Use words to tell him that you want your truck back. No hitting in this room. Hitting hurts."

Center director to teachers in a workshop, "In this center, we use positive discipline. This means that we refuse to hurt children. We NEVER shake children of any age, we NEVER use corporal punishment, and we NEVER say anything that is degrading or demeaning."

Encouraging healthy self-control through limits.   We help children achieve internal control and learn how to work well with others when we encourage them to make choices and help them experience safe consequences for their choices.

Reasonable, fair rules help children develop self-control because they clearly communicate choices to be made and safe consequences for those choices (e.g., having a child paint only on her own paper or choosing another activity).

Good limits help children develop a firm set of values about respectful treatment of others.   Responsible adults set and maintain limits prohibiting degrading or hurtful treatment of others. Examples include rules on humane treatment of animals ("Hold the kitten gently") and forbidding name-calling and making fun of others ("I think Donna feels sad because you called her 'fatso.' No name-calling in this room, Tom").

Good Limits Are Developmentally Appropriate

The National Association for the Education of Young Children (NAEYC) published the booklet *Developmentally Appropriate Practice* (Bredekamp, 1986), which focuses on appropriate practice in several key areas, including guidance. A part of developmentally appropriate guidance is the area of limit setting based on a child's developmental level, that is, setting limits that are suitable for a particular child at a specific age (Toepfer, Reuter, & Maurer, 1972).

Authoritative adults understand how children grow and develop. They are aware of the rapid cognitive, linguistic, motor, and social changes that set the stage for the development of self-control during the first 8 years of life. As children grow and develop, authoritative adults begin to expect different behavior from them. They are ready and willing to examine limits as children get older to make sure that the rules are valid for a child's changing developmental level. For example, an authoritative teacher might permit a 2½-year-old to climb only to the second rung on a rope ladder but allow the same child at age 4 to climb higher because she has greater motor skills and self-control.

Help Children Accept Limits by Setting the Stage and by Clearly Communicating Limits

Be Alert to a Situation, Focus a Child's Attention, and Use Appropriate Nonverbal Cues

Many adults start by making a request (they ask for *task compliance*) and fail to get compliance because they have not paid attention to setting the stage so that a child can accept the limit (Schaffer & Crook, 1980; Stayton, Hogan, & Ainsworth, 1971). Other adults, who believe that children are naturally compliant (Haswell, Hock, & Wenar, 1981; Lytton, 1977; Lytton & Zwirner, 1975; Minton, Kagan, & Levine, 1971), are adept at tuning in to a situation and orienting a child properly. Here are some practical hints for helping children accept reasonable limits:

▼   *Observe what the child is doing before stating a limit.* Is a child reading the last two pages of a book? Does she have headphones on? If Carly is reading when lights are blinked and clean-up announced to the group, she will very likely try to finish the book before putting things away.

▼ *Decrease the distance between you and a child.* Walk over to the reading area, for example, and then bend or stoop so that you can talk directly to Carly (Satir, 1976).

▼ *Get a child's attention.* Touch Carly on the arm and look at her directly but in a nonthreatening way. The use of nonthreatening nonverbal cues and appropriate physical contact is essential with toddlers (Schaffer & Crook, 1980) and is highly recommended with preschoolers, especially those who have not been very compliant (Kramer, 1977).[2]

▼ *Direct a child's visual attention to a specific object or task.* Show Carly the puzzle piece you are holding and then point to the puzzle table. (This is called *orientation compliance;* its purpose is to properly orient the child before stating a limit or making a request.)

▼ *Have the child make contact with a specific object.* Put the puzzle piece in Carly's hand. Walk with her to the puzzle table and pull the puzzles she worked with toward her. (This is called *contact compliance;* its purpose is to help the child tune in to the task at hand before she is asked to do anything specific.)

▼ *Make your specific request (ask for task compliance).* Carly is much more likely to comply with your request because you have properly oriented her; that is, suggest that she put the puzzle pieces away when she is at the puzzle table holding the puzzle pieces rather than when she is sitting in another area listening to a story when you blink the lights and announce cleanup time.

▼ *Work with a child if it seems appropriate.* As Carly works on her puzzle, you can work on one, too, and then you can both place the finished puzzles on the shelf or on a puzzle rack.

State Limits Effectively

Our goal in the art of child guidance is to be helpful to children. Helping them comply with necessary limits means that we must clearly communicate enough information so that they are able to carry out a suggestion:

▼ *Speak naturally, but speak slowly enough that the child hears everything you say.*

▼ *Use concrete words and short sentences when stating limits.* "Put your puzzle in this first slot of the puzzle rack" tells Carly exactly where the finished puzzle goes and is a more effective thing to say than "Put it over there." Avoid using

---

[2] A note on appropriate physical contact: it is a source of comfort to a young child and is a part of the style of sensitive, supportive, encouraging adults (Sroufe & Ward, 1980). Appropriate physical contact reassures a child, is never imposed on a child, and is given in response to the child's needs. With recent concern about child abuse in child care centers, it would be prudent for center personnel to be clear about the center's policy of appropriate physical contact between staff and children. This policy must also be clearly communicated to and discussed with parents (Phyffe-Perkins & Birtwell, 1989).

PROBLEM FOR YOU TO SOLVE: Tell This Child What to Do

Try your hand at telling a child what you want her to do rather than what you don't want her to do. Change the following statements. Be positive. Be polite. Be firm.

1. "Stop banging on the piano!" (What do you want the child to do?)
2. "Don't pick that flower." (What do you want the child to do? Give an alternative.)
3. "Stop flapping your arms so I can braid your hair."
4. "Stop making so much noise while the baby sleeps."

---

abstract words or phrases like "in a little while," "be a good boy," or "knock it off."

▼ *Tell a child exactly what to do rather than what not to do, and be as positive as possible.* It is more helpful to say "Use this tissue to clean your nose" than "Don't pick your nose!"

▼ *Use suggestions whenever possible.* Suggestions are statements phrased as a request or a question: "I have an idea, Jenny. Let's write what we want to buy at the store on this piece of paper and take it with us today." They result in compliance more frequently than more restrictive commands (Forehand, Doleys, Hobbs, & Resick, 1976; Lytton, 1979; Minton et al., 1971; Peele & Routh, 1978).

▼ *Use nonrestrictive, self-responsible commands when you think it is necessary to use a command.* For example, "I want you to put the puzzles away now, Carly." This type of command tends to elicit much more compliance than do more restrictive commands like, "Carly, get over to the puzzle table and put the puzzles away right now." Restrictive commands seem to arouse anger and foster noncompliance because they simply give an order (Green, Forehand, & MacMahon, 1975).

▼ *Give choices when appropriate.* For example, "Do you want to put the cat or dog puzzle together first, Carly?" Avoid giving a choice when the child really has no choice, for example, "Do you want to put away the puzzles, Carly?" Use *when-then* statements if appropriate. "When you put away the puzzles, then you can read the other story." (Carly will get to listen to the other story only when the puzzles are put away.)

▼ Have you been clear? Get feedback. When it seems necessary, *ask a child to tell you what you have said.* You will discover if you have been clear or if you need to restate your limit. Avoid just asking if she understands—the word *understand* is too abstract.

Time and Pace Suggestions Well

Good *timing* and *pacing* of limits helps children accept and comply with limits (Schaffer & Crook, 1980). You have good *timing* if you are focused and remain aware of what children are doing before stating a limit. You have good *pacing* of instructions and suggestions if you give instructions at a rate the child can easily deal with or if you ask a child to work at a speed that matches her developmental capabilities.

Here are suggestions for timing and pacing your limits properly:

▼ *Issue only a few suggestions at a time.* "Hang your painting. . . . Now, wash the part of the table on which you worked. . . OK . . . nice and clean. . . . Now, wash your hands and hang up your apron."

▼ *Avoid giving a chain of limits.* Children tend not to remember and therefore not comply with a rapid-fire series of commands.

▼ *Allow enough time for the child to process the information and carry out the limit.*

▼ *Allow enough time for the child to complete a task before issuing another suggestion.*

▼ *Repeat a limit if necessary, but do it effectively.* Avoid restating the limit every 5 seconds or simply stating the limit again in exactly the same way, because this tends to result in noncompliance (Forehand et al., 1976).

▼ *Look for ways to restate the limit more effectively.* For example, if Carly ignores your request you might try calling her name again, picking up one of the toys, handing her the toy, and then repeating the request.

Give Reasons for Rules and Limits

Children comply more easily with a limit when they understand the rationale behind it.

▼ *Give short, simple, concrete reasons* along with the limit.

▼ *Decide when to state the reason*—either before or after stating the limit, or after a child complies with the limit.

Examples   State the rationale before you state the limit: "Each person needs a clean space for painting. Use this sponge to wipe your part of the table." A child may tend not to argue about the rule if she hears the reason first and the limit second.

State the rationale after you state the limit: "I want you to wipe your own spot so that each person who paints has a clean space."

State the rationale after the child complies with the limit: "Thanks for cleaning your spot, Linda. Now George has a clean space when he paints."

▼ *Decide whether you need to repeat the rationale* if you restate the limit. Avoid playing the "why game" with children. A child's goal in the why game is to distract you from following through with the limit by repeatedly asking "Why?" Ignoring their "Why?" is one of the most helpful things you can do for them. Or you can say, "I think you're having fun asking me why and I'll tell you why one more time and then the game is over" (Seefeldt, 1993). Repeating the rationale is a good idea when you want to emphasize the reason for the limit, perhaps when children are first learning a limit.

Example   Teacher to children before going out to the playground on the second day of school, "Tell me our safety rule about how many children are allowed on the sliding board at one time . . . That's right . . . only one at a time so that nobody gets hurt."

CASE STUDY PROBLEM SOLVING: Setting Limits

Help Jenny's mother (see opening case study) deal more effectively with this problem by using good limit setting. Focus on limit setting here. You will have a chance to use other strategies elsewhere in the chapter.

1. Jenny's mom could have set a limit on what they would be buying at the store before going to the store by doing and saying . . . (Be specific and follow the guidelines for limit setting.)
2. Suppose Mom had set the limit well and then wanted to quickly remind Jenny about it just before they got out of the car. She could have said, in a good-natured and low-key way:
3. Now suppose that Mom had simply forgotten to state the limit before getting to the store, and then Jenny began her whining. Jenny's mother could have then stated the limit by saying . . .

Teach More Appropriate Behavior and Give Signals or Cues for Appropriate Behavior

Teaching More Appropriate Behavior

Mr. Cunningham was concerned because most of the children in his group of 4-year-olds did not wash their hands after using the bathroom or before they ate. And his reminders after they forgot to wash their hands did not seem to be working. To achieve his goal of getting the children to willingly wash their hands, he decided *to teach the more appropriate behavior*—handwashing—rather than nag about not washing hands. He focused on modeling the more appropriate behavior (Krumboltz & Krumboltz, 1972).

Example   Mr. Cunningham made up a puppet play showing handwashing before lunch and after using the bathroom. He invited one of the mothers, who was a nurse, to model correct handwashing, and small groups of children practiced handwashing with her. Finally, he taught an action song about handwashing to the whole group.

"This is the way we wash our hands, wash our hands, wash our hands . . ." Adults teach children appropriate behavior.

Giving Cues for the Appropriate Behavior

Mr. Cunningham realized that his group might not remember to wash their hands, even though they had learned how. So, he decided to give *signals* or *cues* to teach the children to remember to wash their hands, but he gave the signal just *before* they should wash hands rather than waiting until they had forgotten (Krumboltz & Krumboltz, 1972).

   Example   At the end of group time Mr. Cunningham reminded the children to wash their hands for snack time by having them sing the action song and then sending them to the bathroom. The aide was there to cue those children who went to the bathroom to wash hands afterward. In the next few days he made the cues more subtle by reminding children with handwashing motions as they exited the toileting area.

Put picture on mirror

CASE STUDY PROBLEM SOLVING: Teaching and Cuing More Appropriate Behavior

Suppose that Jenny's mother had been working on changing Jenny's whining by teaching her some new behavior that is different from whining, such as asking for things in a normal, conversational tone of voice. She has modeled a *normal* voice for Jenny.

1. Mom can easily teach Jenny to remember to use a normal voice by using this signal or cue before they get out of the car:
2. Mom wants to use cuing when they are in the store if reminding Jenny is necessary, but she wants to cue her daughter in a matter-of-fact, low-key way. Be prepared to role-play what this would look like.

Support Children in Using More Appropriate Behaviors

1. *The new behavior might be rewarding all by itself.* Consider teaching new behaviors that a child will find attractive enough to want to continue without any other reward (Krumboltz & Krumboltz, 1972).

   Example   Paul did not wipe his paint smock when he painted. His teacher made a new job for the job chart and assigned that job to Paul for two days. The new job entailed being the person who ran the paint smock wash. This person was in charge of checking all the smocks to make sure they were clean, and was also responsible for the new sponge and bucket.

2. *Consider adding external support* (Goetz, Holmberg, & LeBlanc, 1975). This strategy comes from the social learning model of child guidance and is described in greater detail in chapter 10. Effective praise and token systems are practical and positive ways to encourage new behavior (see Hitz and Driscoll [1988] for a good discussion of praise and encouragement).

   Examples   Jenny's mother used a token system to encourage Jenny to ask for things in a normal tone of voice. She devised a simple chart, and for each time Jenny asked for something in a normal tone of voice Jenny got to place one of her favorite stickers in the appropriate day's spot. Her mom asked her what she would like to trade for a completed card (three days of at least two stickers), and Jenny said she would like to rent a video at the store.

   Mom encouraged Jenny with effective praise—specific, sincere, and nonjudgmental: "You used a normal voice for asking for your juice, Jenny. Thanks!"

Change Something About a Situation

Positive discipline often involves asking yourself the following question: "What can I do about this situation that will help this child be safe or help her behave more appropriately?" For example, "Do I want to keep telling these two children to stop fighting over the blocks, or can I change something to help them accept the idea of cooperating?" There are a number of ways to change a situation to prevent or stop potentially dangerous or inappropriate behavior: increase options, decrease options, and change the physical environment.

Increase Options Available to the Child

▼ *Introduce new ideas to children engaged in an activity.* For example, some children have built a block train and have begun to fight over who will be the conductor. Present this as a problem they can solve. Help them decide who will be passengers and who will be the conductor, and then help them decide on a rotation method.

▼ *Introduce new materials into an activity.* Bring out a basket of rolling pins and cookie cutters after children at the play dough table have made the dough and seem to be ready for an expansion of the activity.

▼ *Forestall predictable problems.* Identify the times in your group's schedule when things tend to go wrong and forestall these problems whenever possible.

   Example   Mrs. Winslow knew that some children awoke from nap before the others but still had to be quiet. Instead of just asking them to sit quietly, she increased their options by developing special quiet time activities. She forestalled the problem by gathering a special group of toys and books for quiet time and then brought these materials out only after the nap. The children chose one of these activities.

Decrease Options Available to the Child

▼ *Limit choices.* Making wise choices is a skill that develops over time. We are helpful when we teach young children how to make choices from only a few alternatives.

Increasing options. This teacher put out the rollers after the children had played for a while with the play dough.

Example   Mrs. Winslow knew that Diane had difficulty zeroing in on one activity, so she helped Diane focus her attention and limited her choices by asking, "I know how much you like to paint and to play with the flannelboard. Which of those two things would you like to do first today?"

▼ *Change activities.* This may involve a moderate change like the one in the example below, or a more drastic change, such as dropping an activity or leaving an area completely.

Example   Mrs. Winslow tried to figure out why her group had such trouble settling down and going to sleep. After changing the type of song sung before nap from an active song to a quiet, soothing, relaxation exercise, the children were able to relax and go to sleep more easily.

Manage the Physical Environment Effectively

Guide children effectively by managing the environment well. For example, organize the physical space well; provide materials and equipment simple enough for the child to use easily; make it easy for the child to clean up and organize her things; and make the environment attractive and sensory rich but not overstimulating. (This topic is dealt with in more detail in chapter 4.)

Ignore Behavior When It Is Appropriate to Do So

Julie, 4 years old, used a wheedling, whiny voice when she wanted something. Her teacher felt irritated by the high-pitched, nasal sound, and since she wanted Julie to ask for help in a normal tone, she decided to ignore the whining and encourage Julie to speak in a normal voice.

This teacher used positive discipline by teaching, cuing, and then supporting Julie's new, more appropriate behavior. She also knew that it is just as important for her to stop paying attention to certain inappropriate behaviors, such as whining. *Ignoring behavior* (also called *extinction*) involves withdrawing reinforcement for a specific behavior or no longer paying attention to the behavior. Ignoring certain behaviors weakens the inappropriate behavior because the child stops getting reinforced for it. And, because the payoff is eliminated, there is no reason for the child to continue with it.

Some Behaviors Should Not Be Ignored

It is irresponsible to ignore such dangerous behaviors as running into the street, hitting other children, hurting animals, or playing with an electrical outlet.

1. *Do not ignore a child's behavior that endangers anyone, including the child.* Authoritative adults do not hesitate to forbid certain classes of behavior, including dangerous, aggressive behaviors. A responsible, supportive adult teaches that these potentially harmful behaviors will not be tolerated. Adults who ignore aggression give tacit approval to this behavior, and the

PROBLEM FOR YOU TO SOLVE: Change Something About These Situations

Change something about each situation so that you could help the child behave more appropriately or so that you could prevent a problem. First, say whether you would *increase* options, *decrease* options, or *change the physical environment.*

The Problem: Tim's parents had been sitting in the booth at Burger Palace for 15 minutes. They had finished eating and were talking to each other. Three-year-old Tim wiggled off the bench, ran around, and then crawled under the table. His dad scooped him up and told him, "Now, you sit here and be quiet." Five minutes passed, and Tim, who had missed his morning nap, started screaming in frustration. His dad grabbed Tim's arm to try to quiet him, but Tim continued screaming. Dad finally slapped him.
My Solution: I would change this situation by . . . (Note: Tim must be supervised constantly, so, sending him to the restaurant's outdoor playground is not an option.)

The Problem: Dad was frustrated when 10-month-old Richard kept zooming (a fast crawl!) right to the uncovered electrical outlets. He said "No-no," every time his son approached the outlet.
My Solution: I suggest that Dad change this situation by . . .

The Problem: John, 4 years old, has been working for 20 minutes in the sandpile constructing a "canal" for water (he has no water yet) when you glance over and notice that he is tossing sand into the air.
My Solution: In addition to stating a safety rule, I would change this situation by . . .

aggression will usually increase, which can also lead other children to think that adults will not protect them from aggressive outbursts.

2. *Do not ignore a child who damages or destroys property* or acts in a way that could damage or destroy property. Again, ignoring such destructive behavior conveys adult approval. Instead, give children a clear message of disapproval for destructive behavior.

3. *Do not ignore children when they treat someone rudely, embarrass someone, are intrusive, or cause an "undue" disturbance.* Young children do some of these things because they might not know a better way of behaving, and some older children may act this way because they have been permitted to. With younger children our job is to teach that better way, not to ignore inappropriate behavior. Older children must learn that some adults value politeness and respecting boundaries and will set limits that convey these values.

Guidelines for Ignoring Behavior

Adults who employ this strategy successfully and humanely use the following guidelines:

1. *Tell the child that you will ignore a specific behavior whenever it occurs.* Julie's teacher has a right to try to stop giving attention to and to decrease an irritating behavior like whining, but she also has an obligation to act self-responsibly. She should tell Julie that she is irritated by the whining and that she will no longer pay attention to Julie when she asks for something with a whine: "Julie, I'm not going to pay attention to you when you whine. I won't look at you, and I won't talk to you when you whine."

2. *Realize that it takes time to effectively use the ignore strategy* because adults have given lots of attention to the very behaviors they want to eliminate.

Example   Later that afternoon, Julie, in her high-pitched voice, asked her teacher for paint. Her teacher followed through with her plan to stop giving attention and to stop reinforcing whining. Julie was surprised, even though the teacher had explained the procedure, because previously the teacher had reinforced Julie's whining by paying attention to it and giving her what she wanted.

Julie did not stop whining after being ignored only one time. Like most children whose irritating behavior is being ignored for the first time, she tried even harder to recapture the teacher's attention by whining even more insistently. Her teacher was prepared for Julie's "bigger and better" whine. She knew that she would have to carry out the procedure at least one or two more times before Julie finally realized that she would not get what she wanted by whining.

3. *Decide to thoroughly ignore the behavior.* This is difficult because the adult has decided to change her own customary behavior. In order to help herself stop paying attention to and encouraging the whining, the teacher wrote the following list of reminders:

    "Don't mutter to myself under my breath."

    "Don't make eye contact."

    "Don't communicate with this child verbally or with gestures."

4. *Teach and encourage more acceptable behavior.* Go beyond *ignoring* a behavior to teaching children how to behave appropriately. Julie's teacher realized that she was eliminating the payoff (the reinforcement of the whining) but that Julie needed to be firmly reminded of a better way to ask for what she wanted. She said, "Julie, you're whining. I'll pay attention to you when you speak in a normal voice." Julie used a normal voice later in the day to ask for a turn stirring a cake, and the teacher responded, "Sure, Julie. You asked for a turn with a normal voice."

PROBLEM FOR YOU TO SOLVE: Should I Ignore This Behavior?

Look over this list and decide which of the behaviors you, as a parent or teacher, should not ignore. Which could you safely ignore? Give reasons for your choices. Think about the types of behaviors that should not be ignored.

1. A child in your class calls another child a creep. Ignore?

   Yes   No   Reason:

2. A 3-year-old girl smashes another child's play dough structure. Ignore?

   Yes   No   Reason:

3. Another child smashes his own play dough structure. Ignore?

   Yes   No   Reason:

4. The children in your group leave small trucks on the stairway to the outside play area. Ignore?

   Yes   No   Reason:

5. Jordan bites Mitchell. Ignore?

   Yes   No   Reason:

6. "I don't want to nap. Why do I have to nap?" a 4-year-old said to the aide at transition to nap. Ignore?

   Yes   No   Reason:

CASE STUDY PROBLEM SOLVING: Help Jenny's Mother Ignore Behavior

This time help Jenny's mom ignore certain behaviors. Suppose that Mom had set limits before going into the store and that she had restated the limit when Jenny said she wanted a thermos.

1. Explain why it would have been appropriate to have ignored Jenny's whining and arguments once appropriate limits had been clearly stated.

2. Tell Jenny's mom specifically how to effectively use the *ignore* strategy in this case. List the essential things that you would tell her to do—or not to do.

3. Warn Jenny's mom about how Jenny is likely to react to the ignore strategy the first time it is used, and offer her advice on how to deal with this.

4. Give her some advice on how to deal with other adults in the store who might indicate that she "should do something to that kid to stop her squealing!"

Redirect Children's Behavior—Divert and Distract the Youngest Children

Diverting and *distracting* are forms of redirection in which an adult immediately does something to distract a child from the forbidden or dangerous activity and then involves the child in a *different* activity.

Authoritative, responsible caregivers understand that they perform most of an infant's or young toddler's ego functions. For example, they remember things for the child and keep the very young child safe because an infant's or young toddler's concept of danger is just emerging. Authoritative adults accept responsibility for stopping very young children from doing something by setting limits that discourage certain behaviors, but they do so in a way that avoids being drawn into a power struggle.

Diverting and distracting the youngest children accomplishes both of these tasks. An adult who has told a child not to do something can avoid getting drawn into a power struggle by *immediately* doing something to distract the child from the forbidden activity and steering her toward a different activity.

Example   Mary, 16 months old, walked over to the bowl of cat food, picked up a piece, and started to place it in her mouth. The babysitter told her, "Put the cat food back in the bowl, Mary" (a short, clear, specific limit). Then the babysitter picked Mary up and said, "You know, I think it's time for Sesame Street."

CASE STUDY ANALYSIS: Using Diversion and Distraction

The teacher in one of the chapter opening case studies has attempted to redirect behavior through *diversion and distraction*.

1. Identify the behaviors that the adult thought she had to prohibit in each instance: for Yer? for Janie? for the two toddlers?

2. The teacher successfully used diversion and distraction when she encouraged each child to get involved with a *different* activity. Say how she did this with each infant or toddler.

3. I think this adult effectively used diversion and distraction, as evidenced in the child's behavior. Here are at least two examples:

Redirect Children's Behavior—Make Substitutions when Dealing with Older Children

Substitution is a form of redirection in which an adult shows a child how to perform an activity or type of activity in a more acceptable and perhaps safer way.

Tony's dad used diversion *and* distraction *when he scooped Tony up to get him away from the kitchen where pots were bubbling on the stove: "Oh, Tony, look at the puppet."*

Substitution is an excellent strategy to use when you are faced with inappropriate behavior in children who are at least in Piaget's preoperational stage, approximately age 2 to age 6. It is also a good strategy to use with older children because it acknowledges the child's desire to plan and engage in a specific activity. But first the adult must accept the responsibility of developing the substitutions to demonstrate the first step in the process of problem solving (Crary, 1979).

Example   Martin, age 4, dressed for easel painting, aimed his brush at Jerry's picture. The teacher stepped in and said, "Paint on one of these pieces of paper, Martin, not on Jerry's. Which size do you want to use?" She then led Martin to the other side of the easel.

Children may test adult commitment to substitution by trying the inappropriate activity again—later in the day, the next day, or with a different person.

Example   Martin swung around from his side of the easel to try to paint on his friend's painting. The teacher said, "Paint on *your* paper, Martin." Martin eventually accepted the substitution because the teacher resisted getting drawn into a power struggle and continued to make the substitution calmly and with goodwill.

CASE STUDY ANALYSIS: Using Substitution

In the following statements, show how Mike's teacher (see chapter opening case study) used substitution effectively.

1. The teacher showed Mike how to perform the same activity in a more acceptable way when she . . .
2. Mike tested the adult's substitution when he . . .
3. The teacher used positive discipline when she responded to Mike's testing of her substitution by . . .

Listen Actively

Active listening is a positive discipline strategy that comes from the theories of Carl Rogers and which is taught in Gordon's (1970, 1978) Parent Effectiveness Training (P.E.T.) program (see chapter 10 for a detailed description of this strategy). Active listening is the skill that responsible adults use when a child *owns a problem*, when something is troubling a child, and when the adult can best help a child by listening actively and responsively to the feelings implied in the child's words.

Active listening involves focusing on what the child says, not interrupting, not offering solutions, listening for the feelings in the words, suspending judgment, avoiding preaching, and then feeding back your perception of the feelings.

PROBLEM FOR YOU TO SOLVE: Using Substitution

Look over these problem situations and use the material just presented to think of substitutions that are both appropriate for the child and acceptable to you.

1. Sylvia fingerpainted on the window because, she says, she likes how the sun shines on the colors.
2. Mickey poured pineapple juice on one of the plants because "the plant needs a drink."
3. Jake pulled a chair over to the shelf holding the record player and twisted all the knobs, trying to see how they worked.
4. Pat wiped his nose on his sleeve.
5. Sarah scribbled with markers on paper, but the paper was on the tablecloth and marks strayed to the cloth.
6. Steven rode his tricycle on the newly seeded part of the lawn.

Example   Janelle was about to be vaccinated. She jumped off the examination table and scooted under it. The doctor knelt down, peered under the table, and said, "Looks like you'd rather hide than have this vaccination, right?"

"I don't like needles."

"Sounds to me like you really don't like them."

"They hurt!" More quietly, "They hurt my arm."

Think of how an authoritarian adult would have dealt with Janelle's behavior. This behavior would very likely have been perceived as misbehavior and would have been punished in some way. In many cases children try to tell us through their behavior that something is wrong in their world. We will discover what is wrong only if we take the time to listen actively. And, we discover through active listening that a child can change her own behavior with our assistance.

Use I-Messages

I-messages are also based on the theories of Carl Rogers and are taught in Gordon's P.E.T. program. An I-message is a positive discipline strategy used by an adult when a child has done something that interferes in some way with that adult's needs. The essential element is the adult's acknowledgment that she, the adult, owns her own feelings of irritation, annoyance, sadness, anger, or fear. She does not accuse the child of causing these feelings, but she does take responsibility for communicating these feelings to the child in a respectful, nonaccusatory way. The goal is to give the child the opportunity to change her behavior out of respect for the adult's needs.

Effective I-Messages Have Three Parts

When Ms. Ahmann blinks the lights for cleanup, 3-year-old Matthew heads for the bathroom and leaves whatever he has been working on to somebody (usually Ms. Ahmann) else to put away. She realizes that it is *her* problem, that she is annoyed and that she should let Matthew know in a nonaccusatory way. She uses an I-message.

1. *I-messages give data about the child's behavior but avoid accusing a child:* "Matthew, when I blink the lights for cleanup, I have seen you leave the block area and go to the bathroom every day this week . . ."

2. *I-messages tell the child how his behavior tangibly affects the adult:* ". . . and that has meant that *I* have had to put away the things that you are working with . . ."

3. *I-messages tell the child how the adult feels:* ". . . and I feel really irritated because I don't have enough time to get ready to read our story."

CASE STUDY PROBLEM SOLVING: Helping Jenny's Mother Use an I-Message

Suppose that Jenny's mom had set good limits and clearly told Jenny that they have just enough time to buy the lunchbox and still get to the bank before it closes. Jenny started whining anyway, and they missed getting to the bank. Mom now has to make an extra trip to the bank. Show Jenny's mom how to use an I-message by writing exactly what you think she should say in each section.

1. Mom should name the exact behavior that is causing her a problem:

2. Mom should then say how the behavior is tangibly affecting her (not how she feels, but the actual effect on her time, energy, plans):

3. Then Jenny's mom has to actually say how she feels, because Jenny's whining has tangibly affected her. (Remember, the goal is not to induce guilt but simply to say how she feels. Jenny did not cause the feeling.) Mom owns that feeling and says: "I feel _____ because now I _____."

4. This is a public place. Take Jenny's perspective and say whether Mom should try to deliver this I-message in private. Why or why not?

Use Natural and Logical Consequences

A well-delivered I-message implies that an adult accepts responsibility for her own feelings. But, after infancy, children also have a responsibility for their behavior (Maccoby & Martin, 1983), and we can use the *consequences* strategy to let a child know what her part is in a problem and how she can change things.

Natural and logical consequences support children in accepting responsibility for their own behavior. Consequences encourage children to choose appropriate behavior because they know what the consequences of their behavior will be before they choose the behavior. Knowing the consequences helps children learn from the natural or social order of events (Dinkmeyer & McKay, 1988).

The positive discipline strategy of using consequences comes from the work of the Adlerians (see chapter 10), and this skill is taught in the parenting course known as Systematic Training for Effective Parenting (S.T.E.P.).

Natural Consequences

Examples   Susan refused to eat lunch. The natural consequence of choosing not to eat lunch was hunger well before afternoon snack time.

Tom took off his mittens when making snowballs. The natural consequence was cold hands.

Notice that each result (consequence) followed the child's behavior inevitably (naturally), without an adult's intervention. There are some natural consequences that responsible adults would *never* allow to occur if they could prevent them, because such consequences bring great bodily harm to children, such as getting hit by a car while playing near or in a busy street; getting burned after touching a barbecue grill, iron, or stove; or getting shocked by electricity while playing with electrical outlets. They would, instead, substitute safe logical consequences.

Logical Consequences

Logical consequences are safe consequences that would not have occurred naturally and are designed by an adult. The natural consequence of running into a busy street is getting hit by a vehicle, but a logical consequence is to choose to play inside the house. Logical consequences are most effective when

▼ *the adult has delivered an I-message* so that the child is aware of the exact nature of the issue.

▼ *the consequence is "logically" related to the unsafe or inappropriate behavior.* You will have used punishment, and not consequences, if the consequence is unrelated to the behavior.

    Example   Tim's dad has to move Tim's bicycle and toys from the driveway before he can park his car. He uses logical consequences when he stated an I-message and then said, "Tim, I can't park the car with all the toys lying around. So I'll put them in the shed if you decide not to pick them up tomorrow." (He would have used punishment if he had said, "You either pick up those toys or there will be no baseball game for you on Saturday!")

▼ *the consequence is one the adult can really accept and that the child would likely view as fair even though she might be unhappy about it at first.* Tim's dad could accept putting the toys in the shed for a short time but would probably not have been able to accept running over the toys with the car or giving the toys away. Tim would probably view Dad's actions as fair. (Note: some authoritarian adults could accept giving away the toys or running over them, but this a mean-spirited, negative strategy often employed by parents who psychologically abuse their children.)

▼ *the consequence is well timed.* All discipline strategies are more effective when they are timed well. Adults guide children most effectively when they accept a child's choice and then allow the consequence to occur as soon as possible after the child chooses.

Steps in Using Logical Consequences

The following steps for using logical consequences are based on Dinkmeyer and McKay (1988).

1. *Respectfully restate expectations and tell the child how to change things.* Give the child a safe choice. This is a critical part of using consequences. Remind

the child of the limits and give specific suggestions about how to change things. Offer alternatives. You design the safe consequences. Adults usually are feeling irritated when they have to apply logical consequences, and it is easy to turn irritation into sarcasm. So state the choices in a way that conveys your respect along with your message. You will be more effective if your tone of voice is friendly, firm, and nonthreatening.

Example   "We're in the gym to play a game, Penny. I expect you to listen for directions. You can listen to the directions and play with us or you can see how the game is played while you sit on the sidelines. You choose."

2. *Allow the child to make a choice.* You can accept either choice because you have designed these choices to be safe and they do not degrade the child.

3. *Tell the child that you accept her choice* by allowing safe consequences to occur. Take action.

Examples   (Penny continues to be disruptive.) "I see that you've decided to wait for us on the sidelines and see how to play the game. You can try again the next time we have gym."

(Penny settles down and joins the group.) "I see that you've decided to play the game with the class. We sure like to have you playing."

CASE STUDY PROBLEM SOLVING: Logical Consequences

Jenny's mother has just been self-responsible when she delivered her I-message. Now, show her how to use logical consequences to support Jenny in making choices about her behavior and in her developing sense of self-responsibility. Remember, they must buy the lunchbox today.

1. What were Jenny's mother's expectations about Jenny's behavior while they were shopping for the lunchbox?

2. Jenny's mom should restate this expectation/limit by saying this to give Jenny a choice:

3. Show Jenny's mom what to say that shows her acceptance of Jenny's choice.

   a. What she would say if Jenny had continued whining?

   b. What she would say if Jenny had stopped whining?

Teach Children How to Resolve Conflicts and Do Problem Solving

Conflict between two people or within a group is almost inevitable. Relationships do not have to be severed because of conflict, but can actually become stronger if people learn to resolve conflict through good problem solving. Responsible, authoritative caregivers adopt this perspective and accept the challenge of supporting young children in learning how to recognize and manage conflict creatively rather than merely punishing behavior that frequently accompanies conflict between children (e.g., conflict over possessions) (Marion, 1993, 1994; Smith, 1982).

You will study Gordon's method (1970, 1978) of conflict resolution called the *no-lose* method in chapter 10. This method involves teaching children five steps in resolving a conflict, from identifying and defining the conflict to following up and evaluating how well the solution worked. This is a direct method of positive discipline because it focuses on teaching skills in problem solving.

Teach Children to Recognize and Responsibly Manage Strong Emotions

Harry is 4 years old and is often rejected by the other children, largely because he has such a difficult time dealing with anger. He strikes out at other children if they take something from him or if they frustrate him in some way. His teacher sought help from her director and a child development consultant in developing a guidance plan that would help Harry. The teacher's immediate concern—that Harry got so angry that he hit somebody—was to protect the other children and to stop Harry's aggression. Her long-term goal was to help Harry deal effectively with the issues that triggered his angry outbursts.

They developed a positive discipline plan that included several of the strategies described in this chapter. In addition, they thought Harry needed special help in recognizing and dealing effectively with the strong emotion of anger (Marion, 1993, in press). (See chapter 7 for specific guidelines on dealing with anger.)

Teach Children to Withdraw from Certain Situations (*Not* Time-Out) *Articles in packet*

Withdrawing from situations when necessary is a skill that a person can use throughout her lifetime, and teaching the skill of withdrawing is a positive discipline strategy. The main purpose of this strategy is to teach children how to take themselves out of situations when they lose control, are extremely angry, or endanger their own or someone else's safety. It gives children time to get their autonomic nervous system under control (Hole, 1981).

A secondary purpose in teaching withdrawal from certain situations is for adults to recognize that developmentally appropriate guidance/discipline involves attention to the special needs of specific children. Harry's teacher recognized that Harry's level of self-control was not very good when he was angry, but she felt uncomfortable with merely putting Harry in time-out, thinking that he needed something other than that punishment. So, she decided to help him by gradually transferring management of his emotion of anger to him by teaching him how to withdraw from anger-arousing situations.

Guidelines for Withdrawing/Cooling Off

1. *Identify and teach the child to focus on a specific behavior.* In Harry's case they focused on Harry's hitting, which followed his anger episodes.

2. *Give the child information about when and why you will request that she withdraw.* Demonstrate respect for a child. Harry's teacher had a dual obligation: first, to prevent Harry from threatening or hurting other children, and second, an equally great responsibility to Harry—to act self-responsibly.

Example   Harry's teacher said, "You sure get angry. Angry enough that you hit the other children. I can't let you hurt them, and I want you to figure out when you are getting angry. I'll help you figure out those times [she will actually perform the ego function of monitoring an emotion]. When you feel like you're getting angry, I want you to play the *get away game* instead of hitting somebody."

3. *Demonstrate, explain, and make sure a child understands the process.* She clearly explains and demonstrates to Harry how to play the *get away game* to take himself out of an anger-arousing situation.

Example   "Let's figure out a good place for you to *get away* by yourself when you *feel the motor in your chest*" [Harry had described anger as a R-R-R-R feeling (teacher asked, "Like a motor?") in his chest]. Harry decided that he would *get away* and watch the fish swim in the tank.
"You can tell me that the *motor is starting up* and that you would like to *play the get away game* by going to the fishtank."
"Or, I will tell you that I think your anger motor is starting up and that it is time to play the *get away game*."
"Then you'll go to the fishtank" (both walk to the tank).
Harry's teacher decided to also sit with him when he *got away* because she believed that Harry would benefit from learning how to relax. She taught him how to do deep-breathing exercises as a way to relax, regain control, and diffuse some of the energy of his anger.

4. *Follow through.* Help the child identify the target behavior when it occurs.

Example   "Hey, you! Give that to me!" was all the teacher heard before she saw Harry's arm swing up in preparation for a hit. She went quickly to him, catching his arm. She stooped and talked quietly to Harry: "Harry, your *anger motor* is going. I want you to come with me and do the *get away game*. Let's do that right now." An adult is much more respectful if she reminds a child about the procedure, especially the first time that it is used.

5. *Help the child withdraw every time that the targeted behavior appears.* You will be most helpful if you use strategies consistently. Inconsistent discipline is not helpful and often makes behavior like Harry's hitting even worse. The teacher kept her hand on Harry's shoulder, "Let's get to the fishtank, take deep breaths, and watch the fish."

6. *Teach the child to withdraw as soon as possible after the target behavior occurs.*

7. *Teach and encourage more appropriate behavior when the child returns to an activity* after her withdrawal/cooling off. This is crucial. In addition to teaching stress management with breathing exercises, the teacher also taught Harry the skill of verbalizing his frustration and telling someone what he wants (Marion, 1993, 1994).

Whatever happened with Harry? Progress was slow but steady, and hitting episodes and anger outbursts decreased gradually. After several weeks of encouraging Harry to get away when he felt anger, the teacher observed him as he played in the block area, a place where he had previously had lots of unfriendly, angry interactions. She watched him look surprised and annoyed when John took one his blocks. She gave a silent cheer when Harry stopped for a few seconds, scrunched up his mouth, closed his eyes, and then said, "That's *my* block, John. You can use it later. I have it now!" He did not need to physically remove himself to regain control. He had made an important transition—thinking about what to do instead of reacting to anger.

Help Children Save Face and Preserve Their Dignity

Our ultimate responsibility is to help children save face and preserve their sense of dignity no matter what positive strategy we use. Authoritarian adults degrade children by using negative discipline and continue to humiliate the child by telling others about what the child did in front of the child, by saying "I told you so," or by saying something like "Now, let this be a lesson to you," to the child.

Use your perspective-taking skills. Put yourself in a child's place and think about how it would feel to have an adult telling you that you have to calm down or that you've done something wrong. How would you want this adult to treat you after the telling is over? With dignity.

This means that once you are done with the positive discipline strategy you let the episode go, let it become history, and allow the child to get on with things. No speeches or reasoning are necessary. This is especially important when a child has become enraged and has lost control and you have helped her regain control.

CASE STUDY PROBLEM SOLVING: Preserving Jenny's Dignity

Jenny's mom has successfully helped Jenny deal with her extremely high level of frustration by withdrawing with her to the bathroom and helping Jenny regain control (holding her hands, encouraging her to breathe deeply, washing her face with a cool cloth, and saying little besides "It'll be OK"). Mom believes that they are ready to leave the bathroom. She realizes that the customers were curious, and she doesn't want Jenny to feel embarrassed.

1. I believe that Mom would be most effective if she said the following to Jenny before leaving the bathroom (remember: no speeches, no preaching, no reminding of limits now. Remind her later. This is the time to let Jenny know that this episode is *over*):

2. I believe that, under the circumstances, Jenny should have a choice about whether to continue shopping this day, even if they think they should buy the lunchbox. I would offer her this choice (this is *not* logical consequences) by asking:

3. Be prepared to say how your choices would help Jenny preserve her dignity.

EFFECTS OF POSITIVE DISCIPLINE

Positive discipline has a powerful effect on a child's development and on the relationship between adult and child.

Positive Discipline Helps Children Feel Safe and Secure

Responsible adults believe that children control their own behavior best when they are not afraid of being hurt, when they feel safe and secure. Adults who rely on positive discipline usually believe that they have a responsibility to keep children safe but also to teach children the rules of the culture.

These adults believe that it is possible to fulfill their responsibility without using raw power. They do not use force, and they do not threaten children. They understand that using power or instilling fear is inhumane and actually an ineffective way to deal with another person. Authoritative adults know that threatening or hurting children does not stop inappropriate behavior.

Positive Discipline Encourages Children to Be Self-Responsible

The positive discipline strategies described in this chapter focus on teaching, not punishment. Authoritative adults use strategies that show that they refuse to use sarcasm or degrade children. Authoritative adults use strategies such as I-messages, which acknowledge their adult responsibility for their actions. They are nonjudgmental as they explain the consequences of a child's choice of behaviors. Children learn to take responsibility for their own actions when they experience positive discipline because the adults in their lives have modeled self-responsible behavior through positive discipline.

Positive Discipline Fosters Healthy Self-Control

The long-range goal in guiding children is the achievement of healthy self-control. We want children to be able to control themselves 5, 10, or 20 years from now. The ability to control one's self is nurtured through interaction with warm, supportive adults who use positive discipline strategies.

Careful observation of adults using positive discipline shows that they model self-control, tell children that self-control is expected of them, tell children how to control themselves, and then reinforce self-control. It should not surprise us, then, that these children achieve self-control more easily than children who are threatened, hit, or ridiculed (Parke & Deur, 1972). More recently, a research group at Louisiana State University has found that children of authoritative parents showed self-control on the playground by exhibiting fewer disruptive behaviors than children of authoritarian parents (Hart, DeWolf, Wozniak, & Burts, 1992).

Positive Discipline Arouses Empathy

Adults influence children by telling them how their behavior affects somebody else. Responsible adults credit children with the ability to think and, with guidance, to figure out how to behave appropriately and understand why people act in certain ways.

Piaget (1970) posits four ways in which children gradually become less egocentric and more empathic. One of these factors of development is social interaction, a process by which a child is confronted with the ideas of other people. When we confront a child with another point of view we encourage her to look at things from someone else's perspective. This cognitive developmental skill begins to develop in early childhood but does not develop automatically. Adults can help children learn to understand that other viewpoint by taking the time to explain the other person's perspective (Selman, 1976).

Positive Discipline Builds Positive Self-Esteem and a Strong Core of Personal Values

Competence, confidence, and a sense of worthiness are the cornerstones of positive self-esteem. One of our goals as early childhood educators is to help each child discover how wonderful she is and also to help her understand and believe in the rights of others to dignified, fair treatment.

Negative discipline (hitting, ridiculing, sarcasm, shaming, threatening) humiliates children, damages their egos, and ultimately diminishes their self-esteem. Negative discipline also affects a child's value system; for example, she is taught to use power unfairly when dealing with others.

Like all humans, children are motivated by a need to be competent and to know that they can do things well, whether it is fingerpainting, making and keeping friends, or training a puppy (White, 1959; White, Kaban, Shapiro, & Attonucci, 1976). Positive discipline helps children feel competent and confident enough to behave appropriately (Bishop & Rothbaum, 1992). It takes time and effort to use positive discipline, and children who experience positive discipline view themselves as worthy of the adult's efforts. Positive discipline also teaches children that others have rights and to value fair, dignified treatment of other people.

SUMMARY OF KEY CONCEPTS

1. *Discipline* is any attempt to control or change a child's behavior, and an adult's style of discipline tells us a lot about that person. Discipline is a process affecting both adults and children, and can be either negative or positive. Authoritarian adults believe that discipline is the same thing as punishment; authori*tative* adults believe that discipline means teaching and guiding through positive examples.

2. *Positive discipline* is a disciplinary style that respects children and treats them with dignity. Positive discipline focuses on teaching and not on punishment. Positive discipline is helpful and gives children enough of the right type of information that they need for learning and practicing appropriate behavior.

3. Authoritative adults are skillful in using a cluster of positive discipline strategies. They learn and practice a large number of strategies because

they know these will better equip them to deal with a variety of issues and not be locked into using only one or two strategies.

4. Authoritative adults tend to be clear about their values, the limits they set with children based on those values, the behavior they model, the instruction they give, and the types of behaviors they encourage.

5. Positive discipline has powerful effects on a child's development and on the relationship between adult and child. Positive discipline helps children feel safe and secure, encourages self-responsibility, fosters self-control, arouses empathy, and builds positive self-esteem and a strong core of personal values.

OBSERVE CHILD GUIDANCE IN ACTION
Identify Positive Discipline Strategies

Observe adults and children together in several different settings. Use the following format to write brief descriptions of the interactions. Be specific and write only what you see or hear; for example, what the adult and child said or did. Avoid writing your opinion. After recording several examples, pick out the positive discipline strategies. To make your observation easier to read, use a single page for each example.

Date: _____

Setting: _____

Approximate age of child: _____

Describe what the child did or said. (Include direct quotes.)

Describe what the adult did or said. (Include direct quotes.)

Describe the outcome.

Name of the positive discipline strategy:

REFERENCES

Bishop, S., & Rothbaum, F. (1992). Parents' acceptance of control needs and preschoolers' social behaviour: A longitudinal study. *Canadian Journal of Behavioural Science*, *24*(2), 171–185.

Bredekamp, S. (Ed.) (1986) *Developmentally appropriate practice*. Washington, DC: NAEYC.

Brown, B. (1979). Parents' discipline of children in public places. *The Family Coordinator*, *28*(1), 67–73.

Canter, L. (1988). Assertive discipline and the search for the perfect classroom. *Young Children*, *43*(2), 24.

Crary, E. (1979). *Without spoiling or spanking*. Seattle, WA: Parenting Press.

Dekovic, M., & Janssens, J. (1992). Parents' child-rearing style and child's sociometric status. *Developmental Psychology*, *28*(5), 925–932.

Dinkmeyer, G., & McKay, G. (1988). *S.T.E.P.: Parents handbook*, Circle Pines, MN: American Guidance Service.

Erikson, E. H. (1963). *Childhood and society* (2nd rev. ed.), New York: Norton.

Forehand, R., Doleys, D., Hobbs, S., & Resick, P. (1976). An examination of disciplinary procedures with children. *Journal of Experimental Child Psychology, 21*, 109–120.

Goetz, E. M., Holmberg, M. C., & LeBlanc, J. (1975). Differential reinforcement of other behavior and noncontingent reinforcement as control procedures during the modification of a preschooler's compliance. *Journal of Applied Behavior Analysis, 8*(1), 77–82.

Gordon, T. (1970). *P.E.T.: Parent effectiveness training.* New York: Peter H. Wyden.

Gordon, T. (1978). *P.E.T. in action.* Toronto: Bantam.

Green, K., Forehand, R., & MacMahon, R. (1979). Parental manipulation of compliance and noncompliance in normal and deviant children. *Behavior Modification, 3*(2), 245–266.

Grusec, J., & Kuczynski, L. (1980). Direction of effect in socialization: A comparison of the parent's versus the child's behavior as determinants of disciplinary techniques. *Developmental Psychology, 16*, 1–9.

Hart, C., DeWolf, M., Wozniak, P., & Burts, D. (1992). Maternal and paternal disciplinary styles: Relations with preschoolers' playground behavioral orientations and peer status. *Child Development, 63*, 879–892.

Haswell, K., Hock, E., & Wenar, C. (1981). Oppositional behavior of preschool children: Theory and intervention. *Family Relations, 30*, 440–446.

Hitz, R., & Driscoll, A. (1988). Praise or encouragement? *Young Children, 43*(5), 6–13.

Hole, J. (1981). *Human anatomy and physiology.* Dubuque, IA: W. C. Brown.

Kramer, P. E. (1977). Young children's free responses to anomalous commands. *Journal of Experimental Child Psychology. 24*, 219–234.

Krumboltz, J., & Krumboltz, H. (1972). *Changing children's behavior.* Englewood Cliffs, NJ: Prentice-Hall.

Lytton, H. (1977). Correlates of compliance and the rudiments of conscience in two-year-old boys. *Canadian Journal of Behavioral Science, 9*, 242–251.

Lytton, H. (1979). Disciplinary encounters between young boys and their mothers and fathers: Is there a contingency system? *Developmental Psychology, 15*, 256–258.

Lytton, H., & Zwirner, W. (1975). Compliance and its controlling stimuli observed in a natural setting. *Developmental Psychology, 11*, 769–779.

Maccoby, E. E., & Martin, J. A. (1983). Socialization in the context of the family: Parent-child interaction. In P. Mussen (Ed.), *Handbook of child psychology* (Vol. 4). New York: Wiley.

Marion, M. (1991). *Guidance of young children* (3rd ed.). New York: Merrill/Macmillan.

Marion, M. (1992). Keynote address at the annual conference of the Oregon Association for the Education of Young Children, Portland, October.

Marion, M. (1993). Responsible anger management: The long bumpy road. *Day Care and Early Education.* April 4–9.

Marion, M. (1994). Encouraging the development of responsible anger management in young children. *Early Child Development and Care, 97*, 155–163.

Minton, D., Kagan, J., & Levine, J. (1971). Maternal control and obedience in the two-year-old. *Child Development, 42,* 1873–1894.

Minuchin, S. (1974). *Families and family therapy.* Cambridge, MA: Harvard University Press.

Parke, R. D., & Deur, J. L. (1972). Schedule of reinforcement and inhibition of aggression in children. *Developmental Psychology, 7,* 266–269.

Peele, R. A., & Routh, D. K. (1978). Maternal control and self-control in the three-year-old child. *Bulletin of the Psychonomic Society, 11*(6), 349–352.

Phyffe-Perkins, E., & Birtwell, N. (1989). Comprehensive child abuse prevention: Working with staff, parents, and children. Presentation at the Annual Conference of the NAEYC, Atlanta, November.

Piaget, J. (1970). Piaget's theory. In P. Mussen (Ed.), *Carmichael's manual of child psychology.* New York: Wiley.

Pulkkinen, L. (1982). Self-control and continuity from childhood to adolescence. In P. B. Baltes & O. G. Brim (Eds.), *Life-span development and behavior* (Vol. 4). New York: Academic Press.

Rollins, B. C., & Thomas, D. L. (1979). Parental support, power, and control techniques in the socialization of children. In W. R. Burr, R. Hill, F. Nye, & I. Reiss (Eds.), *Contemporary theories about the family* (Vol. 1). New York: Free Press.

Satir, V. (1976). *Making contact.* Millbrae, CA: Celestial Arts.

Schaffer, H. R., & Crook, C. K. (1980). Child compliance and maternal control techniques. *Developmental Psychology. 16,* 54–61.

Seefeldt, C. (1993). Parenting. Article in St. Paul Pioneer Press. Sunday, May 23.

Selman, R. L. (1976). Social-cognitive understanding: A guide to educational and clinical practice. In T. Lickona (Ed.), *Moral development and behavior.* New York: Holt, Rinehart, & Winston.

Smith, C. (1982). *Promoting the social development of young children.* Palo Alto, CA: Mayfield.

Sroufe, L. A., & Ward, M. J. (1980). Seductive behavior of mothers of toddlers: Occurrence, correlates and family origins. *Child Development, 51,* 1222–1229.

Stayton, D. J., Hogan, R., & Ainsworth, M. D. S. (1971). Infant obedience and maternal behavior: The origins of socialization reconsidered. *Child Development, 42,* 1057–1069.

Toepfer, D., Reuter, J., & Maurer, C. (1972). Design and evaluation of an obedience training program for mothers of preschool children. *Journal of Consulting and Clinical Psychology, 32*(2), 194–198.

White, B. L., Kaban, B., Shapiro, B., & Attonucci, J. (1976). Competence and experience. In I. C. Uzgiris & F. Weigmann (Eds.), *Moral development and behavior.* New York: Holt, Rinehart, & Winston.

White, R. W. (1959). Motivation reconsidered: The concept of competence. *Psychological Review, 66,* 297–323.

4

Effective Design and Management of Physical Environments for Children: Indirect Guidance

Chapter Overview

After reading and studying this chapter, you will be able to

▼ *Identify* characteristics of developmentally appropriate physical classroom
  environments for 3- to 8-year-old children.

▼ *Describe* and *give a rationale for* each type of classroom activity area.

▼ *Analyze* a case study to decide how well a teacher managed a small-group
  area.

▼ *Explain* how to create an attractive, sensory-rich activity area and how to
  design good boundaries for activity areas.

▼ *List* criteria for developmentally appropriate activities and *analyze* a case
  study to decide whether a teacher's activities are developmentally appropriate.

▼ *Summarize* research findings on the impact of the physical environment on
  cognitive development of infants and toddlers.

▼ *Explain* how these findings can help teachers of infants and toddlers make
  decisions about designing the physical environment.

▼ *List* activity areas appropriate for infants and toddlers.

▼ *Explain* how these areas meet the developmental needs of infants and toddlers.

"Human caregivers have the ability to create just the right
kinds of experiences . . . materials, warmth, and involvement to fit
the infant's needs at any given point in development."
(Fogel, 1984, p. 276)

CASE STUDY: Mr. Fox's Classroom

Background

Mr. Fox teaches a group of 22 four-year-olds in a child care center sponsored by a major manufacturing plant. He has organized his room into areas, based on his overall goals. The children nap in a separate room.

Areas

On arrival each day, children find areas ready for play, and Mr. Fox encourages each child to choose an area. On Monday he used the following setup.

Reading/language arts area: There were four new library books on the rack, plus a flannelboard with figures for retelling a story heard the previous week. He set out a tape recorder and a set of pictures illustrating a story on the table.

Science/math area: He placed a homemade game focusing on the concept of larger/smaller "sets" on the table (he has lots of these homemade items, all packaged, labeled, and stored for easy retrieval). The computer screen showed a seriation game on which several children had been working for two days. He placed several other math-related games on shelves, along with the games used throughout the day. He hoped to encourage interest in butterflies by rearranging things in the science area, so he placed a butterfly display introduced on the previous Friday on the science table along with a new book about butterflies and a magnifying glass.

Dramatic play area: Children found a "backyard" complete with a small picnic table, umbrella, toy lawn mower set on a green carpet, and hand gardening tools along with artificial plants. Mr. Fox planned to leave the new area up for several days.

Block area: To follow up a visit to the bus barn of the bus station, he set out large pictures of buses, a real bus driver's hat, and a steering wheel set in a large wooden block in the block corner.

Art area: "Squish-squash, closely watch . . ." Mr. Fox arranged four chairs around a small table and placed one lump of smooth, white play dough in front of each chair. The children had made white dough on Friday, and today's focus was to add one drop of red food coloring to each lump of white dough and to encourage squishing, squashing, observing, and describing color changes. The easel was set up with cups of red and white paint. And, as always, there were lots of other art materials neatly arranged in see-through plastic tubs on the art shelf.

Manipulative toy area: The school invests a little each year in small, manipulative toys and a good storage system, so Mr. Fox has access to lots of these items. On Monday he placed three old, frequently used, but well cared for puzzles on the table and set two tubs of small, interlocking blocks on the floor. The children could also choose from among seven or eight other manipulative toys stored neatly on low, open shelves.

There are several factors that go into making a developmentally appropriate, supportive classroom environment: an adult's knowledge of child development and degree of responsiveness, the use of positive discipline, the setting of good limits, and the ability to communicate well with children. Another factor is how well adults manage the physical environment itself (Bredekamp, 1986; Day, 1983; Phyfe-Perkins, 1980; Prescott, 1984).

A well-designed and well-managed physical environment helps children become independent and to take initiative (Howes, 1991; Jones & Prescott, NAEYC film #806; King, Oberlin, & Swank, 1990; Marcu, 1977). A poorly designed and poorly managed physical environment for children sets the stage for many discipline problems (Heimstra & McFarling, 1974; Marcu, 1977; Marion, 1991; Mehrabian, 1976: Olds, 1977; Phyfe-Perkins, 1980).

This chapter focuses on the effects of environmental design on the behavior of young children and offers practical suggestions for developmentally appropriate classroom design. The first major section of the chapter focuses on classrooms for children who are between 3 and 8 years old, and the second focuses on environments for infants and toddlers.

DESIGNING DEVELOPMENTALLY APPROPRIATE PHYSICAL CLASSROOM ENVIRONMENTS FOR 3- TO 8-YEARS-OLDS

Adults influence children by providing and managing physical settings and materials. Developmentally appropriate physical environments foster positive adaptive behavior and promote the development of self-control and mastery by encouraging children to move and to control their environment. A well-designed, safe physical environment allows children to interact with the objects and people in that environment, with adults setting reasonable, fair limits on movement to protect children's safety.

Authoritative adults act self-responsibly—they realize that they alone are responsible for their adult behavior. Self-responsible caregiving and teaching include structuring and managing a physical space well. The focus in this section is on helping you act in a professionally self-responsible way by helping you recognize a developmentally appropriate physical environment in an early childhood classroom.

Organize the Environment into Activity Areas

Imagine that you've just stepped into your first classroom, a classroom in a child care center. The room contains an assortment of furniture: tables, chairs, bookshelves, and so on, and it is up to you to arrange this space. Realizing that a well-arranged physical space with clear limits helps children regulate their own behavior, you decide to divide the space into a number of different areas that support your overall curriculum goals. Each of the classroom areas will have different general characteristics: some will be small, some large; some will have seating, others will not. Each area will be used for different activities. Your classroom will contain a private area, several learning centers or small-group areas, and a large-group area. This section describes different types of classroom activity areas.

Private Space

A *private space* is a small, semienclosed space with room for only one or two children, visually isolated from other children but easily supervised by adults (Bowers, 1990, Marion, 1991). There are no chairs or tables or special materials in the private area. Figure 4.1 shows the private area Mr. Fox developed.

Why is a private space necessary? Because healthy systems acknowledge the right to privacy and the right to choose or limit contact with others. A developmentally appropriate child care center pays attention to not only what the group of children needs but also to what individuals may need. Like adults, children need breaks from large groups, but we must make a special effort to teach children how to take these breaks and to pace their interactions. Well-designed private spaces can help us

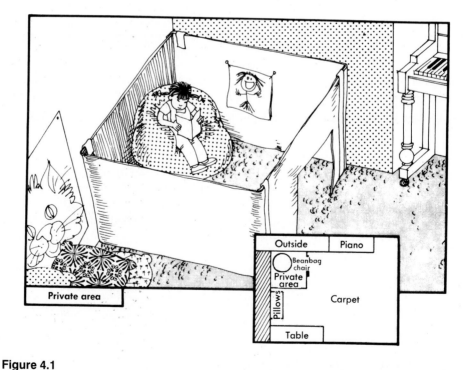

Figure 4.1

The private space in a classroom

Source: Alward, K. R. (1973). *Arranging the Classroom for Children.* San Francisco: Far West Laboratory for Educational Research and Development. Reprinted by permission.

teach children to focus on learning when they can and should be alone without being disturbed (Bredekamp, 1986). Children who are allowed to pace their interactions and control the degree of contact with others tend to be more independent and cooperative than children who are not permitted such control (Stallings, 1975).

You can manage the private space well by setting clearly defined limits on how both you and children may use the space. Make sure that every adult who works in your room knows that the private space is a place of refuge and relaxation and should never be used as a time-out/punishment area. Make sure each child knows that he can retreat to this spot to be alone and will not be disturbed. Teach children the strategies for politely telling another person that he does not wish to be disturbed when in the private area. Set limits prohibiting group play in the private area.

Small-Group Learning Center

A *small-group learning center* is a permanent or semipermanent space large enough for five or six children (see Figure 4.2). This is the most flexible type of space because of the seating arrangement. You can place a table and chairs in one of these centers if needed, as you saw in Mr. Fox's art area (case study). Or,

Figure 4.2
A small-group learning center
Source: Alward, K. R. (1973). *Arranging the Classroom for Children.* San Francisco: Far West Laboratory for Educational Research and Development. Reprinted by permission.

you may design a center that does not need a table, such as his block area. You may also decide to arrange a center so that children can work either at a table or on the floor, as in Mr. Fox's manipulative center. Each small-group area has a specific purpose, and this requires storing materials related to the activity in the area. Store materials you want children to have access to within their reach, but store materials you do not want children to have access to out of their reach, for example, in closed cabinets or on higher shelves. Clearly communicate an area's special function by separating it well from other areas in the room.

The actual centers that you design will, of course, depend on your school's overall goals. Examples of well-defined small-group areas include the following: math and science, a "manipulative" area (puzzles and other small-muscle equipment), reading and language arts, dramatic play, block center, and a creative arts area (see Figure 4.2 and figure below). You will do some problem solving with Mr. Fox's permanent small-group area for dramatic play, which he placed next to the block area (below).

CASE STUDY PROBLEM SOLVING: Decide How Well Mr. Fox Managed a Small-Group Area

This is Mr. Fox's dramatic play area set up with the kitchen equipment. The small inset drawing shows an overhead view.

Dramatic play area

Outside
Toy kitchen
Clothes
Table
Carpet
Shelves

Analyze the small-group area by answering the following questions.

1. Explain how this center is large enough to accommodate five children at one time.
2. Explain how Mr. Fox allows children access to some materials but makes sure that some materials are not accessible to them.
3. How will the children know where to return the materials when they finish working with them?
4. What would you do, specifically, to improve on how the clothes are stored in this area?
5. Explain how Mr. Fox used good boundaries and how he limited the traffic going through the area.
6. Name two things done to keep the slightly higher noise level in the area from distracting others.

When he was first hired, the dramatic play area contained a kitchen set, which is typical equipment in "housekeeping" areas. After noticing his 4-year-olds losing interest in playing only with kitchen equipment, Mr. Fox concentrated on changing the area to rekindle interest in dramatic play. Parent volunteers, with his guidance, developed prop boxes (Myhre, 1993) and collected some great dress-up clothes. The "office," the "backyard" (see case study), the "gardening" center, and the "fix-it shop" were all hits. Boys and girls working in the fix-it shop wore special shirts and checked books and puzzles for needed repairs, inspected trikes for squeaks needing oiling, examined dolls for necessary bathing and clothes washing, and inspected animal housing for necessary cleaning and repair. Then they carried out these tasks under a parent's supervision.

Large-Group Area

The *large-group area* is a space large enough to accommodate most or all of the children for large-group activities (Alward, 1973). This space should be large, open, and flexible to accommodate group participation in many activities: music, language arts, creative dramatics, stories, nutrition education, dance, and other activities that fit in with a school's goals. Therefore, specific materials are usually not stored in the large-group area but are brought there by the teacher (see Figure 4.3). Many teachers do store items there that help them manage the large-group area well, such as individual pieces of carpeting that can be arranged in seating patterns and indicate to children where they are to sit before group begins. Some teachers keep the daily calendar there, or the puppet who introduces the activity for the day.

Develop Enough Activity Areas

Consider the number and age of the children in the classroom when deciding how many of each type of area to include in the room. Provide one third more

Figure 4.3
Large-group area. Things for large-muscle activities have been set up in this area today.
Source: Alward, K. R. (1973). *Arranging the Classroom for Children.* San Francisco: Far West Laboratory for Educational Research and Development. Reprinted by permission.

spaces than there are children so they can change activities without having to wait. For example, in a classroom of 20 five-year-olds you would need about 27 work spaces (one third more spaces than children). These 27 spaces might consist of two small, private spaces, four or five small-group areas, and a large-group area. Table 4.1 shows how many of each type of space are needed, depending on the number and age of the children. Avoid filling your classroom with so many activity areas that children are overstimulated, frustrated, and unable to move around easily (Mehrabian, 1976; Olds, 1977; Sommer, 1974).

Arrange Activity Areas Logically and Regulate Traffic Flow

Logically separate one area from others, but make it easy for children to move between areas. Areas themselves should be designed so that young children can easily move around in them without disrupting others. Plan pathways carefully using furnishings that define and enclose the centers. Well-defined boundaries—shelves, walls, bulletin boards—indirectly cue children about the traffic pattern in the room (Kritchevsky & Prescott, 1977). For example, shelves separating the block and dramatic play areas regulate traffic flow between areas.

Table 4.1
Number of activity areas needed based on ages and numbers of children in class

		Number of Children in Class			
Area	Ages of Children	1–9	10–14	15–24	25–29
Private area	3–4	1	1	1	2
	5–6	1	1	1	1
Small-group area	3–4	1	3	4	5
	5–6	2	2	4	6
Large-group area	3–4	1	1	1	1
	5–6	1	1	1	1

Adapted from Alward (1973).

Make pathways wide enough for wheelchairs, long enough to make moving between areas easy, and short enough to discourage running. Regulate traffic by making only one entrance to a center, and develop a closed circuit around the room with the pathway so that children may stop off at each center if they wish (Bowers, 1990).

Be Conscious of Noise Level in Activity Areas

Wachs and Gruen's work (1982) showed that very young children's cognitive development is enhanced when their physical environment is relatively quiet.

PROBLEM FOR YOU TO SOLVE: How Many Activity Areas Would I Need If . . . ?

Use Table 4.1 to decide how many activity areas you would need in each classroom.

1. How many small-group areas are needed for a class of
   fourteen 5-year-olds? _____
   fourteen 3- and 4-year-olds? _____
   twenty-seven 5½-year-olds? _____
   twenty-five 3-year-olds? _____
   twenty 4-year-olds? _____
2. How many private spaces are needed for a group of
   fourteen 5-year-olds? _____
   twenty-five 4-year-olds? _____
3. Explain whether Mr. Fox's classroom contains enough of each type of area.

Strive for a classroom in which quiet, purposeful, enthusiastic, and even vigorous interaction is the norm. Children should not have to endure excessive noise that disrupts their learning.

Some classroom areas are best for relatively quiet activities, such as private spaces and small-group areas for language arts and reading, science and math, puzzles, and other small-table toys. Other areas encourage more vigorous activities: dramatic play, blocks, climbing, music, creative arts, and large-group area. Expect these areas to be somewhat noisier than areas where children play less vigorously.

Logically arrange areas so that quieter areas are placed near other quiet areas and so that they are well separated from areas encouraging more active play. Placing the dramatic play area near the block area is appropriate because both are high activity areas and dramatic play can flow so easily from one to the other. Books next to blocks would not be as appropriate an arrangement.

Combine your well-designed physical environment with appropriate, clearly communicated limits on noise level. Teach children about having fun without disrupting other people, about everyone's right to a quiet place in which to work, and that one of your basic classroom values is respect for the rights of others.

Create Boundaries for Areas

Creating proper boundaries for activity areas is not trivial and may well be one of the most appropriate things you do for children from chaotic, disorganized homes. People in *un*healthy systems tend to violate the psychological and physical boundaries of others. One of the clearest marks of a healthy system, however, including a developmentally appropriate classroom, are clear and distinct boundaries. These boundaries include psychological boundaries and the physical boundaries within the classroom itself. On a practical level this means that activity areas should be very clearly defined and properly separated from one another.

Children tend to be less disruptive when they understand where one area ends and the next begins (Olds, 1977). Clear boundaries, along with well-organized materials, also help children know where each piece of equipment belongs and encourage them to put things in their proper areas.

Be creative when separating areas. Use shelves, movable or permanent dividers, bulletin boards, pegboards, or cloth hanging from ceiling to floor (see Figure 4.4 and the insets of the earlier figures).

Create Attractive, Sensory-Rich Activity Areas

"Soft" architecture describes an environment responsive to the needs of the users of that environment (Sommer, 1974). This concept has been applied to work with animals in zoos, such as the one in Apple Valley, Minnesota, or the San Diego Zoo, where developers work diligently to provide each species with an

Figure 4.4
Activity areas need good boundaries.
Source: Alward, K. R. (1973). *Arranging the Classroom for Children.* San Francisco: Far West Laboratory for Educational Research and Development. Reprinted by permission.

environment like their natural habitat. There are no bars or typical "cages" in these zoos.

The concept of "soft" architecture has also been applied to early childhood education settings. It is fairly easy to "soften" a seemingly hard, cold classroom with tile floors, formica tables, concrete walls, curtainless windows, and harsh lighting to make it more responsive to the young children who spend a large part

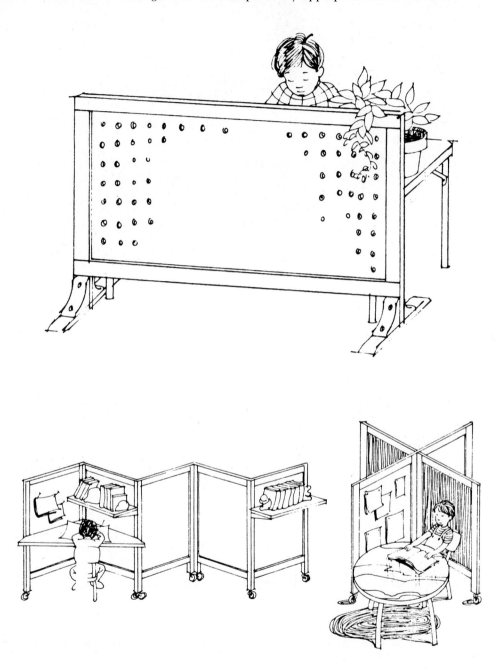

Figure 4.4, *conti   ied*

of their day there. Turn a room like this into a soft, safe, serene, but lively refuge by following these guidelines.

Strive for a Sensory-Rich but Uncluttered Classroom

Many early childhood teachers do a good job of adding interesting items to the classroom, but it is also important to weed out items that have served their purpose. A cluttered, disorderly room is unpleasant and distracting. Eliminating clutter helps children focus on new material because the number of stimuli to which they must attend is decreased.

Example   Mr. Fox realized that lots of his children were fascinated by all the butterflies in their area, so he planned a unit on butterflies. After adding a beautiful book on butterflies, two large, color photographs, and several real butterfly models to the science area, he was puzzled at the children's lack of interest. A close look at the science corner showed that the butterfly book was on the table with old cups of seeds, the rock collection, a magnet, and a magnifying glass. The pictures had been pinned to a somewhat cluttered bulletin board, and the butterflies had been dwarfed by a large, green plant. After clearing the science table and the bulletin board, Mr. Fox set out only "butterfly" things—the collection of butterflies, books, and the magnifying glass. He arranged the pictures of butterflies attractively on the bulletin board so that they were the central focus. He also placed a picture of butterflies on the door of his classroom with a note to parents to "join us in learning about butterflies."

Modify the Lighting

Skillful use of lighting is an indirect method of guidance. Many schools are equipped with bright lights, and although it is desirable to have adequate lighting, it can also be boring, stressful, and overstimulating to be in a harshly lighted room for an extended time. Classrooms are often equipped with only one or two light switches, giving adults only two options: all the harsh lights on or all of them off. Teachers can request that dimmer switches be installed so that they can control the intensity of lighting in different sections of the room. (Be prepared to justify this minor expense to your administrator.)

Example   In spite of a developmentally appropriate group time and well-stated limits, Mr. Fox noticed that some children had difficulty staying focused on the activity. He brought up his dilemma to the other teachers, discussed the problem, and decided to try to guide the children indirectly by changing the lighting. After school one day Mr. Fox and the other teachers experimented with the three banks of lighting. During group time the children really only needed the lights on in the section where they sat, so Mr. Fox turned the lights in the other two sections down but not off, helping the children focus on the activity in the area with brighter lighting.

Take advantage of natural lighting as well. Windows at eye level or with a "step-up" allow children to view their larger world and allow natural light into the classroom. Some researchers consider sunlight, in moderation, vital to health and well being (Olds, 1987), so teachers should admit sunlight into the room. Blocking out natural light will also be desirable at times, and inexpensive shades or curtains work well.

Modify Ceiling Height or Floor Level

No. You don't have to be a carpenter! Think about ways to create safe, cocoonlike spaces for the children that help them define the areas in their classroom. Many schools, for example, build inexpensive platforms or pits in parts of the rooms to clearly separate one area from the next. Children use platforms or pits for a variety of activities (see Figure 4.5). My university lab school also used the space *under* a platform to house the manipulative/writing areas.

Further define an activity area by draping strips of cloth across and between dowels hung from the ceiling. This strategy softens an area and room and actually makes the ceiling appear to be lower. This strategy is especially useful when a private, quiet, semienclosed activity area is desired.

Example   Mr. Fox, in his first year at his school, was disappointed that the children did not seem to enjoy the reading area. He drew a floor plan of his reading area and decided that he needed to make some changes. A major change was to use bookshelves to better separate the reading area from other areas. He added a fluffy carpet and large reading pillows that are designed to lean against a wall, and thoroughly cleaned the table, chairs, and shelves. He then added to the

Figure 4.5
A platform set in a corner against the wall
Source: Alward, K. R. (1973). *Arranging the Classroom for Children.* San Francisco: Far West Laboratory for Educational Research and Development. Reprinted by permission.

cozy feeling by suspending cloth across two rods hanging from the ceiling. The children loved it, and reading activity soared!

Modify the Sensory Environment

Make your classroom pleasant and attractive by creating visual, auditory, olfactory, and textural interest.

Create visual interest.   Sommer and Davis (cited by Sommer, 1974) found that students and faculty think college classrooms are more pleasant, comfortable, relaxing, and cheerful when a few decorative items such as posters or plants are added to the room. Enhance the aesthetic appeal of your early childhood classroom by keeping it clean and by adding well-chosen, inexpensive items such as paintings, posters, safe green plants, photographs of the children, cloth hangings, and artwork.

Create auditory interest.   Teachers and children should be able to work in a room where quiet, purposeful interactions are the norm (Wachs & Gruen, 1982). Think about the limits you will set to achieve this end: talking is just fine, but yelling is not allowed. When loud talking, screaming, or yelling occurs too frequently, it might be wise to reexamine both the physical setup of the room and the classroom limits.

How pleasant and relaxing it is for children to be able to hear their favorite composer's music when they arrive at school. Other sounds—new musical instruments, a gerbil gnawing a box or scratching around in his bedding, a mobile tinkling, or the hum of the computer—can help create a pleasant, relaxing atmosphere if the children are tuned in to the sounds and are not distracted by unnecessary noise.

Create olfactory interest.   Scary, hurtful, fun, and joyful memories are often triggered by aromas—the disinfectant smell of the hospital, the fragrance of the lilac bush as we brushed by it, the garden after a rainfall, fresh oranges shared with a friend on a summer day.

Think of all the ways you could make your room pleasant through attention to fragrance. Eliminate unpleasant odors by maintaining cleanliness. Add pleasant aromas to your classroom. Bake bread, muffins, and cookies, and vary ingredients, urging children to identify aromas. Put peppermint extract in the play dough, inexpensive scented soap in the bathroom, safe flowering plants in the room or yard. Can you think of other ways to add safe, inexpensive, pleasant aromas to the classroom?

Create textural interest.   Putting carpeting on the floors or walls and covering bulletin boards with cork or burlap are two things you can do almost immediately. Then, the fun begins when you hang children's large collage of cloth scraps or when you create a *touch* wall with an expanse of corrugated paper and other materials, or when you hang fabric wall hangings. Developmental appropriateness means attending to the needs of individual children, and children with impaired sight will benefit from a room rich in textures.

Plan Developmentally Appropriate Activities

Children more easily develop self-control, independence, competence, and prosocial behavior in well-organized classrooms that contain developmentally appropriate activities (Stallings, 1975). Use the following criteria to decide whether activities in a classroom are developmentally appropriate:

1. Does this classroom contain a wide, but not overwhelming, variety of age-appropriate activities that occur throughout the day?
2. Does this classroom contain activities that occur at the same time each day?
3. Does this classroom contain activities requiring active involvement of the children?
4. Does this classroom encourage children to choose their own activities?

CASE STUDY ANALYSIS: Are Mr. Fox's Activities Developmentally Appropriate?

Use the criteria just presented to decide how well Mr. Fox's classroom meets the criteria for developmentally appropriate activities.

1. There was a wide, but not overwhelming, variety of age-appropriate activities that occurred throughout the day.
   Examples:
2. His classroom contained activities that occur at the same time each day.
   Examples:
3. His classroom contained activities requiring the active involvement of the children.
   Examples:
4. He encouraged children to choose their own activities.
   Examples:

Summary: Activities in a classroom do indeed affect self-control, independence, and competence. Explain *how well* Mr. Fox's classroom is likely to foster these positive traits.

Provide Developmentally Appropriate Materials

Adults influence children by providing materials and equipment (see chapter 2). Adults who provide a moderately rich assortment of exploratory materials encourage competent, independent behavior in children (Stallings, 1975; Wachs & Gruen, 1982; White & Watts, 1973). Professionals choose materials that reflect the developmental level of the children and the goals of the school or learning center, but there are general criteria for organizing any type of material chosen (Olds, 1977).

Take Leadership in Gathering Materials

Adults in healthy systems take a clear leadership role, and this applies to early childhood settings when teachers take leadership in gathering materials for activities. It is the adult's responsibility to think through items needed and to gather or help children collect things needed for specific projects.

An excellent management strategy is to list *all* materials that you will need for an activity. Exactly what do children need for a "paper" collage? A backing of some sort, paper to be cut or torn, scissors if cutting, paste, a pen for writing names, and a place to store collages while they dry. Making this list is not a waste of time because when this strategy is used consistently it becomes an automatic skill. This does not mean, however, that you never ask the children to do problem solving, such as "How can you make this collage without scissors? You need little pieces of paper but you don't have scissors. What can you do?"

Provide Correctly Sized Items That Work Well

Children with positive self-esteem believe that they have some control over events in their lives. The early childhood period is an important time in the development of self-esteem because of hundreds of almost imperceptible ways in which teachers help children acquire this healthy sense of control.

Example   Mr. Fox realizes that a good way to help children achieve a sense of control over their environment is for them to be able to use equipment and materials by themselves as much as possible and without a lot of help from him. He supplies small scissors and cuts dress-up clothes to fit them. Paint aprons are small and easily managed by his 4-year-olds. He placed a step in front of one of the sinks so that every child could use faucets unaided, and clipped clothespins at the children's height so that they could hang their own paintings. He pasted outlines of blocks on shelves where he expected children to place specific blocks. He also believes that equipment that is clean and works well will foster a sense of control—scissors are stripped of paste, paintbrushes scrupulously clean, easels clean, trikes oiled, items repaired, and blocks sanded.

Organize and Display Materials Well

Organize materials logically (e.g., items for creative arts should be stored in the creative arts area). If you expect children to routinely clean certain things, such as easels, paintbrushes, and their spots at tables, then organize sponges, water, and soap so that children can use them easily. If you expect them to help with setting tables for lunch, organize an area where they have easy access to napkins, cups, and sponges. Make the effort to think through how you can inexpensively organize items used in the manipulatives area (e.g., plastic dishpans? baskets? recycled heavy cardboard boxes?). Bowers (1990) gives excellent suggestions for organizing equipment.

Display books so that the front cover is visible. Keep puzzles on puzzle racks and resist stacking puzzles on top of each other. Children find it much easier and less frustrating to remove a puzzle from a rack than from a pile. Display blocks by arranging them according to size and stacking them neatly on shelves. Cue children about the arrangement by painting the outline of the block on the shelf. Store crayons, paper, paste, and scissors in attractive, convenient containers and place them on low, open shelves in the art area.

Decide Which Materials Should (or Should Not) Be Accessible to Children

Independence is fostered if children can easily reach materials needed for a certain task, so display materials to which children should have access on low, open shelves or in other logical places. Materials that children are not allowed to use should not be available to them. For example, teacher supplies and scissors should be stored out of reach.

Encourage Children to Personalize Activity Areas

Help children put their imprint on their classroom. There are lots of ways for you to encourage children to claim ownership or to "personalize" their space (Vergeront, 1987). For example, observe a few classrooms and "savor the flavor" of the rooms in which each child's artwork is joyfully displayed. You will see all sorts of matted or unmatted two-dimensional artwork (easel, sponge, spatter, screen paintings; drawings done with chalk, markers, crayons). You may also be lucky enough to observe how teachers display three dimensional work, such as mobiles, stabiles, and play dough structures. A very nice side effect of displaying artwork is that parents learn about children's stages of development through their paintings, drawings, and sculptures.

Developmentally appropriate practice means attending to the needs of individuals. Some children do not do the usual "art" work, but you can still display their work in other areas. Observe each child carefully and vow to find his strength; then simply make a record of his progress in his chosen activity. Display these along with the typical matted artwork to show that you value the work of each and every child.

Examples   Take photos of blockbuilding to show the same stagelike progression as more typical artwork. Display the photos to show parents this child's work over time.

Collect a booklet of stories by your budding writer.

Make a chart summarizing the scientific observations of a child whose main interest lies in things like magnets.

DESIGNING DEVELOPMENTALLY APPROPRIATE PHYSICAL ENVIRONMENTS FOR INFANTS AND TODDLERS

"It is impossible to think about the infant at any age without at the same time considering the child's environment" (Fogel, 1984, p. 276).

Brief Summary of Infant/Toddler Development

Developmentally appropriate physical environments are based on the developmental level of the children using them. This brief summary of development during the first 3 years of life is based on Fogel's work (1984). Very young infants, up to 3 or 4 months, are involved in getting bodily and physiological systems in order. Parents and teachers spend a lot of their time with new infants holding and rocking the baby, giving them tactile stimulation, and helping them establish a schedule of eating, sleeping, playing, and exercising.

Continued development in several areas enables infants to cope somewhat more easily with more complex stimulation. Rapid perceptual and motor development in infancy allows the infant to engage in one-on-one interactions, to play with any of hundreds of "things" in his environment, and to experience the pleasure of these new abilities.

Infants are partners in social interaction from the moment they are born, but cognitive development during the first year or so of life enables infants to "sense" their status as partners in social interaction and realize that they "cause" things to happen. Emotional development is tied to cognitive development and, like cognition, shows dramatic changes during the first year. By 10 to 12 months, infants are better able to use complex "feeling," or affective, states to adapt to more intense or confusing stimulation, although their ability *is* still limited.

By his first birthday, an infant has a better sense of the permanence of objects, that is, that Mom and Dad do not disappear when he cannot see them. He now understands the value of words and has become a real "communicator." Emotional development over the next few years means that toddlers will develop fears and some anxiety, but, as Fogel says, have play, dreams, and understanding caregivers to help them deal with these uneasy feelings.

Ever-changing cognitive and emotional development allow toddlers to begin to see themselves as separate individuals and to be conscious of the "self," a phenomenon that grows as infants and toddlers interact with others. Motor skills advance, enabling toddlers to act in an increasingly autonomous way. Development during this period and in the next few years allows toddlers to experience the joy of living, to begin to understand the world around them, and to develop feelings of competence and confidence.

Adults: Architects of Environments for Infants and Toddlers
The Physical and Caregiving Environments

There are two types of environments—the *physical environment* and the *caregiving environment*—for children from birth to age 3 (Fogel, 1984). The two are difficult to separate because caregivers have such a crucial role in structuring the physical environment for infants. The *physical environment* includes all objects and situations, such as how clean and safe the home or center is; the types of toys and how available they are; the size and nature of the home or center; the adequacy of nutrition, health care, and sanitary practices; and the variety of objects and settings that the baby experiences. The *caregiving environment* includes caregiver behavior as the caregiver interacts with baby.

Adults support the development of children in the first 3 years of life by knowing each infant or toddler as an individual and by designing the physical environment to be safe, cozy, and appropriate for the care and education of each child in the group (Fu, 1984). Responsive teachers of infants take a lot of responsibility for infants because infants are not equipped to function on their own. Responsive teachers understand that babies cannot control themselves, cannot remember things, and are limited in how they tell us what they need. Responsive teachers anticipate what babies need and know when and how to gradually adjust the support and how to transfer control to the child as he reaches certain stages of development.

Examples   Mrs. Goldberg, head teacher in the infant room, realizes that babies cannot stop crying just because somebody tells them to. But she knows that babies cry for lots of different reasons and that there are some things she can do to help a baby who is crying (see *Special Focus: Why Does Baby Cry?*).

SPECIAL FOCUS: Why Does Baby Cry?

▼   *Hungry.* Babies often cry when they're hungry. If it has been at least two hours since he was fed, see if he is hungry.

▼   *Lonely.* If a baby calms and stays calm as soon as you pick him up, he missed you! A baby's need for closeness is real. You can't spoil a baby by cuddling him when he needs it.

▼   *Cold/Hot.* Feel the baby's back or tummy to see if he is too cold or too hot. Adjust his clothing to make him comfortable. Dress a baby as warmly as you dress yourself, or one layer warmer.

▼   *Overstimulated.* Give him calm and quiet. Rocking him in a dimly lit room may help.

▼   *Undressed.* Put a cloth on his tummy until you redress him.

▼   *Startled.* A baby may move suddenly, startle, and cry. Wrapping a blanket securely around him and holding him securely may calm him.

▼   *Wet diaper.* Some babies don't mind; others do.

▼   *Pain.* A baby might be ill or uncomfortable because a pin is pricking him or because his clothes have sharp tags or zippers.

▼   *Sleepiness.* Some babies need to fuss a bit before sleeping.

Source: Parenting the First Year. Wisconsin Children's Trust Fund, 110 E. Main St., Suite 614, Madison, WI. Adapted from the newsletter for the first month of life.

Ms. Corelli, head teacher in the toddler room, understands that her children have not yet achieved self-control and that her job is to model self-control and to gradually transfer control to them as they progress through toddlerhood. She does this when setting limits by giving positively worded statements like "Hit this ball," rather than just restricting a toddler and saying what *not* to do.

The Physical Environment Affects Cognitive Development
Problem Solving in Infants and Toddlers

An infant or toddler's cognitive development is affected by how well his care-givers manage the physical environment. For example, children in their second and third years have better problem-solving skills and engage in more exploratory behavior when teachers and parents provide certain types of objects for them (Fogel, 1984).

Implications

▼   *Provide a variety of safe inanimate objects for infants.*

▼   *Provide objects that are responsive to an infant's actions,* such as busy boards, nesting blocks, and shape sorters.

Provide infants with safe toys that are responsive to their actions.

Spatial Relations in Infants and Toddlers

Young children develop better spatial relations and perspective taking in well-organized and peaceful environments.

Implications

▼ *Avoid noise, confusion, and overcrowding in environments for infants and toddlers.*

▼ *Organize the physical environment well.* Develop activity areas to meet the developmental needs of infants and toddlers.

How Infants Plan Strategies

A child's ability to figure out new ways to do things and to plan effective strategies is related to the type of play materials parents and teachers provide (Wachs, 1982; Wachs & Gruen, 1982).

Implication

▼ *Provide age-appropriate play materials for infants and toddlers.*

Timing of Stimulation for Infants and Toddlers

Wachs found that certain forms of environmental stimulation were more effective for development if they were introduced at specific ages during infancy and toddlerhood.

Implication

▼ *Introduce certain forms of environmental stimulation at specific ages* (see *Special Focus: Time Environmental Stimulation Well for Infants and Toddlers*).

Activity Areas for Infants and Toddlers

Infants and toddlers learn through experimentation and repetition, and teachers encourage their learning by providing a safe, stimulating, and emotionally supportive environment. "Routines are the curriculum" (Bredekamp, 1986), and sensitive teachers take advantage of routine situations such as eating, bathing, diapering, and dressing to help very young children feel safe and learn at the same time.

Well-organized infant and toddler rooms contain activity areas but are not just scaled-down versions of classrooms for children 3 to 8 years old. Infants and toddlers should be able to practice sensorimotor activities in a well-designed space: clean, spacious bathing and dressing areas; crawling, scooting, walking in safe, open areas; pushing, pulling, rolling, emptying, and filling safe, clean toys; climbing on safe structures; gazing at objects at their level; and doing messy, active things like fingerpainting or the swish-swish of a water table.

SPECIAL FOCUS: Time Environmental Stimulation Well for Infants and Toddlers

Birth to 6 Months

▼   Provide a variety of things for the baby to look at.

▼   Provide lots of physical contact. Some babies do *not* like to cuddle, so tune in to what the individual needs.

▼   Avoid overcrowding, excessive noise, and confusion.

▼   Pay attention to and respond to the baby's social signals.

6 to 12 Months   (Continue above. Emphasize following)

▼   Plan a variety of appropriate activities.

▼   Assure primary caregiver interaction with the baby.

▼   Let the infant have lots of "floor freedom."

▼   Give the infant a variety of safe objects.

▼   Place objects within the baby's reach.

▼   Provide objects that "respond" to the baby's actions.

12 to 24 Months   (Continue above. Emphasize following)

▼   Provide verbal stimulation.

▼   Encourage exploration.

▼   Avoid restricting or forcing the child to do things. But, set reasonable, developmentally appropriate limits.

▼   Assure a predictable but flexible physical environment and time schedule.

24 to 36 Months   (Continue above. Emphasize following)

▼   Respond to the toddler's verbal signals.

Source: Adapted from Wachs & Gruen (1982).

Rattle, Reach, and Roll: Activity Areas for Infants

Well-designed and maintained diapering, dressing areas

Comfort corner (soft spot)

Pleasant eating area

Rattle, reaching, and sensory areas

Manipulative area

Interaction-game area

Exercise mat

Water table

Reading

Explorers: Activity Areas for Toddlers

Well-designed and maintained eating, toileting, dressing, and sleeping areas

Music corner

Private space

Block corner

Dramatic play

Creative arts

Large muscle area

Sand/water table

Play dough table

Reading

Comfort corner (*soft spot*)

Small muscle

Sources: Cataldo, 1983; King et al., 1990; Marion, 1991; Miller, 1984; Wilson, 1990. King et al., Miller, Wilson, and Bredekamp (1986) give excellent suggestions on specific and developmentally appropriate activities for these centers.

SUMMARY OF KEY CONCEPTS

1. There are two types of environments for children—the *physical* and the *human* (or caregiver/teacher). The two are intertwined because adults play such a crucial role in setting up the physical environment. Several human environmental factors are essential to a developmentally appropriate physical classroom environment. This chapter has focused on how adults design and manage the physical environment.

2. Developmentally appropriate physical environments foster positive adaptive behavior, confidence, and competence in young children. There are several characteristics of a *developmentally appropriate physical classroom environment:* it

has an adequate number of well-designed and well-arranged activity areas; it is clean, attractive, relatively quiet, and sensory-rich but not excessively stimulating, cluttered, or confusing; activities are developmentally appropriate, and materials for activities are arranged and displayed well; and children are encouraged to personalize the room.

3. Designing a developmentally appropriate environment for infants and toddlers requires that adults understand development of children from birth to age 3. Teachers are then equipped to make knowledge-based decisions about design and management of physical environments for infants and toddlers. Well-designed and well-managed physical environments for infants and toddlers have a positive effect on cognitive development of children using those environments.

4. Well-organized infant and toddler rooms contain activity areas and follow many of the same principles outlined for classrooms for older children, but the developmental level of children from birth to age 3 calls for modifications in the type of activity areas provided.

OBSERVE CHILD GUIDANCE IN ACTION
Observing the Arrangement of Space in a Classroom

The goal of the observation is to observe the space and to give positive feedback.

1. Draw a simple floor plan of a classroom for children from birth to age 8. Include the toilet area for children, doors to the outside and to hallways, small-group learning centers, large-group area, private areas, and boundaries between areas. Label each area clearly.

2. Use the following form to explain how this classroom meets the criteria for effective arrangement of each of these areas.

Name: _____

Setting: _____

Date: _____

Number of children: _____

Ages of children: _____

Private Area. Positive feedback: explain how the private space in this classroom meets the criteria for private spaces.

Large-Group Area. Positive feedback: explain how the large-group area in this classroom meets the criteria for large-group areas.

Small-Group Learning Centers. Number of centers: _____ Positive feedback: Explain how the small-group learning centers in this classroom meet criteria for this type of activity area.

3. Make positive suggestions for changes that would make this classroom even better. Show your recommendations graphically by drawing a second-

floor plan, this time with suggestions clearly indicated. (For instance, if you note that the classroom does not have a private space, decide where you would put it and draw it on your "after" floor plan.)

REFERENCES

Alward, K. R. (1973). *Arranging the classroom for children*. San Francisco: Far West Laboratory for Educational Research and Development.

Bowers, C. (1990). Organizing space for children. Texas *Child Care Quarterly*, Spring, 3–10, 22.

Bredekamp, S. (Ed.) (1986). *Developmentally appropriate practice*. Washington, DC: NAEYC.

Cataldo, M. (1983). *Infant and toddler programs: A guide for very early childhood education*. Reading, MA: Addison-Wesley.

Day, D. E. (1983). *Early childhood education: A human ecological approach*. Glenview, IL: Scott Foresman.

Fogel, A. (1984). *Infancy: Infant, family, and society*. St. Paul, MN: West Publishing.

Fu, V. (1984). Infant/toddler care in centers. In L. Dittmann (Ed.), *The infants we care for*. Washington, DC: NAEYC.

Heimstra, N. W., & McFarling, L. H. (1974). *Environmental psychology*. Monterey, CA: Brooks/Cole.

Howes, C. (1991). Caregiving environments and their consequences for children: The experience in the United States. In E. Melhuish & P. Moss (Eds.), *Day care for young children*. New York: Routledge.

Jones, E., & Prescott, E. *Environments for young children*. Washington, DC: NAEYC, Film #806.

King, M., Oberlin, A., & Swank, T. (1990). Supporting the activity choices of two-year-olds. *Day Care and Early Education*, *17*(2), 9–13 and 67–70.

Kritchevsky, S., & Prescott, E. (1977). *Environments for young children: Physical space*. Washington, DC: NAEYC.

Marcu, M. (1977). Environmental design and architecture: The friendly environment versus the hostile environment. *Children in Contemporary Society*, *11*(1), 3–5.

Marion, M. (1991). *Guidance of young children* (3rd ed.). New York: Merrill/Macmillan.

Mehrabian, A. (1976). *Public places and private spaces: The psychology of work, play, and living environments*. New York: Basic Books.

Miller, K. (1984). *More things to do with toddlers and twos*. Chelsea, MA: TelShare Publishing.

Myhre, S. (1993). Enhancing your dramatic play area through the use of prop boxes. *Young Children*, *48*(5), 6–19.

Olds, A. R. (1977). Why is environmental design important to young children? *Children in Contemporary Society*, *11*(1), 58.

Olds, A. R. (1987). Designing settings for infants and toddlers. In C. S. Weinstein & T. G. David (Eds.), *Spaces for children*. New York: Plenum Press.

Phyfe-Perkins, E. (1980). Children's behavior in preschool settings: The influence of the physical environment. In L. G. Katz (Ed.), *Current topics in early childhood education* (Vol. 3). Norwood, NJ: Ablex.

Prescott, E. (1984). The physical setting in day care. In J. Greenman (Ed.), *Making day care better*. New York: Teacher's College Press.

Sommer, R. (1974). *Tight spaces: Hard architecture and how to humanize it*. Englewood Cliffs, NJ: Prentice-Hall.

Stallings, J. (1975). Implementation and child effects of teaching practices in followthrough classrooms. *Monographs of the Society for Research in Child Development, 40* (78).

Vergeront, J. (1987). *Places and spaces for preschool and primary (Indoors)*. Washington, DC: NAEYC.

Wachs, T. D. (1982). Early experience and early cognitive development: The search for specificity. In I. Uzgiris & J. Hunt (Eds.), *Research with scales of psychological development in infancy*. Champaign: University of Illinois Press.

Wachs, T. D., & Gruen, G. E. (1982). *Early experience and human development*. New York: Plenum.

White, B. L., & Watts. J. C. (1973). *Experience and environment: Major influences on the development of the young child* (Vol. 1). Englewood Cliffs, NJ: Prentice-Hall.

Wilson, L. C. (1990). *Infants and toddlers* (2nd ed.). New York: DelMar.

Part Two

Special Topics in
Child Guidance

This section concentrates on topics of special interest to early childhood educators—stress, self-esteem, anger, aggression, and prosocial behavior.

Chapter 5. Helping Children Cope With Stress. This chapter describes stress and what happens to children when they cannot cope with potential stressors. You will learn what you can do to eliminate stressors or to buffer their effects on children—and on you.

Chapter 6. Helping Children Develop Positive Self-Esteem. This chapter focuses on developing a positive evaluation of the self as well as developing a clearly defined set of personal values. Teachers can help children do both.

Chapter 7. Responsible Anger Management: The Long, Bumpy Road. A 1993 report from the American Psychological Association notes that one of the most effective ways to decrease violence is to teach people how to recognize, accept, and responsibly manage angry feelings. Case studies in this chapter give you a chance to try out specific practical strategies for smoothing the bumpy road for children—and yourself.

Chapter 8. Understanding and Coping With Aggression in Children. This chapter is a companion to the previous one. It will help you understand how some children become excessively aggressive and how you can best deal with their aggression while also protecting others. You will solve problems and analyze case studies as you practice effective strategies for decreasing aggression.

Chapter 9. Prosocial Behavior: Nurturing the Roots of Concern for Others. One of our tasks as early childhood educators is to nurture the roots of compassion, generosity, helpfulness, and cooperation in the children we teach. When we nurture these positive traits, we actually give children an alternative to aggression—a truly fine gift. You will practice strategies for enhancing prosocial behavior when you analyze this chapter's case studies.

5

Helping Children
Cope With Stress

Chapter Overview

After reading and studying this chapter, you will be able to

▼ *Define* and *explain* stress for children as a child–environment relationship.

▼ *Identify* two major categories or sources of stress for children and *give examples* for each category.

▼ *List* the stages of the stress response, *summarize* the elements of each stage, and *identify* stages of the stress response evident in a case study.

▼ *Describe* the effects that chronic stress may have on physical health.

▼ *List* properties of optimal coping and *summarize* what each implies about a person who has these skills.

▼ *Explain* how young children's developmental limitations hamper their ability to automatically know how to cope with stress.

▼ *List* and *give examples of* guidelines for helping children cope with stress.

▼ *Analyze* a case study in which a teacher attempts to buffer the effect of stress for a child.

> *"Growing up means meeting a variety of challenges,*
> *many of which can cause stress."*
> (McCracken, 1986)

CASE STUDY: Winnie's New School

Wednesday, 5:30 P.M.

Mr. Moore waited for Winnie, a new child in his class, and her dad to arrive. "Hello Winnie. I'm pleased to meet you," said Mr. Moore. To her father he said, "Please come in and we'll all look around Winnie's new classroom. Here's where you hang your coat. I've printed Winnie's name on her locker already." He showed her the pictures of the children in the class and took her picture to place with the others. He pointed out areas in the classroom, and then they toured the playground. Mr. Moore showed Winnie the children's bathroom. She practiced turning on faucets, using the soap dispenser, and getting paper towels. She and Dad looked at the toileting area, which was in a room right next to the classroom. "You can go to the bathroom whenever you want to," said Mr. Moore. "We have snack here at your new school, but we usually have juice in a cup." (She had milk in a carton at her other school.)

Mr. Moore asked Winnie about her favorite activities (play dough), books, snack (crackers and cheese), and song. Then they looked in the nap room, and Winnie discovered that she already had a cot with her name on it. Mr. Moore told Winnie that they would have blue play dough tomorrow.

Privately, Dad told Mr. Moore, "This room is different from her old one where she did lots of workbooks and coloring books. She used to cry because the teacher made the children wait for lots of things, like using the toilet. I'm relieved that I got transferred to this part of the state. I'll do whatever I can to help her adjust to her new school." Mr. Moore replied, "I have a book on moving. You can borrow it if you'd like. Winnie might like to read it with you."

Thursday Morning

Winnie stood next to her locker while all the new faces swirled around her. Mr. Moore decided to let her watch the other children for a while, but brought her a piece of the play dough to squish while she looked. Soon he brought Justin over to her and said, "Justin, Winnie would like to play with some of our play dough equipment. Will you please show her where the rollers and cookie cutters are?" Snack that morning was cheese and crackers, Winnie's favorite. Mr. Moore explained the playground rules to Winnie when they went outside, and at naptime Winnie knew that she had a cot with her name on it.

CASE STUDY: Daniel and the Math Workbook

At Home

Dan's father, Tom, fresh from yet another argument with Mom, walked into the family room, where 5½-year-old Daniel sat with a bowl of popcorn on the sofa. "Move!" said Dad. Daniel jumped off, knocking over the bowl of popcorn. Knowing what was coming, he tensed and shut his eyes. Dad said, "Here we go again. Pick up this popcorn! I wish you'd never been born."

Mom walked in. "What a mess. You know what he did today, Tom? He picked seven new green onion plants . . . said they were *weeds*. He said he was helping you with the garden." Dad to Dan, "Dummy! I'm going to make sure that you're in the 'dummy room' at school." Dan cried as he lay trying to go to sleep that night.

Next Day at Kindergarten

One of the many developmentally *in*appropriate practices Dan's teacher uses is a math workbook that all the children do in a group. Teacher, "Open your workbooks to page 54. Hurry up about it." Daniel, exhausted from problems at home and a poor night's sleep, looked left, then right, puzzled about what 54 looked like or even where to look on the page. He seemed to panic as the children next to him found the page. The teacher droned on as Dan sat rigid. "Daniel, pick up that pencil and get to work!" He picked up the pencil, bent over a page, tears dripping onto the book. He still had not found page 54.

WHAT IS STRESS?

Zimbardo (1982) believes that humans have several fundamental needs—security, bonding, status, meaning, and mastery—and that stress results when conditions threaten the achievement of these needs.

There are several ways of looking at the concept of stress. One view is that stress is a *life event* that is generally considered stressful, such as moving, starting a new job, having a parent die, or going through a divorce. Zegans (1982) believes that these life events may well result in stress but that the life event is not in itself a stress. Other researchers believe that stress is solely a *response* that sometimes occurs after an event (Tache & Selye, 1978), such as ulcers, headaches, and an inability to concentrate.

Stress results for children when they cannot cope effectively with some internal or external demand. This definition, then, views stress as a *relationship* between a child and her environment. She feels stress because she does not have the resources with which to cope effectively with some event and therefore is overwhelmed by it (Holroyd & Lazarus, 1982).

Many people believe that moving is a stressful life event for preschool children (Jalongo, 1986b), and most adults acknowledge that preschool children are affected by moving. Using our definition, however, it is Winnie's (see case study) evaluation of the move and of her ability to cope with it that eventually places moving in the "stressful" or "not stressful" column.

SOURCES OF STRESS FOR CHILDREN

Internal Sources of Stress

Some events with which children cannot cope are *internal;* that is, they come from within the child (Honig, 1986). Internal sources of stress include things like pangs of hunger in an infant who is being neglected; shyness (Zimbardo & Radl, 1981; Zimbardo, 1982); or headaches (Sargent, 1982). Emotions may also be internal sources of stress. Anxiety, anger, jealousy, guilt, and even joy are potentially stressful for children if parents and teachers do not help them understand and deal with these emotions. Children do not automatically understand and know how to deal with an emotion like guilt (Marion, 1993, 1994).

Examples   John was happy about the family trip to the beach, but the feeling was apparently overwhelming and stressful because his mom said he just "lost it and got overexcited."

Peter's family is tension ridden, with constant bickering, loud arguments, and even physical violence when Dad slaps Mom around. Peter is puzzled and confused by his family dynamics, and the hostility in his family is threatening his security. He gets absolutely no help from his parents in coping with his fear and anxiety. He is overwhelmed and in a state of stress. Lately, he has had terrible pains in his stomach, which his doctor has diagnosed as ulcers.

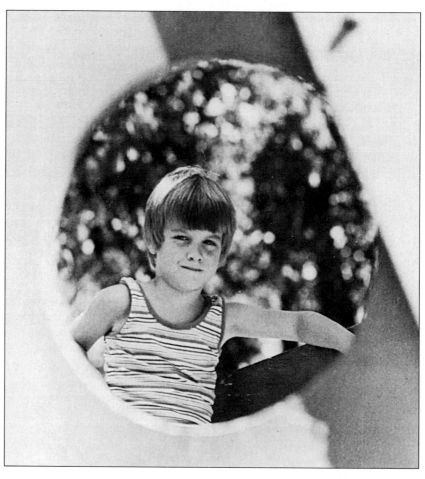

Young children are the target of many **external** *sources of stress.*

External Sources of Stress

Other potential sources of stress for children are *external;* that is, they come from the child's environment. Boundaries that separate infants from parents can evoke stress (Pollowy, 1977). In overcrowded houses or apartments, the degree of quarreling and the extent to which parents hit their children is likely to increase (Edwards & Booth, 1977). Other external sources of stress include divorce (Skeen & McKenry, 1986); joint custody arrangements (McKinnon & Wallerstein, 1987); moving (Matter & Matter, 1987); going to a new school with new children, some of whom might be aggressive (Furman, 1986; Kostelnik, Whiren, & Stein, 1986); poor quality day care (Matlock & Green, 1990); daily hassles for parents (Crnic & Greenberg, 1990); child abuse (Gale, Thompson, Moran, & Sack, 1988; Garbarino, Guttman, & Seeley, 1986; Kiser, Ackerman, Brown, & Edwards, 1988; Martin & Elmer, 1992); social interactions in which anger plays a part (Fabes & Eisenberg, 1992; Marion, 1993, in press); negative discipline (Defares, 1987; Marion, 1991); illness and hospitalization (Bull & Drotar, 1991; Fassler, 1986; Stuber, Nadar, Yasuda, & Pynoos, 1991); "hothousing," or developmentally inappropriate expectations for achievement (Burts, Hart, Charleworth, Fleege, Mosley, & Thomasson, 1992; Elkind, 1987; Gallagher & Ooche, 1987; Hills, 1987; Hyson, Hirsh-Pasek, Rescorla, & Cone, 1991; Minuchin, 1987; Zuckerman, 1987); death (Furman, 1986); and blended families (Skeen, Robinson, & Flake-Hobson, 1986).

Acute and Chronic Stress

Some stress is *acute.* It occurs quite suddenly but tends to subside as suddenly as it arose, like a visit to the emergency room to have a broken arm set or a visit from the firefighters to put out a fire. The impact of the event on a child depends on how the child appraises the event and on how others deal with the event. The trip to the emergency room to have a broken arm set will have little impact if parents buffer the experience for a child. On the other hand, one instance of being sexually molested can have a long-lasting impact if parents and professionals deal with the incident poorly.

Some stress is *chronic;* that is, it goes on and on. The effects of chronic stress seem to accumulate to cause problems even for children who are well adjusted (Honig, 1986). Chronic illness, child abuse, irresponsible or inept parenting, long-term bitterness after divorce, and daily hassles are a few examples of chronic stress.

STAGES OF THE STRESS RESPONSE

Children go through a series of stages in response to a stressor, and each stage places different demands on a child's body (Zegans, 1982).

Alarm

A child stops what she is doing and "orients" toward or focuses on the potentially stressful event.

Example   Ben, 5½ years old, sat in the barber's chair for his first barbershop haircut. He looked around the shop, closely following the barber's activities and keeping an eye on Dad.

Appraisal

A complex stage, *appraisal* involves reviewing what this event meant in the past ("Dad has always cut my hair before") and making an assessment of how to cope ("I've visited here with Dad, and he's here with me now"). In older children, personality traits such as positive self-esteem influence what the event means and whether children think they can cope ("Dad says I'm brave").

Searching for a Coping Strategy

Children have a better chance of coping successfully when they believe they can control or master the event (Levine, Weinberg, & Ursin, 1978). Controlling or mastering an event depends, first, on whether the child is familiar with this event, and second, on whether she can generate successful coping strategies. The following possibilities were outlined by Zegans (1982).

1. *The stressor is familiar, was actively encountered in the past, and a good coping strategy was used in past.* Dad took Ben to the barbershop whenever Dad got

Child life specialists are trained to help children adjust to the potentially stressful experience of going to the hospital, particularly during the holidays.

haircuts, and Ben got to sit in the big chair on his own or with Dad. The barber showed Ben the things used in haircutting, such as a comb, scissors, and towel.

2. *The stressor is familiar and was actively encountered in past, but the coping strategy failed* because it was applied incorrectly or was not a good strategy in the first place. John's father also took John to the barbershop, but when John was in the chair he said to the barber, "Now it's time for the big scissors!"

3. *The stressor is familiar, but it was passively encountered in the past;* that is, the child has had only a secondhand experience of the event, and the secondhand source of information has an impact on her level of emotional or physiological arousal.

   Example   John's secondhand experience with barbershops was from a brother who told him that the barber uses BIG scissors that get ". . . real close to your ears! You have to sit still while he cuts!" At the barber's John sat still in the chair and didn't cry, but he wet his pants when he saw the scissors.

4. *The stressor is totally unfamiliar.* In this case the child does not have a coping strategy, and her level of physiological or emotional arousal depends on whether she thinks a coping strategy is available. Adults can be helpful in these cases when they

   ▼   alter the situation and eliminate the stressful event. When Ben's family moved (something they had never done before) they did not know anyone in their new neighborhood. Dad took Ben for a "get acquainted" walk and met the new neighbors.

   ▼   buffer the impact of the stressful event by helping a child control the meaning of the unfamiliar event. Ben's first trip to the emergency room had all the earmarks of a "stressful event" when his parents ran to the car with him seconds after he fell off the swing and broke his arm. A neighbor called the emergency room. In the car, Mom cradled him and spoke soothingly, realizing how frightened he was. "Remember the hospital, Ben? We're going there now, to a special room called the emergency room. A doctor is waiting for you and she'll take a special picture so she can see your arm's bone. Then she'll fix the bone. Mommy and Daddy will stay with you. And then we'll all come home. It'll be OK."

CASE STUDY ANALYSIS: Daniel's Stages of Stress Response

Stage of Alarm

1. I could tell that Dan was clearly in the stage of alarm at home when he . . .

2. At school he went through the stage of alarm when he . . .

3. I think that Dad and Mom's behavior is likely to result in negative self-esteem for Dan because . . .

Stage of Appraisal

4. Dan's behavior seemed to indicate that he appraised the incidents at home and at school as things he could not cope with. Specific behavior(s) that support this conclusion were . . .

5. Suppose that a child with positive self-esteem also had problems finding the workbook page. Describe how she would have demonstrated confidence in her ability to cope with the potentially stressful event.

Stage of Searching for a Coping Strategy

6. I could tell that Dan was familiar with Dad's abuse because . . .

7. Dan coped with his father's outbursts by . . .

8. How might Dan's coping strategy *make sense* in view of his inability to do anything about this psychologically abusive behavior?

Summary: Explain how the climate of fear and anxiety in Dan's home seems to be affecting his emotional and intellectual functioning.

EFFECTS OF STRESS

Common effects of stress are depression, crying, poor concentration, sweaty palms, racing heart, dry throat, headaches, and ulcers. These are symptoms that something is wrong in our world. Our body's major goal in responding to stress is to maintain constancy, or *homeostasis*. Our body's responses are controlled by our brain, which receives messages about the stressful event from all parts of our body. The brain's task is to prepare our body for either "fight" or "flight" by increasing breathing rate, heart rate, and blood pressure; by dilating air passages; by shunting blood to skeletal muscles; and by increasing production of certain hormones. The number of white blood cells also decreases; since these cells protect us from infections, a child who is chronically stressed may have a lowered resistance to infectious diseases (Hole, 1981).

Stress, then, can cause disease in a number of ways (Zegans, 1982). Our immune system response can be decreased or exaggerated (Stein, Keller, & Schleifer, 1981); our body might produce either too much or far too little of certain hormones (Lipton, 1976); and our sleep patterns are often interrupted, which has a negative effect on a variety of our body's functions (Weitzman, Boyar, Kapen, & Hellman, 1975).

COPING EFFECTIVELY WITH STRESSORS
What Is Coping?

Coping is a search for resources inside or outside oneself to come to terms with stressors (Haan, 1982). There are a multitude of ways to deal with stressful events

(Cohen & Lazarus, 1979). A person can seek information, take direct action (run away or argue), inhibit action (Dan in the case study did this), or use intrapsychic processes (deny or avoid the problem). One of the major characteristics of abusive families is that they deny the abuse (Tower, 1993).

Haan (1982) believes that coping does not necessarily mean a person will have a happy or successful outcome. Some situations, like the abuse that Dan experienced, do not allow the person a "successful" solution.

Aspects of Optimal Coping

Haan (1982) identified five aspects of optimal coping.

1. *Openly examining options*. This implies the ability to look at different options and consider at least two things at one time. It also requires the ability and willingness to "keep an open mind" and take a perspective that is different from one's usual way of looking at things.

2. *Creating flexible and inventive options*. This implies flexible thinking and a certain level of creativity in problem solving. It also implies an ability to categorize or classify groups of options.

3. *Being reality based and understanding how one's reactions will affect the situation*. This implies a knowledge and experience base from which to draw the understanding.

4. *Being able to think purposefully*. Thinking purposefully brings together our conscious and preconscious thoughts and implies an ability to "think about thinking."

5. *Being able to control negative or disturbing emotions*. This implies an awareness and acceptance of such emotions and an ability to effectively manage the emotions.

HOW CHILDREN COPE WITH STRESSORS

Infants, toddlers, and preschoolers, or even kindergartners and first or second graders, given their level of cognitive development, are not able to cope effectively with potential stressors on their own. They have difficulty considering two things at one time, and they operate at a very low level of perspective-taking.

The children we teach have limited classification skills. They obviously have a limited knowledge and experiential base and are not able to understand another person's motives. They tend to believe what important adults tell them and have a desire to please those adults. There is a real power differential between adults and children, and this works against children when they are confronted with certain potential stressors, such as sexual abuse.

Young children cannot "think about thinking," and this means that they will not think about their "conscious and preconscious" thoughts. Dan in the case study will not understand that he is denying the pain his Dad and Mom cause him, because he cannot understand the concept of denial. Young children *have* emotions, but they tend not to understand them or be able to deal with them. The research on anger tells us that children are not able to understand or deal with anger until a certain age, and then only if they have had good models and instruction in managing anger (see chapter 7).

HOW TEACHERS CAN HELP CHILDREN COPE WITH POTENTIALLY STRESSFUL EVENTS

Coping abilities develop gradually as infants and young children interact with their environment (Fogel, 1982). Therefore, your adult role in helping children develop good coping skills for stress is a crucial one. Early childhood teachers actively support children in developing many parts of their personalities (e.g., self-control and positive self-esteem) because we realize that these things do not develop automatically. Children also need developmentally appropriate support if they are going to cope effectively with stressful events (Dimidjian, 1985).

CASE STUDY ANALYSIS: Buffering Winnie's Move

Decide how well Mr. Moore has buffered the effect of moving to a new school for Winnie. He has attempted to follow suggestions recommended by Jalongo (1986a, 1986b).

1. Mr. Moore was *flexible* and allowed Winnie time to observe before she was expected to participate when he . . .
2. He treated both Winnie and her Dad courteously when he . . .
3. Mr. Moore provided *continuity* and pointed out similarities between her old and new schools when he . . .
4. Mr. Moore attempted to help Winnie feel "at ease" in and learn the routines of her new classroom by . . .
5. Winnie's old classroom was a stressor for her because . . .
6. Mr. Moore promoted peer interaction for Winnie when he . . .
7. Mr. Moore supported Winnie's dad in his efforts to smooth the transition to the new school when he . . .

Summary: I would rate this teacher's overall attempt to help Winnie adjust to this unavoidable but potentially stressful event as: Excellent, Good, Adequate, Barely Adequate, Quite Bad

SPECIAL FOCUS: Guidelines for Supporting Children in Coping With Stress

1. *Learn and model responsible stress management* (Honig, 1986; McBride, 1990). Children need teachers to model calm, thoughtful approaches to dealing with daily hassles.

2. *Create a low-stress classroom environment.* Anticipate and prevent stress whenever possible. For example, prevent the stress that accompanies developmentally inappropriate practices by purposively designing an appropriate classroom with appropriate activities and materials. Use positive discipline.

3. *Acknowledge and learn about the variety of stressors in children's lives.* Learn strategies that are helpful with specific stressors such as moving or going to the hospital.

4. *Give emotional support through reflective listening.* This is also called *active listening* and is described in chapter 10. When children are embroiled in a stress-producing event, we can best help by listening to their problem without judging, evaluating, or ordering them to feel differently.

5. *Do "mental muscle" training for stress with children* (Furman, 1986). Buffer the impact of stressful events by helping children control the meaning of the events. Give children opportunities to discuss their concerns in order to prepare them for stresses of new experiences.

6. *Teach coping skills.* Make up situations and then give instruction in how to deal with the issue. For example, "What could you do if you wanted to paint but somebody stepped up to the easel just before you did?"

7. *Teach creative relaxation*, a stress reduction technique for children (Campbell & Perkins, 1993; Humphrey, 1984). Children who can actively control their bodies by deliberately relaxing one or more body parts have a strategy that can be used when they are under stress. For example, a child who is very angry can be encouraged to cool down and decrease the stress accompanying the anger by taking deep breaths and by stretching her arms out like tight rubber bands and then bringing the rubber bands back to hang limply next to her body. After cooling down, the child will be more receptive to working on the anger-arousing issue.

8. *Be proactive.* Invest a part of your professional service time in "primary" prevention of stress, that is, in preventing some stressors from ever occurring. Go beyond your classroom to protect children. For example, prevent the stress of child abuse by preventing child abuse. Protect children by reporting suspected child abuse (teachers are *mandated* reporters). Join other teachers and take an active role in reviewing laws on abuse and neglect. Prevent stress from inept parenting by teaching positive discipline to parents through parent education.

SUMMARY OF KEY CONCEPTS

1. Children experience *stress* when they cannot cope effectively with some internal or external demand, when they are overwhelmed by an event because they lack resources with which to cope.

2. Some sources of stress for children are *internal*, such as emotions. Emotions such as anxiety, anger, or even joy are potentially stressful when a child's parents or teachers do not help the child understand and deal with them. Other potential sources of stress for children are *external*, and these include moving, divorce, child abuse, inept parenting, and illness. Stress may be *acute* or *chronic*.

3. Children go through three stages in responding to a potentially stressful event. First is the stage of *alarm*. Second is the stage of *appraisal*, in which the child makes a decision about what this event means for her and whether she thinks she can cope. Third is the stage of *searching for a coping strategy*, and success at this stage depends on whether the child can generate successful coping strategies.

4. The human body's responses to stress are aimed at maintaining constancy, or homeostasis. The body's response to stress is actually a warning signal, and exposure to chronic, severe stress can cause disease and other problems.

5. *Coping* is the search for resources inside or outside ourselves to come to terms with stressors. Optimal coping requires several abilities that young children do not have, but teachers can help children cope with potentially stressful events by preventing stress whenever possible, by creating low-stress classroom environments, by learning about the stressors in children's lives, and by buffering the impact of potential stressors.

OBSERVE CHILD GUIDANCE IN ACTION
Helping Children Cope With the Stress of Hospitalization

The goal is to observe how hospitals buffer the stress of hospitalization for children. Invite a *child life specialist* to class and interview her about how the hospital helps children cope with stress. Some sample questions:

How does the hospital buffer the stress of being admitted to the hospital when the admission is not an emergency? When the admission is an emergency?

Is a child life specialist available in the emergency room?

How does the child life specialist help children understand new or different procedures once the child has been admitted?

How important is play in buffering the effects of stress?

RESOURCES TO HELP YOU UNDERSTAND SPECIFIC STRESSORS

Campbell, J., & Perkins, M. *Vital choices for children*. Funded through the Office of the State Attorney General of Illinois. Available from Campbell or Perkins, Dept. of Curriculum and Instruction, Southern Illinois University at Carbondale, Carbondale, IL 62901–4610. This is a drug abuse prevention curriculum for use in early childhood settings. Level A is for prekindergarten through kindergarten; level B is for grades 1 through 3.

Childswork/Childsplay. (1993). *Helping kids deal with stress*. King of Prussia, PA: Center for Applied Psychology. This is a catalog of games, posters, books, and toys. Items focus on coping effectively with a variety of stressors.

McCracken, J. B. (1986). *Reducing stress in young children's lives*. Washington, DC: NAEYC. This a fine collection of articles on a variety of stressors affecting young children. Each article explains the nature of the stressor and then gives positive, concrete suggestions for helping children deal with it.

REFERENCES

American Psychological Association. (1993). *Violence and youth report*. Washington, DC: APA Commission on Violence and Youth.

Bull, B., & Drotar, D. (1991). Coping with cancer in remission: Stressors and strategies reported by children and adolescents. *Journal of Pediatric Psychology*, *16*(6), 767–782.

Burts, D., Hart, C., Charleworth, R., Fleege, P., Mosley, J., & Thomasson, R. (1992). Observed activities and stress behaviors of children in developmentally appropriate and inappropriate kindergarten classrooms. *Early Childhood Research Quarterly*, *7*, 297–318.

Campbell, J., & Perkins, M. (1993, November). *Vital choices for children*. A presentation at the annual convention of the National Association for the Education of Young Children, Anaheim, CA.

Cohen, F., & Lazarus. R. (1979). Coping with the stresses of illnesses. In G. C. Stone, F. Cohen, & N. E. Adler (Eds.), *Health psychology*. San Francisco: Jossey-Bass.

Crnic, K., & Greenberg, M. (1990). Minor parenting stresses with young children. *Child Development*, *6*(5), 1628–1637.

Defares, P. (1987). Stress and parent-child interactions. *Gedrag-and-Gezondeid-Tijdschrift-voor-Psychologie-and-Gedondheid*, *15*(1), 14–24.

Dimidjian, V. (1985). Helping children in times of trouble and crisis. *Journal of Children in Contemporary Society*, *17*(4), 113–128.

Edwards, J., & Booth, A. (1977). Crowding and human sexual behavior. *Social Forces*, *55*, 791–808.

Elkind, D. (1987). *Miseducation: Preschoolers at risk*. New York: Knopf.

Fabes, R., & Eisenberg, N. (1992). Young children's coping with interpersonal anger. *Child Development*, *63*(1), 116–128.

Fassler, D. (1986). The young child in the hospital. In J. B. McCracken (Ed.), *Reducing stress in young children's lives*. Washington, DC: NAEYC.

Fogel, A. (1982). Affect dynamics in early infancy: Affective tolerance. In T. Field & A. Fogel (Eds.), *Emotion and early interactions*. Hillsdale, NJ: Erlbaum.

Fogel, A. (1984). *Infancy*. St. Paul, MN: West Publishing.

Furman, E. (1986). What nursery school teachers ask us about: Psychoanalytic consultations in preschools: Stress in the nursery school. *Emotions and Behavior Monographs*, No. 5, 53–68.

Gale, J., Thompson, R., Moran, T., & Sack, W. (1988). Sexual abuse in young children: Its clinical presentation and characteristic patterns. *Child Abuse and Neglect*, *12*(2), 163–170.

Gallagher, J., & Ooche, J. (1987). Hothousing: The clinical and educational concerns over pressuring young children. *Early Childhood Research Quarterly*, *2*(3), 203–210.

Garbarino, J., Guttman, E., & Seeley, J. (1986). *The psychologically battered child*. San Francisco: Jossey-Bass.

Haan, N. (1982). The assessment of coping, defense, and stress. In L. Goldberger & S. Breznitz (Eds.), *Handbook of stress: Theoretical and clinical aspects*. New York: Free Press.

Hills, T. (1987). Children in the fast lane: Implications for early childhood policy and practice. *Early Childhood Research Quarterly*, *2*(3), 265–273.

Hole, J. (1981). *Human anatomy and physiology*. Dubuque, IA: Wm. C. Brown.

Holroyd, K., & Lazarus, R. (1982). Stress, coping, and somatic adaptation. In L. Goldberger & S. Breznitz (Eds.), *Handbook of stress: Theoretical and clinical aspects*. New York: Free Press.

Honig, A. S. (1986). Research in review: Stress and coping in children. In J. B. McCracken (Ed.), *Reducing stress in young children's lives*. Washington, DC: NAEYC.

Humphrey, J. (1984). Creative relaxation: A stress reduction technique for children. In J. Humphrey (Ed.), *Stress in childhood*. New York: AMS Press.

Hyson, M., Hirsh-Pasek, K., Rescorla, L., & Cone, J. (1991). Ingredients of parental pressure in early childhood. *Journal of Applied Developmental Psychology*, *12*(3), 347–365.

Jalongo, M. R. (1986a). Using crisis-oriented books with young children. In J. B. McCracken (Ed.), *Reducing stress in young children's lives*. Washington, DC: NAEYC.

Jalongo, M. R. (1986b). When young children move. In J. B. McCracken (Ed.), *Reducing stress in young children's lives*. Washington, DC: NAEYC.

Kiser, L., Ackerman, B., Brown, E., & Edwards, N. (1988). Post-traumatic stress disorder in young children: A reaction to purported sexual abuse. *Journal of the American Academy of Child and Adolescent Psychiatry*, *27*(5), 645–649.

Kostelnik, M., Whiren, A., & Stein, L. (1986). Living with he-man. In J. B. McCracken (Ed.), *Reducing stress in young children's lives*. Washington, DC: NAEYC.

Levine, S., Weinberg, J., & Ursin, H. (1978). Definition of the coping process and statement of the problem. In H. Ursin (Ed.), *Psychobiology of stress*. New York: Academic.

Lipton, M. (1976). Behavioral effects of hypothalamic polypeptide hormones in animals and man. In E. J. Sachar (Ed.), *Hormones, behavior and psychopathology*. New York: Raven.

Marion, M. (1991). *Guidance of young children* (3rd ed.). New York: Merrill/Macmillan.

Marion, M. (1993). Responsible anger management: The long bumpy road. *Day Care and Early Education*, April 4–9.

Marion, M. (1994). Encouraging the development of responsible anger management in young children. *Early Child Development and Care, 97,* 155–163.

Martin, J., & Elmer, E. (1992). Young children grown up: A follow-up study of individuals severely maltreated as children. *Child Abuse and Neglect, 16*(1), 75–87.

Matlock, J., & Green, V. (1990). The effects of day care on the social and emotional development of infants, toddlers and preschoolers. *Early Child Development and Care, 64,* 55–59.

Matter, D., & Matter, R. (1988). Helping young children cope with the stress of relocation: Action steps for the counselor. *Elementary School Guidance and Counseling, 23*(1), 23–29.

McBride, A. (1990). The challenges of multiple roles: The interface between work and family when children are young. *Prevention in Human Services, 9*(1), 143–166.

McKinnon, R., & Wallerstein, J. (1987). Joint custody and the preschool. *Conciliation Courts Review, 25*(2), 39–47.

Minuchin, P. (1987). Schools, families, and the development of young children. *Early Childhood Research Quarterly, 2*(3), 245–254.

Pollowy, A. (1977). *The urban nest.* Stroudsburg, PA: Dowden, Hutchinson & Ross.

Sargent, J. (1982). Stress and headaches. In L. Goldberger & S. Breznitz (Eds.), *Handbook of stress: Theoretical and clinical aspects.* New York: Free Press.

Skeen, P., & McKenry, P. (1986). The teacher's role in facilitating a child's adjustment to divorce. In J. B. McCracken (Ed.), *Reducing stress in young children's lives.* Washington, DC: NAEYC.

Skeen, P., Robinson, B., & Flake-Hobson, C. (1986). Blended families. In J. B. McCracken (Ed.), *Reducing stress in young children's lives.* Washington, DC: NAEYC.

Stein, M., Keller, S., & Schleifer, S. (1981). The hypothalamus and the immune response. In H. Weiner, M. Hofer, & A. Stunkard (Eds.), *Brain, behavior and bodily disease.* New York: Raven.

Stuber, M., Nadar, K., Yasuda, P., & Pynoos, R. (1991). Stress responses after pediatric bone marrow transplantation: Preliminary results of a prospective longitudinal study. *Journal of the American Academy of Child and Adolescent Psychiatry, 30*(6), 952–957.

Tache, J., & Selye, H. (1978). On stress and coping mechanisms. In C. D. Spielberger & I. G. Sarason (Eds.), *Stress and anxiety* (Vol. 5). Washington, DC: Hemisphere.

Tower, C. (1993). *Understanding child abuse and neglect.* Boston: Allyn & Bacon.

Weitzman, E., Boyar, R., Kapen, S., & Hellman, L. (1975). The relationship of sleep and sleep stages to neuroendocrine secretion and biological rhythms in man. *Recent Progress Hormone Research, 31,* 399–446.

Zegans, L. (1982). Stress and the development of somatic disorders. In L. Goldberger & S. Breznitz (Eds.), *Handbook of stress: Theoretical and clinical aspects.* New York: Free Press.

Zimbardo, P. (1982). Shyness and the stresses of the human condition. In L. Goldberger & S. Breznitz (Eds.), *Handbook of stress: Theoretical and clinical aspects.* New York: Free Press.

Zimbardo, P. G., & Radl, S. (1981). *The shy child.* New York: McGraw-Hill.

Zuckerman, M. (1987). The high-tech child in historical perspective. *Early Childhood Research Quarterly, 2*(3), 255–264.

6

Helping Children Develop Positive Self-Esteem

Chapter Overview

After reading and studying this chapter, you will be able to

▼   *Explain* the self as a cognitive structure.

▼   *Define* self-esteem.

▼   *List, explain, and give an example* of the three building blocks of self-esteem.

▼   *Explain* how social interaction affects the development of self-esteem.

▼   *Tell in your own words* how adult acceptance and support affect a child's self-esteem.

▼   *List, explain, and give examples* of specific adult practices that affect a child's self-esteem.

▼   *Analyze* two case studies and other adult-child interactions for practices that enhance or demean self-esteem.

▼   *Acknowledge* the importance of helping children develop a strong moral compass as well as positive self-esteem.

"Sticks and stones may break our bones, but words will break our hearts."
(Fulghum, 1988, p. 18)

CASE STUDIES: Self-Esteem

Jimmy and Frank

Both 4-year-olds are in Mr. Miles's class. When Mr. Miles set up a balance beam for large muscle activities, he encouraged Jimmy to try the new balance beam unassisted and then praised him for the effort. But, when Frank stepped up to the beam the teacher said, "Hold it. You'd better let me help you." In fact, Mr. Miles tells Frank to be careful about some physical activity nearly every day. Lately, Jimmy seems more and more willing to try new activities, but Frank has begun to avoid the playground equipment. When he and his dad went to the park Frank's dad was puzzled to hear Frank say, "Nah . . . I don't want to climb on the bars. I can't climb that high."

Mark

Mark is a 5-year-old kindergarten child who has been having trouble with the concept of higher and lower numbers. His teacher told his mom that some simple card games would help him, and she agreed to try some. Granddad asked if he could help Mark, and Mom agreed. While playing card games, Grandpa said, "You should concentrate more. Then you could get them right. That one is wrong. . . this one is wrong . . . that one is wrong." Mark replied, "But look, I got *these* right!" Grandpa replied, "But you got all the others wrong, and that's what you should worry about."

You know the old saying, "garbage in, garbage out."

Figure 6.1

Poor computer programs result from careless programming. Similarly, negative self-esteem in children results from degrading, demeaning adult behavior.
Source: Stone, M. *Data Processing: An Introduction,* by Spencer. Reprinted from INFOSYSTEMS, copyright © 1978 by Hitchcock Publishing Company.

THE NATURE AND DEVELOPMENT OF SELF-ESTEEM

Children develop *self-esteem* largely because of the attitudes of adults who are important to them. The process of forming self-esteem is remarkably similar to the process a computer uses to develop information "output." Computer programmers feed, or "input," data into the computer. Significant adults feed data to the child through words, facial expressions, and actions, telling a child what the adult's attitude toward the child is. The adult data say things like:

"You sure have lots of friends!"

"You're so gentle with Sam [the puppy]. I'll bet he feels safe with you."

"I like being with you."

"It's OK to feel angry when somebody takes something that belongs to you."

"It was thoughtful of you to whisper when you walked past the baby's crib when she was sleeping."

"That game was fun. Let's play it again sometime."

"You tell funny jokes. Grandma would love to hear that one!"

The adult data can also say things like the following:

"No wonder nobody plays with you!"

"You're really a lazy person."

"Yuck! What muddy colors you used for painting."

"Don't bother me. Play by yourself."

"Grow up! Stop whining because she took your puzzle."

"Why don't you stop cramming food into your face? You're fat enough already."

"You know something? I wish you'd never been born!"

A child takes in the "data" over a period of years and uses it to form an opinion of himself. Computer scientists emphasize, as the cartoon implies, that if input is "garbage" then we can expect output to be "garbage" as well. Similarly, adults who feed a child "garbage" messages that convey demeaning, degrading adult attitudes can fully expect that child's self-esteem to be "garbage," too. *Garbage in, garbage out.*

This chapter focuses on self-esteem, one part of a child's knowledge of the "self." The first section defines self-esteem and describes the process through which it develops. The second major section shows how significant adults affect a child's self-esteem, and illustrates several specific examples of enhancing and demeaning strategies. On the practical side, you will have a chance to analyze the case studies as well as situations in which adults either enhance or demean self-esteem.

What Is the "Self"?

Humans have been fascinated by the idea of a "self" and have pondered its meaning for many centuries. The concept of self develops in the first several years of life. Does one's concept of self occur suddenly or does it unfold gradually, and what is the self that humans come to know?

The self is a structure that develops gradually (Curry & Johnson, 1990; Harter, 1983; Sarbin, 1962). Specifically, it is a *cognitive structure* that a human literally builds or constructs inside his head. The cognitive structure of self is built gradually as the result of experience. Infants gradually learn that they are separate from other people, and this learning occurs as the infant's perceptual system develops during the first year of life. Young children eventually learn that their gender is a part of their "self."

Self-knowledge parallels more general changes in cognitive development. In the case of *gender constancy* ("I am a boy and will always be a boy," or "I am a girl and will always be a girl"), children realize their gender will not change at about the same time they understand *conservation,* the idea that some things remain the same despite apparent surface changes.

A child's set of ideas about himself affects how he behaves (Harter, 1983). For example, a 6-year-old boy who believes that washing dishes is "girl's work" is very likely to refuse to comply when his mother tells him to wash dishes. And a 7-year-old girl who views her *self* as someone who can run fast would more likely enter a race than her friend who believes that she cannot run fast.

Two separate but intertwined aspects of self have been identified (Harter, 1983; James, 1963; Wylie, 1979a, 1979b). One part is an *active observer* and is called the "I." The other aspect of the "self" is the part that is observed by "I" and is called "me." Most research has focused on that part of the self that is observed, the *me,* and this chapter also concentrates on this aspect of self.

What Is Self-Esteem?

Self-esteem is the evaluative part of a person's self-system. Children go through a long process of learning about the self. The observer part of self, the "I," gathers and gives the child information about things like physical appearance, physical abilities, gender, intellectual abilities, and interpersonal skills. Then the child processes this information and decides whether he likes the self. He evaluates and forms an opinion or a point of view about the self he sees (Coopersmith, 1967; Gecas, 1972; Harter, 1983; Rosenberg, 1965).

A child's self-evaluation can be either favorable or unfavorable, positive or negative. Some children like the self that they observe and form positive self-esteem. Others do not like the self and eventually develop negative self-esteem or a low level of self-esteem (Gecas, Calonico, & Thomas, 1974).

Competence, Control, and Worth: The Building Blocks of Self-Esteem

A child's opinion of his self is built as he observes and evaluates several different parts of his self (Coopersmith, 1967; Epstein, 1973; Harter, 1983). These parts are called *dimensions of self-esteem*. A child's level of self-esteem develops as he evaluates *competence, control,* and *worth or significance to others*.

Competence

Competence refers to success in meeting demands for achievement (Epstein, 1973; Gecas, 1971, 1972; Harter, 1981, 1982). Children, like people of all ages, are motivated by a need to feel competent and successful (White, 1959). Children who have positive self-esteem judge themselves as competent in several areas. They achieve success in school and thus have cognitive competence. They are socially competent, that is, they get along well with adults and other children, can make friends easily, and can get their parent's or teacher's attention without whining. They are quite likely to be competent in physical skills and are usually fairly successful in playing games or sports requiring coordination or strength, or in other activities, such as dancing, bike riding, running, or climbing.

Children who judge themselves dumb, lacking friends, or uncoordinated and clumsy often develop negative self-esteem. Children who have negative self-esteem judge themselves as *in*competent in a number of areas. They might view themselves as cognitively incompetent if they do poorly in school, or as socially incompetent if they have trouble making or keeping friends. They might view themselves as clumsy, unable to do well on the playground or in sports.

Motivation for achievement involves learning goals or performance goals (Elliott & Dweck, 1988; Heckhausen, 1981; Maehr & Nicholls, 1980). A child who is primarily oriented toward *learning goals* tries to increase competence, to acquire knowledge or skills, or to master or understand something new. He seeks challenges and reacts to mistakes or failures with mastery-oriented responses; that is, he does not just give up but tries to overcome the problem (Mischel, 1981).

A child who is primarily oriented toward *performance goals* tries to get favorable judgments of his competence or avoid unfavorable judgments of his competence (Dweck & Bush, 1976; Maracek & Metee, 1972; Sigall & Gould, 1977; Wine, 1982). This child dreads mistakes and often reacts to them by giving up a project instead of trying again, practicing, and overcoming the problem.

Some children have the confidence that they can achieve their goals, while others expect that they will not be able to achieve their goals even when they have the capacity to do so (Elliott & Dweck, 1988; Nicholls, 1981). Children who expect to perform well on challenging tasks are able to analyze the skills needed for effective performance (Meichenbaum & Asarnow, 1982). Children who expect to be able to perform well are realistic when analyzing a task and are not overly optimistic (Janoff-Bulman & Brickman, 1981). They do not overestimate the difficulty of a task and don't say "I can't do it" (Diener & Dweck, 1978, 1980; Dweck & Leggett, 1988; Meichenbaum, 1977; Zelniker & Jeffrey, 1976).

Control

Control refers to the degree to which a child feels responsible for outcomes in his life or the degree to which he attributes events to sources beyond his control (Connell, 1980). Gaining and internalizing a sense of control and mastery are

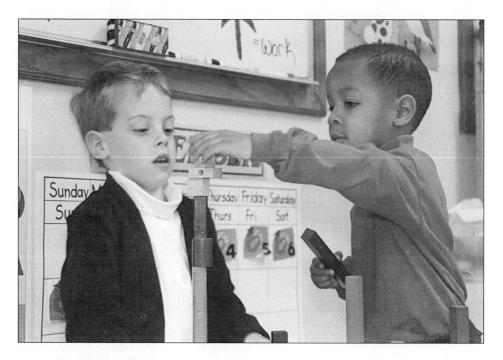

Some children have confidence that they can achieve their goals.

important for all children, and the issue of control is one we all face throughout our lives (Wong, 1992). A child's family system profoundly influences how the child deals with the issue of control. Abusive parents, for example, model a rigid, external type of control that is often imitated by their children (Tower, 1993).

Children with realistic expectations of achieving goals think they have high ability (Nicholls, 1981) and believe they have high control (Harter & Connell, 1981). They believe they can "do it" and that it is their actions that influence whether they achieve a goal. These children believe that expending effort will help them achieve their goal.

Example   When Christine put too many drops of red food coloring in her white play dough mixture she got red dough and not the pink she had wanted. Her teacher suggested adding more white dough to fix the mistake, which Christine set about doing. "Teacher! Look! I fixed it. I made pink!"

Worth or Significance to Others

Worth or significance to others refers to how much children like themselves, judge themselves to be liked or loved by peers and parents, and believe they are accepted by and deserving of attention from others. A child who judges the self to be good, valuable, and well-liked will develop positive self-esteem. The child who judges the self to be bad, unloved, and unworthy of attention frequently develops negative self-esteem.

Self-Esteem Develops in a Social Context

Parents, grandparents, aunts, uncles, brothers, sisters, cousins, neighbors, and teachers make up the child's social environment, and a child's opinion about his competence, control, and worth develops out of close involvement with these persons (Anderson & Hughes, 1989; Curry & Johnson, 1990; Felker, 1974). We can easily see the effects of an infant or toddler's social environment on his developing sense of self. (See *Special Focus: Negative Self-Esteem in Infants and Toddlers*.)

SPECIAL FOCUS: Negative Self-Esteem in Infants and Toddlers

A very young child's behavior reflects the atmosphere at home. Infants or toddlers whose families are dysfunctional or abusive begin to show the following signs of negative self-esteem (Greenberg, 1991; Tower, 1993):

▼   *Highly anxious.* They cry very little on the whole, are passively watchful, and show no expectation of being comforted by abusive/neglectful parents. They show little interest in toys or playing, and crawl and walk later than others their age. Toddlers like this seem to anticipate failure. They participate from the fringes, are frustrated easily, become cranky when faced with challenges, and refuse to try tasks without lots of help and reassurance.

▼   *Compulsive.* If the abuse or neglect is about control, toddlers might become compulsively neat and precise in effort to have *some* control over their lives. "I can't stop Daddy from hitting me, but I can be very, very neat when I play. Everything can be 'just so.'"

▼   *Withdrawn.* They may feel hopelessly inadequate, so highly anxious about failure that they withdraw from or stop trying new things, including relationships. Withdrawal is also a characteristic of abused children who want to avoid further punishment. They are verbally inhibited. Infants who feel like this make very little or no effort to connect with others, including their mothers.

▼   *Overtly hostile.* These children lack control over their lives, and this results in suppressed anger. Many also observe violent parents. Some children act out anger against other young children, animals, or adults, while others turn the anger inward on themselves. Abused toddlers show little compassion and may hurt, belittle, push others around, bully, and grab things from others.

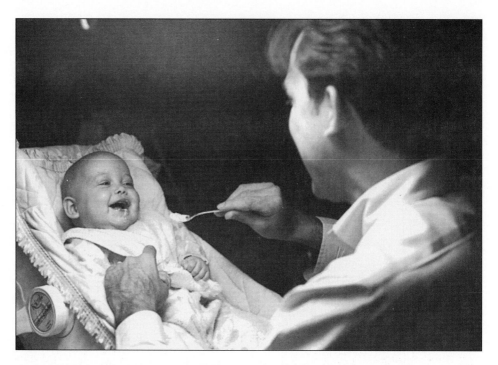

We help infants develop positive self-esteem when we treat them with respect.

Many writers have looked at the development of self in relation to others. Early in the twentieth century, Cooley (1902) explained the development of self-esteem with the metaphor of the "looking-glass self." According to this view, the attitudes children hold about themselves are actually reflections of what they believe others think about them. Mead (1934) also maintained that self-esteem or attitudes toward oneself are much like those held by certain other people in the environment.

Social interaction as a major factor in the development of self-esteem has been an enduring concept, and many modern writers and researchers have relied on this concept (Bandura, 1977; Coopersmith, 1967; Greenberg, 1991; Lewis & Brooks-Gunn, 1979). Bandura believes that a child's sense of competence results from hearing others talk about how well the child does things.

General Process of the Development of Self-Esteem

The following steps describing the general process of the development of self-esteem show that children value themselves as significant others value them.

1. Significant adults have opinions and attitudes about a child's competence or significance.
2. The adult's behavior toward the child shows how he feels.

3.   The child tunes in to the adult's opinion.

4.   The child's self-evaluations begin to match the adult's attitudes.

CASE STUDY ANALYSIS: The Social Context

Explain how Mr. Miles's attitude about Jimmy's and Frank's physical skills and his behavior toward each boy seem to be affecting each child's self-esteem (see case study at chapter opening).

1.   What do you think this teacher's opinion is about each boy's level of coordination?

2.   How is Mr. Miles's opinion reflected in his behavior toward each boy?

3.   How has each child begun to show that his self-evaluation of his physical ability is beginning to match that of this important adult?

THE ADULT'S ROLE IN CHILDREN'S SELF-ESTEEM

Not all adults are "significant" to children during each phase of their development. This is an important concept for caregivers because we must know whose opinion influences children during infancy, toddlerhood, and early and middle childhood. Both parents and teachers are among the significant others who affect children's self-esteem because young children believe that adults possess a superior wisdom and children tend to rely on adult judgments (Harter, 1983; Rosenberg, 1979). Peer opinion becomes increasingly important as children move into middle childhood.

Adults affect a child's self-esteem through two main processes. One is the adult's level of support and acceptance of the child. Adults also affect the level of a child's self-esteem *by using specific practices* as they interact with the child (Hales, 1979a, 1979b). This section focuses on these two mediating processes.

Helping Children Build Positive Self-Esteem

Children need our acceptance and support if they are going to evaluate themselves as competent (Coopersmith, 1967; Hales, 1979a, 1979b; Harter, 1983; Heyman, Dweck, & Cain, 1992; Rogers, 1951; Sheridan, 1991). Gecas (1971) found that children think of themselves as competent, worthy, happy, good, active, friendly, honest, and confident when adults important to them were supportive. White (1975) found that children were academically and interpersonally competent when significant adults communicated genuine interest in them.

Rogers (1951) believed that children need a special type of adult support that he called *unconditional positive regard,* support that is given freely and "without strings" or conditions. When you give unconditional positive regard to a child you do not require the child to earn your interest, time, or concern. Giving unconditional positive regard does *not* mean you are being permissive, and you do not have to accept everything a child does. It is important that we help children develop a clear set of values, among them that some behaviors, such as hurting others, putting oneself in danger, and destroying property, are wrong. For example, you would accept a child unconditionally when you accept all his feelings, including anger, but you would *stop* him from expressing or venting the anger irresponsibly.

Adults use specific practices that affect a child's self-esteem. Authori*tative*, supportive adults use strategies that *enhance*, or help to improve, children's development of positive self-esteem. Nonsupportive adults use strategies that *demean* children and contribute to the development of negative self-esteem.

Strategies That Enhance Self-Esteem

Use Positive Discipline

Positive discipline is related to higher levels of compliance (obedience), helpfulness, and cooperation, and to lower levels of aggression. As you might suspect, the type of discipline used by adults also affects a child's self-esteem. Positive discipline has a significant and positive influence on a child's self-esteem (Coopersmith 1967; Hales, 1979a, 1979b).

Example   "I want you to move the toys back to the sandpit, Sam, and keep them there. James hurt his leg because he landed on the shovel that you left in front of the slide."

Develop Reasonable, Fair Limits, State Them Well, and Enforce Them Firmly (and With Kindness)

Good limits are an essential part of positive discipline and are an expression of an adult's support. Limits are a form of adult control of the child, and the child gradually internalizes limits and develops self-control. In the process he will view himself as competent because he remembers a limit. He will also come to see himself as worthy of the adult's time. Competence and worth are both dimensions of positive self-esteem (Coopersmith, 1967).

Encourage Autonomy and Self-Responsibility

Girls tend to have more positive self-esteem when parents require them to assume responsibilities at home (Hales, 1979a, 1979b). Wallinga and Sweaney (1986) have written a short but helpful article on how parents can teach children how to participate in household tasks. Perhaps children who are responsible for certain tasks think that they are an important part of their family system.

Encourage Credit-Taking

Feedback from adults about how well or how poorly a child has performed a task is an important source of information about the child's competence (Bandura, 1977, 1981). When adults focus on what a child has done well they help a child recognize his competence, and competence is one dimension of positive self-esteem.

Example   Mrs. Herbach, who knew that Sarah recognized and could name a square and a circle but did not know what a triangle was, placed a large square, circle, and triangle on a bulletin board and had the same shapes in a box. "You know the names of some shapes, Sarah. Reach into this box, take out one shape, and put it on top of the same shape on the board. When Sarah correctly matched squares, Mrs. Herbach said, "You're right!" When Sarah matched the triangular shapes Mrs. Herbach simply said, "You've matched the *triangles!*"

Acknowledge Pleasant and Unpleasant Feelings

The real test of support of a child worthy of attention comes when a child is sick, hurt, unhappy, angry, jealous, fearful, or anxious.

Example   Six-year-old Lisa, jealous of her new baby brother, muttered "I wish that stupid baby would go back to the hospital!" Her father responded, "You kind of wish Todd would go back to the hospital, don't you?" He was supportive and treated her concern seriously.

Express Genuine Interest in Children and Their Activities

Engage in joint activities willingly. Adults who show an interest in children believe that a child's activities—whether it is playing with measuring cups, fingerpainting, playing computer games, building a campsite, or playing in sand—are valid and interesting for the child (Kuykendall, 1991). An adult communicates his belief that the child is a person worthy of the adult's attention by demonstrating concern about a child's welfare, activities, and friends.

Coopersmith (1967) found that parents of both high and low self-esteem children spent the same amount of time with their children. He explained this puzzling finding by saying that the mothers of high self-esteem children spent time willingly with their child and seemed to enjoy the interaction. Mothers of low self-esteem children, on the other hand, appeared to spend time with their child grudgingly. Consider Jane's experience with her mother.

Example   While Jane and her mom were making cookies, her mother pointed out the steps in the recipe, explained new cooking terms, and showed Jane how to measure an equal amount for each cookie. She asked Jane if she would like to learn to make another kind of cookie sometime.

Avoid Sexism and Judging Physical Attributes

Example   Mr. Johnson needed help in carrying a bale of hay. He asked for two strong *children* and then chose a girl and a boy.

Respect All Family Groups and Cultures

It is important that children observe teachers who demonstrate respect for various family groups and for different cultures (Beane, 1991).

Examples   Mr. Johnson knows his class well. Several children live in single-parent families. When discussing the topic of families, he showed pictures of each child's family and said, "There are lots of people in some of your families, and some of your families are small."

Mahesh's family was from India. Mahesh announced that he was making puris (an Indian bread) as he worked with play dough. Mr. Johnson replied, "It was nice of your mom to show us how to make puris. It was fun to watch the bread puff as it cooked."

Strategies That Degrade or Demean Children

Nonsupportive Adults Use Negative Discipline

Nonsupportive adults control, are sarcastic, threaten, use harsh punishment, and humiliate children.

Example   Mom to son in car after exiting the grocery store, "You little %&#$! You say that one more time and I'll smash your sassy little face. Do you *hear* me?"

Negative discipline has a negative effect on self-esteem. It leaves children lacking in self-confidence, feeling inadequate and incompetent, and derogating (belittling) themselves (Anderson & Hughes, 1989; Freedman, Carlsmith, & Sears, 1970).

Nonsupportive Adults Do Not Set Limits Well

Some adults set almost no limits, some set too many limits, and many adults do not know how to clearly state even reasonable limits. Poorly defined or poorly stated limits are not helpful to children because the child has no way of knowing whether a behavior is appropriate or inappropriate. He is left to guess and frequently guesses "wrong."

Example   During naptime Leslie decided to get up and walk over to the puzzle table, and another child followed her. The problem was that the teacher had forgotten to tell the children to stay on their cots during naptime.

Nonsupportive Adults Fail to Emphasize Self-Responsibility

They do not take the time necessary to help children assume responsibility. Chores are either not specified or, even if they are specified, there is no penalty for not doing them. Nonsupportive adults also often fail to require children to take responsibility when they have hurt someone or damaged property.

Nonsupportive Adults Are Overly Critical

Constant negative feedback is degrading because it communicates the adult's belief that the child is incompetent. Younger children, who rely heavily on adult opinion, feel incompetent when they are constantly criticized. Children who are criticized by adults and who live in a negative verbal environment tend to judge themselves negatively, including judgments of their goodness (Heyman et al., 1992; Kostelnik, 1988).

CASE STUDY ANALYSIS: Accentuating the Positive

Objective: Explain how Grandpa's behavior is affecting Mark's level of self-esteem (see case study at chapter opening).

1.   I think that Grandpa concentrates more on what Mark can do/cannot do.
2.   Here is a specific example that led me to make this conclusion:
3.   Explain how Grandpa's behavior is likely to affect Mark's opinion of his own level of competence.

Nonsupportive Adults Deny Children the Right to Have Feelings

Denying feelings is akin to denying a child's self because even unpleasant feelings are real and are a part of the child. The implication is that *if my feelings are bad, then I'm bad, too.*

Example   "Janna! You're not angry. You really like the new shirt, don't you?" Janna obviously did not like the shirt and was angry, but this adult is denying her the right to her feelings.

Nonsupportive Adults Do Not Like Spending Time With Children

Example   Marty asked his mother to show him how to make chocolate chip cookies. Feeling obligated, Mom did teach him, but at the same time clearly communicated resentment, annoyance, and irritability by talking quickly and answering Marty's questions abruptly. Marty is likely to conclude that he cannot be very likable because his own mother does not like to do things with him.

Nonsupportive Adults Are Judgmental and Sexist

Examples   Mrs. Olsen told Tom to "sit outside the circle while we play 'Duck, Duck, Goose,' because you'd have trouble running with that brace on your leg."

Mrs. Olsen allows only boys to use woodworking tools and allows only girls to bathe dolls.

Nonsupportive Adults Show Contempt for Some Family or Cultural Groups

Example   Several of the children in Mrs. Olsen's class live in single-parent families. Vernon lives with his grandmother, and another child lives in a foster home. Mrs. Olsen demonstrated her insensitivity when she had children bring in pictures of families. Looking at Vernon's picture of him and his grandmother at the park, the teacher said, "Too bad that you don't have a family, Vernon."

PROBLEM FOR YOU TO SOLVE: How Has This Child Been Demeaned?

For each situation state specifically how someone has been demeaned. Say how the adult could just as easily have done or said something to *enhance*, rather than *demean*, the child's self-esteem.

Situation: The music teacher stared out at the first-grade class and said, "That was terrible. John, come up here. I want all of you to listen to John. He's the only child in this class who can sing!"

Who has been demeaned?
How could the adult have enhanced self-esteem?

Situation: Sam, the class's pet hamster, died during the night, and the aide found Peter crying after he heard the news. "Come on, Peter. Stop crying. You know that big boys don't cry."

How has Peter been demeaned?
In what way has this adult been sexist?
How has the adult demeaned girls as well as boys?
How could this adult have enhanced self-esteem?

Situation: The teacher asked, "Do you want to play with the puzzles or with the blocks, Maria?" Maria chose the blocks. The teacher said, "Well . . . I think you'd better work with a puzzle."

How has Maria been demeaned?
How could this teacher have enhanced self esteem?

Situation: Three-year-old Gerry correctly matched all the colors in the color-matching activity and named two of the six colors. His teacher said, "Well, you have some work to do. You still have trouble with the names of these colors."

How has Gerry been demeaned?
How could the adult have enhanced self esteem?

CHILDREN NEED A MORAL COMPASS

This chapter is not just a collection of "feel good about me" activities. Helping children develop a positive sense of self-esteem takes more than a collection of activities, although activities are important. Damon (1991) notes that too strong an emphasis on the development of self-esteem in young children can lead to self-centeredness if children are not also helped to develop a strong, objective *moral compass* that guides their behavior.

Without this moral referent even children who have positive self-esteem cannot acquire a stable sense of right and wrong. Using positive discipline and requiring children to be self-responsible, along with clear indications that some things are wrong, are excellent ways to help them develop this moral compass. And, while self-esteem is fundamental to mental health, children need other things that are even *more* basic: prenatal care, food, pure water, shelter, and immunizations (Greenberg, 1991; Children's Defense Fund, 1990).

SUMMARY OF KEY CONCEPTS

1. Humans construct a concept of the self. *Self-esteem* is the evaluation that we make of the self, that is, whether we like the thing we know as *me*. The building blocks of self-esteem are *competence, control, and worth*.

2. Self-esteem develops through social interaction with significant others over time. Children tune in to the opinions that adults have of them and may eventually internalize those attitudes. The child develops opinions about himself that closely resemble adult attitudes.

3. Children have a better chance of developing positive self-esteem when important adults are accepting and supportive. Adults also influence a child's self-esteem by using specific strategies as they interact with the child. Supportive adults use strategies that enhance self-esteem, but nonsupportive adults use strategies that demean or degrade children and result in negative self-esteem.

4. We must do more than just plan activities to *help children feel good* about themselves. We must also help children develop a *strong moral compass*, an internal guide with a clear set of values and a stable sense of right and wrong.

OBSERVE CHILD GUIDANCE IN ACTION
Identify Enhancing and Demeaning Practices

Objective. Observe several interactions between adults and children. Point out examples of adult behavior that either enhance or demean self-esteem.

Use this format to record observable data, noting what you actually see or hear. Avoid writing your opinion.

Name: _____

Date: _____

Setting: _____

Approximate age of child: _____

Describe the adult-child interaction and write direct quotes:

Say how this adult either enhanced or degraded self-esteem:

Summarize your findings. From the data you have collected, describe the degree to which this adult supports the development of positive self-esteem.

RESOURCES FOR SPECIFIC ACTIVITIES

Center for Applied Psychology, Inc. (1993). *The building blocks of self-esteem*. This is a catalog of games and other materials for enhancing self-esteem. Available from Center for Applied Psychology, Inc. P.O. Box 1586, King of Prussia, PA 19406 (1-800-962-1141).

Greenberg, P. (1991). *Character development: Encouraging self-esteem and self-discipline in infants, toddlers, & two-year-olds*. Washington, DC: NAEYC. This is a wonderful resource for teachers of infants and toddlers. It contains practical suggestions for fostering self-esteem and self-discipline in very young children.

Katz, L. (1989). *Family living: Suggestions for effective parenting*. Washington, DC: Office of Educational Research and Improvement. Available from ERIC Clearinghouse on Elementary and Early Childhood Education, University of Illinois, 805 West Pennsylvania Ave, Urbana, IL 61801 (catalogue no. 205).

National Black Child Development Institute. (1991). *The spirit of excellence: Resources for black children ages three to seven*. Washington, DC: Author. Available from NBCDI, 1023 15th St. NW, Suite 600, Washington, DC, 20005 ($5.00).

REFERENCES

Anderson, M., & Hughes, H. (1989). Parenting attitudes and the self-esteem of young children. *Journal of Genetic Psychology*, *160*(4), 463–465.

Bandura, A. (1977). Self-efficacy: Toward a unifying theory of behavioral change. *Psychological Review*, *84*, 191–215.

Bandura, A. (1981). Self-referent thought: The development of self-efficacy. In J. H. Flavell & L. D. Ross (Eds.), *Development of social cognition*. New York: Cambridge University Press.

Beane, J. (1991). Enhancing children's self-esteem: Illusion and possibility. *Early Education and Development*, *2*(2), 153–160.

Children's Defense Fund. (1990). *S.O.S. America! A children's defense budget*. Washington, DC: Author.

Connell, J. P. (1980). *A multidimensional measure of children's perceptions of control*. Unpublished masters thesis, University of Denver.

Cooley, C. H. (1902). *Human nature and the social order*. New York: Scribners.

Coopersmith, S. (1967). *The antecedents of self-esteem*. San Francisco: W. H. Freeman.

Curry, N., & Johnson, C. (1990). Beyond self-esteem: Developing a genuine sense of human value. *Research Monograph* (Vol. 4). Washington, DC: NAEYC.

Damon, W. (1991). Putting substance into self-esteem: A focus on academic and moral values. *Educational Horizons*, *70*(1), 12–18.

Diener, C. I., & Dweck, C. S. (1978). An analysis of learned helplessness: Continuous changes in performance, strategy, and achievement cognitions following failure. *Journal of Personality and Social Psychology*, *36*, 451–462.

Diener, C. I., & Dweck, C. S. (1980). Analysis of learned helplessness: II. The processing of success. *Journal of Personality and Social Psychology*, *39*, 940–952.

Dweck, C. S., & Bush, E. S. (1976). Sex differences in learned helplessness: I. Differential debilitation with peer and adult evaluators. *Developmental Psychology*, *12*, 147–156.

Dweck, C., & Leggett, E. (1988). A social-cognitive approach to motivation and personality. *Psychological Review*, 95(2), 256–273.

Elliott, E., & Dweck, C. (1988). Goals: An approach to motivation and achievement. *Journal of Personality and Social Psychology*, 54(1), 5–12.

Epstein, S. (1973). The self-concept revisited, or a theory of a theory. *American Psychologist*, 28, 405–416.

Felker, D. (1974). *Helping children to like themselves*. Minneapolis: Burgess.

Freedman, J. L., Carlsmith, J. M., & Sears, D. O. (1970). *Social psychology*. Englewood Cliffs, NJ: Prentice-Hall.

Fulghum, R. (1988). *All I really need to know I learned in kindergarten*. New York: Ivy Books.

Gecas, V. (1971). Parental behavior and dimensions of adolescent self-evaluation. *Sociometry*, 34, 466–482.

Gecas, V. (1972). Parental behavior and contextual variations in adolescent self-esteem. *Sociometry*, 35(2), 332–345.

Gecas, V., Calonico, J. M., & Thomas, D. L. (1974). The development of self-concept in the child: Mirror theory versus model theory. *The Journal of Social Psychology*, 92, 67–76.

Greenberg, P. (1991). *Character development: Encouraging self-esteem and self-discipline in infants, toddlers, & two-year-olds*. Washington, DC: NAEYC.

Hales, S. (1979a). *Developmental processes of self-esteem*. Paper presented at the Society for Research in Child Development, San Francisco.

Hales, S. (1979b). *A developmental theory of self-esteem based on competence and moral behavior*. Paper presented at the Society for Research in Child Development, San Francisco.

Harter, S. (1981). A model of intrinsic mastery motivation in children: Individual differences and developmental change. In W. A. Collins (Ed.), *Minnesota Symposium on Child Psychology* (Vol. 14). Hillsdale, NJ: Erlbaum.

Harter, S. (1982). The perceived competence scale for children. *Child Development*, 53, 87–97.

Harter, S. (1983). Developmental perspectives on the self system. In P. Mussen (Ed.), *Handbook of Child Psychology* (Vol. 4). New York: Wiley.

Harter, S., & Connell, J. P. (1981). *A structural model of children's self perceptions of competence, control, and motivational orientation in the cognitive domain*. Paper presented at the Meeting of the International Society for the Study of Behavioral Development, Toronto.

Heckhausen, H. (1981). The development of achievement motivation. In W. W. Hartup (Ed.), *Review of Child Development Research* (Vol. 6). Chicago: University of Chicago Press.

Heyman, G., Dweck, C., & Cain, K. (1992). Young children's vulnerability to self-blame and helplessness: Relationship to beliefs about goodness. *Child Development*, 63(2), 401–415.

James, W. (1963). *Psychology*. New York: Fawcett (originally published 1890).

Janoff-Bulman, R., & Brickman, P. (1981). Expectations and what children learn from failure. In N. T. Feather (Ed.), *Expectancy, incentive, and action*. Hillsdale, NJ: Erlbaum.

Kostelnik, M. (1988). Children's self-esteem: The verbal environment. *Childhood Education*, 65(1), 29–32.

Kuykendall, J. (1991). *Early childhood development series*. Fairbanks, AK: Cooperative Extension Service.

Lewis, M., & Brooks-Gunn, J. (1979). *Social cognition and the acquisition of self*. New York: Plenum Press.

Maehr, M. L., & Nicholls, J. G. (1980). Culture and achievement motivation: A second look. In N. Warren (Ed.), *Studies in cross-cultural psychology* (Vol. 3). New York: Academic Press.

Maracek, J., & Metee, D. (1972). Avoidance of continued success as a function of self-esteem, level of esteem certainty, and responsibility for success. *Journal of Personality and Social Psychology, 22*, 98–107.

Mead, G. H. (1934). *Mind, self and society*. Chicago: University of Chicago Press.

Meichenbaum, D. (1977). *Cognitive-behavior modification: An integrative approach*. New York: Plenum.

Meichenbaum, D., & Asarnow, J. (1982). Cognitive-behavior modification and metacognitive development: Implications for the classroom. In P. C. Kendall & S. D. Hollon (Eds.), *Cognitive-behavioral interventions: Theory, research, and procedures*. New York: Academic Press.

Mischel, W. (1981). Metacognition and the rules of delay. In J. H. Flavell & L. D. Ross (Eds.), *Social cognitive development: Frontiers and possible futures*. New York: Cambridge University Press.

Nicholls, J. G. (1981). Striving to demonstrate and develop ability: A theory of achievement motivation. Unpublished manuscript, Purdue University.

Rogers, C. R. (1951). *Client-centered therapy*. Boston: Houghton-Mifflin.

Rosenberg, M. (1965). *Society and the adolescent self-image*. Princeton: Princeton University Press.

Rosenberg, M. (1979). *Conceiving the self*. New York: Basic.

Sarbin, T. R. (1962). A preface to a psychological analysis of the self. *Psychological Review, 59*, 11–22.

Sheridan, M. (1991). Increasing self-esteem and competency in children. *International Journal of Early Childhood, 23*(1), 28–35.

Sigall, H., & Gould, R. (1977). The effects of self-esteem and evaluator demandingness on effort expenditure. *Journal of Personality and Social Psychology, 35*, 12–20.

Tower, C. (1993). *Understanding child abuse and neglect*. Boston: Allyn & Bacon.

Wallinga, C. R., & Sweaney, A. L. (1986). A sense of "real" accomplishment. In J. B. McCracken (Ed.), *Reducing stress in young children's lives*. Washington, DC: NAEYC.

White, B. L. (1975). *The first three years of life*. Englewood Cliffs, NJ: Prentice-Hall.

White, R. W. (1959). Motivation reconsidered: The concept of competence. *Psychological Review, 66*, 297–333.

Wine, J. D. (1982). Evaluation anxiety: A cognitive-attentional construct. In H. W. Krohne & L. Laux (Eds.), *Achievement, stress, and anxiety*. Washington, DC: Hemisphere.

Wong, P. T. (1992). Control is a double-edged sword. *Canadian Journal of Behavioural Science, 24*(2), 143–146.

Wylie, R. (1979a). *The self-concept: A review of methodological considerations and measuring instruments* (Vol. 1, rev. ed.). Lincoln: University of Nebraska Press.

Wylie, R. (1979b). *The self-concept* (Vol. 2). Lincoln: University of Nebraska Press.

Zelniker, T., & Jeffrey, W. E. (1976). Reflective and impulsive children: Strategies of information processing underlying differences in problem solving. *Monographs of the Society for Research in Child Development, 41*(5, Serial No. 168).

7

Responsible Anger Management:
The Long, Bumpy Road

Chapter Overview   COPY

After reading and studying this chapter, you will be able to

▼ *Define* anger and terms associated with anger management.

▼ *Identify* types of interactions that are likely to elicit anger and *describe* children's responses to each.

▼ *Explain* the function of display rules in emotional development and especially in anger management.

▼ *List, explain, and give examples of* developmentally appropriate strategies that will help children manage anger responsibly.

"Unpleasant feelings are like weeds. They don't go away when we ignore them; they grow wild and take over."

(Beattie, 1987, p. 144)

CASE STUDIES: Anger

Julia

Julia's mother likes to think that she hides angry feelings. Julia, 6 years old, watched her mother pretend that nothing was wrong even though Mom clenched her teeth as she related what a friend had done on a shopping trip. When her friend had pressed her for details about what she had done to make Julia's mother so angry, Mom finally "blew up" and, as she said later, "let her [the friend] have a piece of my mind!"

When Julia was angry with her brother for leaving her markers uncapped, her mother said, "Julia! Knock it off! Get to your room and stay there until you can act like a lady."

Darryl

Darryl, 4½ years old, has a father who does not hide anger. In fact, he seems to be angry all the time. Dad argues with people at work and has been passed over for promotions several times. At home the tension is almost unbearable, with Dad lashing out at Darryl, Darryl's mother and two brothers, and anybody else in his way. Dad refuses to discuss feelings and punishes the children when they show any anger.

Darryl's teacher is worried because Darryl deals with angry feelings by threatening, hitting, or calling other children names, and the other children are beginning to avoid him.

Shantal

Shantal, 5 years old, was sitting on the porch with Mom when her father came home from a fishing trip. Dad hadn't caught any fish. Mom said, "Oh, George! It's no big deal." Dad said, "Hey, I was looking forward to grilling some fish for all of us, and I'm a little disappointed that I didn't catch anything. Plus, I'm *irritated* that you would tell me 'It's no big deal.'" Mom said, "Sorry, honey. I know you're disappointed."

The next day at the child care center, when another child took Shantal's necklace in the dress-up area, Shantal looked straight at the child and said, "I'm *irritated* because you took my necklace. Give it back."

UNDERSTANDING ANGER
A Definition of Anger

Anger is an emotion—an *affective state*, or feeling—experienced when needs are frustrated (Campos & Barrett, 1984). Emotions may help people overcome obstacles so that they can get needs met, or emotions can stand in the way of meeting our needs. Emde, Gaensbauer, and Harmon (1976) note that affective states such as anger portend behavior by the age of 9 months. Anger, then, may be said to be the *felt tendency* to retaliate. Anger and aggression are not identical (Lerner, 1985; Miller & Sperry, 1987), but they are closely related in everyday life (Sabini & Silver, 1982).

Anger is a powerful emotion that all human beings experience, one that should serve as a signal that something is wrong. Some children learn to use the energy in anger to help them solve the problem underlying the anger. Other children learn irresponsible approaches to managing this stress-inducing emotion, and not dealing with anger successfully keeps them in a stressful state (Eisenberg, Fabes, Schaller, Carlo, & Miller, 1991).

Causes of and Coping With Anger in Young Children

Social interactions may be considered a source of interpersonal stress for preschool children because these interactions are often sources of anger provocations. Fabes and Eisenberg (1992) identified several types of interactions that seemed to elicit anger. The most frequent was conflict over possessions, followed by physical assault, social rejection, verbal assault, and issues of compliance.

Some people believe that children almost always respond to anger with aggression, but this is not what Fabes and Eisenberg (1992) found. Children's responses to anger varied according to the *cause* of the anger. Children used

Conflict over possessions is often the source of anger for young children.

active resistance when they had a conflict over possessions; that is, they defended themselves in nonaggressive ways.

Example   Jen tried to swipe the scoop from Michael at the water table, but Michael responded with active resistance, "That's mine! You can't have it."

Children angry about being physically assaulted most often react by actively resisting or by venting, but about 18% of children who had been physically assaulted responded with aggressive revenge (Fabes & Eisenberg, 1992). For teachers this means that young children have difficulty coping with their anger in socially constructive ways when somebody has hit, punched, or pushed them (Shantz, 1987; Shantz & Shantz, 1985). Children also actively resisted and vented when they were angry about social rejection, verbal assault, and issues of compliance.

Children used active resistance when angered by another child, but they used venting when angered by an adult. Why this difference in how children responded to anger-arousing interactions? The strategy a child uses to cope with anger depends on whether she can control the situation (Atschuler & Ruble, 1989; Band & Weisz, 1988). Choice of strategy also depends on whether she is aware of the difference in the status between adults and children (Karniol & Heiman, 1987).

A child probably actively resists other children who arouse her anger because she thinks she has some control over the situation. The same child probably vents or blows off steam when angered by adults because she realizes that she has little control over the situation. The adult is in a more powerful position.

Children Learn Display Rules for Anger

Our culture teaches guidelines, or *display rules,* for dealing with emotions (Doubleday, Kovaric, & Door, 1990). A display rule is imposed, for example, when a person feels an emotion but does not display it in facial expression or in verbal response; that is, what she says or how her face looks does not match the emotion she feels.

Example   Shantal watched her father use a display rule for masking anger when he dealt with a clerk who refused to wait on him at first. Shantal heard her Dad say to himself, "O-o-h, it makes me mad when they take so long to wait on me!" Dad masked his anger by not showing anger in his face and by saying to the clerk, "I've been standing here for some time and I really need your help."

We teach two types of display rules, one for controlling or masking anger and another rule for expressing anger. People mask or control anger by either expressing no emotion at all (putting on a "poker face") or by expressing another—what is perceived to be more acceptable—emotion (Gnepp & Hess, 1986).

Children seem to perceive adult consensus about emotional control earlier than they understand adult rules on how to express emotion. That is, children understand that adults feel a certain way about either expressing no emotion at all or that adults think that some other emotion should be expressed (Doubleday et al., 1990).

Underwood, Coie, and Herbsman (1992) wanted to know if these findings would hold when looking at how middle childhood children understood display rules for masking anger. Their research underscored the complexity of the phenomenon of display rules for anger. First, children used display rules more frequently with adults than they did with peers, thus highlighting children's understanding of the power differential between children and adults and the need to mask anger when an adult had caused the anger.

Second, the data also showed a developmental trend, with older children using display rules—masking anger—more frequently than younger children. But, the interesting twist was that older children invoked display rules primarily with adults and not with peers. Children seem, then, to make choices about when they mask their anger and seem to do so with adults but not so much with peers.

Children used more sophisticated reasoning to justify their choices of action with peers than they used with adults. Piaget's (1970) work can help us understand this difference. He suggested that a child's peer interactions, which are based on mutual relations, may foster moral development more than do interactions with adults, in which the power differential is clear to children.

One other finding is important for teachers and parents. There were some gender differences in how children used display rules for anger. Boys were less likely to mask their anger than were girls. Underwood et al. (1992) explained this finding by acknowledging the different socialization received by boys and girls, with boys encouraged to express anger more readily than are girls. This work was done with children between the ages of 8 and 12. Early childhood teachers work with younger children, who are just beginning to learn display rules. Expect them not to understand these rules like older children. Expect less masking of anger from younger children (Malatesta & Haviland, 1982).

Good Reasons for Teaching Responsible Anger Management

Teaching children responsible anger management is an important task for parents and teachers. Children who do not learn responsible anger management are more likely to engage in negative peer interactions, responding to anger with socially *un*constructive coping responses such as venting, escape, and revenge (Fabes & Eisenberg, 1992; Gottman & Katz, 1989; Segal, 1988).

Responsible teachers are realizing that encouraging responsible anger management may also have positive long-term effects. Researchers are finding a connection between chronic hostility and anger and impaired health and damaged relationships. Cynical hostility is marked by frequent anger, and this high level of hostility has consistently been the factor that best discriminates between adults with coronary heart disease and those without coronary heart disease (Baughman, 1992; Williams, 1989). Anger and hostility also make it difficult to function effectively in groups, whether in school or at work. Teaching responsible anger management to young children, then, may help to prevent some of these problems.

Teachers can work on responsible anger management directly with children in their classrooms. But because children exist in a family system (Bronfenbrenner, 1979) as well, teachers will be more successful in helping children deal with anger if they also work with families. We can design specific parent education and support programs on the topic of responsible anger management to help parents understand the nature of this emotion, and we can teach practical strategies for managing anger responsibly.

All of us travel the road of anger management throughout our lives, but it is a very bumpy road for some children. We can help them smooth out the bumps somewhat by adopting some of the positive, developmentally appropriate strategies described in the next section (Marion, 1993, 1994).

DEVELOPMENTALLY APPROPRIATE WAYS TO HELP CHILDREN MANAGE ANGER RESPONSIBLY
Model Responsible Anger Management

Adults influence children through modeling, and adults are powerful models of how to manage anger (Bandura, 1965; Bandura, Ross, & Ross, 1961). Some adults model responsible anger management, while others model irresponsible anger management. Anger may be modeled by targeting it directly *to* children or to another person, animal, or object.

Most of us would acknowledge that a child receiving the aggression from a parent's anger experiences stress. There is another type of anger, called *background anger,* that may be equally stressful for children (Cummings, 1987; Cummings & Cummings, 1988; Cummings, Iannotti, & Zahn-Waxler, 1981; Cummings, Zahn-Waxler, & Radke-Yarrow, 1981, 1984). Background anger is anger between others that a child observes but in which the child is not directly involved.

Examples   Janie, 3 years old, stood on the landing watching and listening to her parents arguing again. Later that day she listened to her mom talk to a store clerk on the phone, heard her mom get increasingly agitated, and finally heard her swear and slam the receiver down.

Darryl, 4½ years old (one of our case study children), watched as his dad cursed at his grandfather for, as Darryl's dad said, " . . . raking the leaves like a jerk!"

Children are aware of others' angry interactions by 1 year of age (Cummings et al., 1981), and by the age of 4 to 5 years children react to background anger with increased stress and with increased aggression toward friends (Cummings, 1987). Cummings's (1987) study involved a relatively benign situation in which children were dealing with friends in a mildly anger-arousing situation. Emery (1982) notes that a more threatening type of background anger, as in a hostile home, may foster pathology in children.

How to Model Responsible Anger Management

▼   *Acknowledge and accept your own angry feelings.* You will show children that you trust yourself and that you think anger is a normal experience.

▼ *Give yourself permission to feel angry when you are angry.* You will be modeling several important things: that you feel the emotional energy of anger, that you do not think that you have to justify your feelings, that anger simply is, and that there is nothing wrong with this or any other emotion.

▼ *Take responsibility for your own feelings. Avoid blaming others for causing your feelings.* In this way you will show children that you understand that anger often covers some other feeling, as in the following example.

Example   John's teacher took responsibility for his adult anger when he said, "I feel scared when you run into the street, John, and then I feel angry." Notice that the teacher does *not* say "You made me angry, John." Nobody makes us feel anything. Yes, John did something that was inappropriate, but it was the adult's angry feeling, and John observes his teacher "owning" the feeling.

▼ *Make decisions about how to deal with anger; avoid simply venting emotional energy. Venting* anger, or *blowing off steam,* is an ineffective way to manage angry feelings. John's teacher knew that it would be much more helpful for John to observe an appropriate way to deal with the situation that was causing the feeling, so he modeled for John how to determine and then to ask for what one needs from the person who is the target of the anger.

Example   He decided to say what he wanted from John by firmly restating the playground limit of staying inside the fenced area. He also used indirect guidance to manage the environment better by moving the handle on the gate up higher so that the children could not reach it from the inside.

Create a Safe Emotional Climate

The scene is a parent education class on anger management. Parents have been asked what happened in their families when they, as children, expressed anger.

"My dad used to get so mad at me when I was angry, even if my anger had nothing to do with my father," said Marv.

"How did you feel when he got mad?" asked the leader.

"It scared me to see him get so mad that I just stopped telling him when I was upset."

The leader asked, "Did you ever talk about what it was that you were angry about in the first place?"

"No. And, you know what? I ended up taking care of Dad by pretending nothing was wrong even if I was seething about something," said Marv. "I've never thought about this before!"

Others noted that their parent criticized or even punished them for being angry or expressing anger. The root of their anger was never dealt with and resolved. They were punished or criticized for *feeling* angry. Their anger was shamed.

The hallmark of a safe emotional climate is that children are permitted and encouraged to acknowledge all their feelings, pleasant and unpleasant. They are not told to hide feelings, and they know that they will not be criticized for having the feeling, whatever it is. If Ted has sad feelings when the gerbil dies, then he knows that he can express them without fear. If James expresses tender feelings by gently stroking his puppy when it visits, nobody laughs or calls him a sissy. If Mary is irritated when somebody takes her puzzle, then she will feel safe in knowing that her teacher will not also become angry just because Mary is mildly irritated.

Help Children Understand What Makes Them Angry

Helping children understand and identify situations that trigger their anger is a major building block in responsible anger management. Helping children recog-

Children in a safe emotional climate are encouraged to acknowledge all feelings, pleasant and unpleasant.

nize signs of anger can alert them to the need to step back and decide how to act rather than just react to the emotional energy. This means that we will help children learn to regulate and manage their feelings, confront the trigger, solve the problem causing the anger, and eventually to let go of the anger.

Example   One teacher planned a discussion about anger triggers for large-group time. "There are a few things that I get *angry* about," said Mrs. Anderson. "Today I was caught in a traffic jam and I was really *irritated* because I was going to be late. Are there some things that seem to make you angry or that irritate you?" Tim said, "I get mad when somebody takes all the crackers before I get one." Julia, "Yesterday, my brother left the caps off my markers, and was I ever mad!"

Help Children Understand Their Body's Reaction to Anger

Children tend to better understand their feeling of anger when they know that there are actually bodily changes brought on by anger, such as increase in heart rate, muscle tightening, dry mouth, and changes in face color or vocal quality. These changes are controlled by the body's autonomic nervous system (Hole, 1981). Tell children that these changes are signals that they *are* angry.

Example   A teacher used a puppet to illustrate the bodily changes accompanying anger. The puppet is confronted by an anger-arousing situation; for example, somebody dumped her dixie cup with her bean plant in it and squashed the plant. The puppet says, "I'm *so angry* about my bean plant! I can tell because my arms and chest are shaking [teacher makes puppet tremble]. Oh dear, my heart is pounding so fast! And my voice sounds funny, too, and my face is warm."

Teach Children How to Deal with the Stress of Anger

Anger is a useful but stressful emotion, and managing anger responsibly returns the body to a normal state. Not dealing with anger keeps our bodies in a stressful state. It is important for adults to teach children not only how to deal with the events that triggered the anger but also with the stress that almost always accompanies anger (Baughman, 1992; Johnson, 1992).

Two of the most helpful stress reduction strategies are relaxation training and deep breathing exercises. Both strategies allow children (and adults) to get the autonomic nervous system under control, gain control of breathing, get the heart rate back to normal, stop shaking, calm down and actually think about the feeling, and refrain from doing anything irrational while in a highly stressed state. (See chapter 5 for more information on stress management.)

State Your Expectations for Responsible Anger Management

Stating expectations for behavior is, like modeling, a basic process through which adults influence children. Authoritative, responsible adults establish limits that honor and protect each person's physical and psychological boundaries. Responsible adults set limits on how angry children can show their anger, and these limits usually include prohibitions against showing angry feelings in destructive ways.

Example   The teacher watched 4½-year-old Darryl (case study child) get ready to hurl a shovel at Bob after Bob ran over Darryl's sand structure. The teacher was quick enough to grab the shovel, and said, "Darryl! No throwing! I won't allow you to hurt children when you're mad." (The teacher then dealt with Bob's aggression.)

Help Children Learn to Use Words to Describe Angry Feelings

Adults rely on speech to teach children how to express themselves, and by the end of toddlerhood (around 2½ years) children show a rudimentary ability to express and justify their anger and aggression verbally.

An interesting finding in Miller and Sperry's (1987) study was that the children did not use labels for emotions like anger. They did, however, talk about different aspects of the event of anger. They accused the perpetrator, asserted their own rights, threatened or insulted the perpetrator, or defended themselves.

Example   Darryl was angry when George wouldn't give him one of the puppets. Darryl said, "I'm gonna get my dad to beat you up! He'll make you give me a puppet."

Darryl fails to label his anger, but he does use language to talk about George's unfairness. Darryl uses *moral talk*, not *emotion talk*, and has, like many children, adopted this style of talk by observing his parents talk about anger-arousing events (Miller & Sperry, 1987).

Example   Darryl's father was angry about how long he had to wait in the drive-through at the bank and said, "Who do they think they are? I ought to go right in there and tell the manager what I think about this place."

Dad uses *moral talk*, but never does use emotion talk to label his feeling. Be helpful to children like Darryl by teaching them *emotion talk*. Do not assume that a child knows how to label a feeling. She might have come from a family where parents tell stories about how they reacted to anger, say, in the grocery store or on the freeway, but never actually discuss angry feelings. Teach children that they can label the feeling of anger, that there are words to describe the feeling they are having.

Example   Teacher, "Darryl, you seem to be feeling very *angry*. You can use words to tell George how you *feel*. Say, 'George, I'm *angry* because you won't give me a puppet.'"

Teachers would never expect children to automatically know the names of each new animal in a zoo unless somebody had told them the name. Similarly, we should not expect children to know the labels for all the feelings they may have unless we help them learn the label.

Help Children Expand Their "Feelings Vocabulary"

Anger is a complex emotion with many levels of emotional energy, ranging from minor irritation to rage. Some children understand that they can use labels for feelings, but they often have a limited vocabulary for describing their feeling of anger. Help this group of children by encouraging them to increase the number of labels or words they can use to describe the specific feeling they are having.

Many children will describe anger as feeling *mad*. Build their feelings vocabulary by adding synonyms to the list—words like *angry, troubled, irritated, bothered, annoyed*—that help them more accurately describe the level of emotion.

Example   "It seemed to *bother* you when Pete took the block again." "I noticed that you seemed *angry* when Amy put a big blob of red paint on your paper." "Mr. Rogers seemed *troubled* when he discovered that the puppy was lost." "That man was *irritated* when his neighbor walked on the fresh cement."

Make a chart (see Figure 7.1) listing all the words describing angry feelings. (You can do the same thing with other feeling words, too.)

Use Appropriate Books and Stories About Anger Management

Anger, a source of interpersonal stress for young children, is a topic for which bibliotherapy would be most appropriate. *Bibliotherapy* refers to using literature to promote mental health (Overstad, 1981). Books dealing with the emotion of anger can help a child deal more effectively with this strong emotion.

Jalongo (1986) notes that reading crisis-oriented books, including those about anger, serves three purposes. First, children get information about anger from well-chosen books on the topic. Second, they are encouraged to make connections between what they hear about this emotion in school and their life outside of school. Third, a child is more likely to view her own feelings of anger as natural and normal when a teacher plans, reads, and follows up on a story about anger.

Picture books about a topic as important as anger should be chosen with great care. A teacher can actually do more harm to a child who is plagued by anger by carelessly choosing and reading a poorly written book. Jalongo (1986) urges us, when we choose books about anger, to follow selection guidelines for choosing any picture book but to be sure that the book meets additional, specific

Figure 7.1
Help children expand their
feelings vocabulary.

Angry

Irritated

Bothered

Annoyed

MAD

SPECIAL FOCUS: Guidelines for Choosing Books on Anger

Evaluate books on anger by answering these questions:

1. Does this book use correct terminology about anger?
2. Does this book clarify or expand vocabulary on anger?
3. Does this book identify the specific event that seemed to elicit the anger?
4. Does this book convey the idea that feeling angry is acceptable?
5. Does this book tell children that they do not need to hide how they feel?
6. Does this book present good strategies for managing the anger responsibly?
7. Does this book tend to show how to manage anger in an optimistic way?

---

selection criteria (given in the *Special Focus* below). (See the short list of children's books on anger at the end of this chapter just before the reference list.)

Keep yourself focused on the topic by developing specific introductory remarks to motivate thinking, and focus children's attention on the topic of anger. Prepare specific comments and questions to use when reading the book.

Prepare a thoughtful follow-up. Avoid merely asking children to relate the chronological events of the story. Instead, focus on the topic of anger by clarifying information presented on how to manage anger responsibly. Concentrate on reviewing concepts or vocabulary relating to anger. Most important, communicate your acceptance of anger as an emotion and your approval of managing anger in a way that does not hurt others or damage property, that solves a problem, and that eventually allows a child to let go of the angry feeling rather than holding onto it.

CASE STUDY ANALYSIS: Anger Management

Analyze the case studies at the beginning of this chapter by completing these sentences.

1. Shantal's family seems to be the most responsible *model* of anger management because . . .
2. I would say that Darryl's home is *not* a safe emotional climate because . . .

3. Shantal is only 5 years old, but she can already recognize and acknowl-
    edge things that arouse her feelings of anger. The main factor in her fam-
    ily's pattern of interaction that has resulted in this ability is . . .

4. Julia's mother's approach to anger management is *irresponsible* because
    . . .

5. Darryl's dad's approach to anger management is also *irresponsible* because . . .

SUMMARY OF KEY CONCEPTS

1. *Anger* is an emotion, an *affective state,* or feeling, experienced when needs
    are frustrated. Anger and aggression are closely intertwined, but they are
    not the same thing.

2. There are several types of interactions that seem to elicit anger in young
    children. How a child responds to anger depends on what caused the anger.
    Some of their responses are ineffective coping strategies.

3. Children learn *display rules* for anger. There is a developmental trend in
    children's understanding and use of display rules, and children use display
    rules differently with adults than they do with their peers.

4. Adults can use several practical and developmentally appropriate strategies
    to help children manage their anger responsibly, such as modeling respon-
    sible anger management, helping children develop *emotion talk*, and reading
    books about anger.

OBSERVE CHILD GUIDANCE IN ACTION
Identifying Anger in Children

Observe adults and children either in a classroom or in a public place, such as a
mall. Use the following format to describe an episode of anger.

Date: _____

Setting: _____

Approximate age of child: _____

Describe the anger episode:

This child's anger arose over: physical assault, social rejection, verbal assault, a
disagreement over a toy, having to do something she did not want to do, or being
stopped from doing something she wanted to do.

The anger was caused by: an adult/another child

This child reacted to the anger with: active resistance, venting, revenge, other (if
"other," describe).

Explain how effectively you believe the adult dealt with the anger episode:

CHILDREN'S BOOKS THAT DEAL WITH ANGER

Barshun, R. N., & Hutton, K. (1983). *Feeling angry*. Elgin, IL: Child's World.

Duncan, R. (1989). *When Emily woke up angry*. Hauppauge, NY: Barron's.

Riley, S. (1978). *What does it mean? Angry*. Elgin, IL: Child's World.

Simon, N. (1974). *I was so mad!* Chicago: A. Whitman.

Watson, J. W. (1971). *Sometimes I get angry*. New York: Golden Press.

REFERENCES

Atschuler, J. L., & Ruble, D. N. (1989). Developmental changes in children's awareness of strategies for coping with uncontrollable stress. *Child Development, 60,* 1337–1349.

Band, E. B., & Weisz, I. R. (1988). How to feel better when it feels bad: Children's perspectives on coping with everyday stress. *Developmental Psychology, 24,* 247–253.

Bandura, A. (1965). Influence of models' reinforcement contingencies on the acquisition of imitative responses. *Journal of Personality and Social Psychology, 1,* 589–595.

Bandura, A., Ross, D., & Ross, S. A. (1961). Transmission of aggression through imitation of aggressive models. *Journal of Abnormal and Social Psychology, 63,* 575–582.

Baughman, D. (1992). Heal thyself: Reducing the risk of heart disease. *Optimal Health, 4*(2), 1, 4.

Beattie, M. (1987). *Codependent no more*. San Francisco: Harper & Row.

Bronfenbrenner, U. (1979). *The ecology of human development*. Cambridge: Harvard University Press.

Campos, J., & Barrett, K. (1984). A new understanding of emotions and their development. In C. Izard, J. Kagan, & R. Zajonc (Eds.), *Emotions, cognition, and behavior*. New York: Cambridge University Press.

Cummings, E. (1987). Coping with background anger in early childhood. *Child Development, 58,* 976–984.

Cummings, E., & Cummings, J. (1988). A process-oriented approach to children's coping with adults' angry behavior. *Developmental Review, 8,* 296–321.

Cummings, E. M., Iannotti, R. J., & Zahn-Waxler, C. (1985). Influence of conflict between adults on the emotions and aggression of young children. *Developmental Psychology, 21,* 495–507.

Cummings, E., Zahn-Waxler, C., & Radke-Yarrow, M. (1981). Young children's responses to expressions of anger and affection by others in the family. *Child Development, 52,* 1274–1282.

Cummings, E., Zahn-Waxler, C., & Radke-Yarrow, C. (1984). Developmental changes in children's reactions to anger in the home. *Journal of Child Psychology and Psychiatry, 25,* 63–74.

Doubleday, C., Kovaric, P., & Door, A. (1990). *Children's knowledge of display rules for emotional expression and control*. Paper presented at the annual meeting of the American Psychological Association, Boston.

Eisenberg, N., Fabes, R., Schaller, M., Carlo, G., & Miller, P. (1991). The relations of parental characteristics and practices to children's vicarious emotional responding. *Child Development, 62,* 1393–1408.

Emde, R., Gaensbauer, T., & Harmon, R. (1976). Emotional expression in infancy: A biobehavioral study. *Psychological Issues, 10* (Whole No. 37). New York: International Universities Press.

Emery, R. E. (1982). Interparent conflict and the children of discord and divorce. *Psychological Bulletin, 92*, 310–330.

Fabes, R., & Eisenberg, N. (1992). Young children's coping with interpersonal anger. *Child Development, 63*, 116–128.

Gnepp, J., & Hess, D. L. (1986). Children's understanding of verbal and facial display rules. *Developmental Psychology, 22*, 103–108.

Gottman, J. M., & Katz, L. F. (1989). Effects of marital discord on young children's peer interaction and health. *Developmental Psychology, 25*, 373–381.

Hole, J. W. (1981). *Human anatomy and physiology*. Dubuque, IA: Wm. C. Brown.

Jalongo, M. (1986). Using crisis-oriented books with young children. In J. B. McCracken (Ed.), *Reducing stress in young children's lives*. Washington, DC: NAEYC.

Johnson, E. H. (1992). The role of anger/hostility in hypertension and heart disease. Speech presented Feb. 25 at the University of Wisconsin-Stout, Menomonie, WI.

Karniol, R., & Heiman, T. (1987). Situational antecedents of children's anger experiences and subsequent responses to adult versus peer provokers. *Aggressive Behavior, 13*, 109–118.

Lerner, H. G. (1985). *The dance of anger*. New York: Harper & Row.

Malatesta, C., & Haviland, J. (1982). Learning display rules: The socialization of emotion expression in infancy. *Child Development, 53*, 991–1003.

Marion, M. (1993). Responsible anger management: The long bumpy road. *Day Care and Early Education*, 4–9.

Marion, M. (1994). Supporting the development of responsible anger management in children. *Early Child Development and Care, 97,* 155–163.

Miller, P., & Sperry, L. (1987). The socialization of anger and aggression. *Merrill-Palmer Quarterly, 33*(1), 1–31.

Overstad, B. (1981). *Bibliotherapy: Books to help young children*. St. Paul, MN: Toys 'n Things Press.

Piaget, J. (1970). Piaget's theory. In P. Mussen (Ed.), *Carmichael's manual of child psychology*. New York: Wiley.

Sabini, J., & Silver, M. (1982). *Moralities of everyday life*. Oxford, England: Oxford University Press.

Segal, J. (1988, August). I'm so angry! *Parents*, pp. 107–110.

Shantz, C. (1987). Conflicts between children. *Child Development, 58*, 283–305.

Shantz, C. U., & Shantz, D. W. (1985). Conflicts between children: Social-cognitive and sociometric correlates. In M. Berkowitz (Ed.), *New directions for child development* (Vol. 29). San Francisco: Jossey-Bass.

Underwood, M., Coie, J., & Herbsman, C. (1992). Display rules for anger and aggression in school-age children. *Child Development, 63*, 366–380.

Williams, R. (1989, February). Curing type A: The trusting heart. *Psychology Today*, pp. 40–42.

8

Understanding and Coping With Aggression in Children

Chapter Overview

After reading and studying this chapter, you will be able to

▼ *Define* aggression and *list and describe* different forms of aggression.

▼ *Explain* age and gender differences in aggression.

▼ *Explain*, from a systems or ecological perspective, how children become aggressive.

▼ *List, discuss, and give examples* of specific practices that prevent or control aggression.

"You first learn violence within the family." Violence "is learned
early and learned very well . . . violence is preventable."
(APA, 1993)

CASE STUDY: Mrs. Moffett's Class

Early Morning

It was October, and Mrs. Moffett's kindergarten class had been together for six weeks. She looked over to the easel just in time to see Thomas pinch the skin on Nathan's arm in an attempt to get Nathan to give up his spot at the easel. Nathan did not give up his spot. Instead, he shoved Thomas, who then punched Nathan. Mrs. Moffett raced over to the easel, grabbed both boys, marched them over to the *time-out* corner, and plopped them both in "the chair." She smiled as she turned around, thinking that she had solved the problem. When time-out finally ended, she told both boys, "Now you two know what will happen if you fight again!" She did not talk to them about more positive ways to get what they wanted.

Later That Same Day

Mrs. Moffett was astounded to see Nathan and Thomas fighting again. Once again, she put them both in time-out, but this time she yelled at them first.

UNDERSTANDING AGGRESSION

A Definition of Aggression

Aggression is any intentional behavior that results in injury to another person or to an animal, or damage to or destruction of property (Bandura, 1973; Berkowitz, 1973; Caldwell, 1977; Feshbach, 1970; Parke & Slaby, 1983).

Examples   A man tied a dog to his pickup truck and dragged the dog until it was mutilated and dead (an actual event in Menomonie, Wisconsin, in 1992).

A 5-year-old watched his mother beat his brother with a belt.

The same 5-year-old, when angered, hit another child at school.

One child kicked down another child's block structure.

The element uniting all forms of aggression is the infliction of harm on a person, animal, or object. Very few people would disagree with the idea that things like hitting, killing an animal by dragging it, beating a person with a belt, biting, vandalizing a school, and kicking constitute aggression because they are such obvious forms of aggression. There are other more subtle forms of aggression as well, including threats, sexual harassment, sarcasm, or undermining another person's plans.

Aggression may well be one of those behaviors that is *in the eye of the beholder* (Duhs & Gunton, 1988). Connor (1989) discovered that not everybody agrees on what constitutes aggression. She showed 14 videotaped incidents of the play behavior of 4- and 5-year-old children to male and female college students, preschool teachers, and preservice preschool teachers. In the videos, children played with three different types of toys: regular toys such as dolls and trucks, miniature war toys such as "action" characters, and war toys such as commando sets and cowgirl guns.

Whether observers thought any of the types of play constituted aggression depended on whether that person had engaged in war toy play, the person's gender, and whether he worked in a preschool setting. The point is that not everybody will agree on what aggression is. If you work in an early childhood setting, it would be a good idea to come to agreement on what the staff will consider aggression. The staff will be much more likely to deal with aggressive behavior consistently and effectively if you all share the same definition.

Forms of Aggression

This section describes three forms of aggression: *instrumental, hostile,* and *accidental.* Early childhood teachers will see instrumental aggression fairly often but will see hostile aggression far less frequently. Several factors influence how a person is able to show or manifest aggression, and these will be discussed in the material on the different types of aggression.

Instrumental Aggression

Instrumental aggression is aggression aimed at obtaining or getting back some object, territory, or privilege (Hartup, 1974). This type of aggression is linked to simple goal blocking. A child who has a goal of some sort and is hampered in reaching the goal does something aggressive to achieve the goal.

Example   Janet announced that she wanted a pink cookie at snack time (her goal). She anxiously watched the basket pass from one child to the next. Unable to wait any longer (there was only one pink cookie left), she reached across the table and grabbed the basket from Jessica (instrumental aggression), took a pink cookie, and then gave the basket back to Jessica.

This is a common form of aggression during the preschool years. Hartup's subjects, who were 4 to 6 years old, had a much higher rate of instrumental aggression than did older subjects. Cummings, Iannotti, and Zahn-Waxler (1989) found a decrease in the frequency of aggression, initiation of aggression, and average length of aggression between 2 and 5 years of age. Children between 1 and 3½ years of age, then, have most of their conflicts over space and resources (toys and other equipment), and there tends to be little hostility involved (Dawe, 1934). They push their way into line, grab things from others, yell "It's *my* turn!," bite (quite common in very young children), or ignore the fact that somebody else is working with crayons or markers when they themselves want to draw.

Does this mean that early childhood teachers should let children meet their goals by pushing, grabbing, or biting? Certainly not. Children should not be allowed to use aggression to get what they need or want. If Janet is allowed to grab a basket and take the cookie, then she will have been rewarded for aggression. In the cookie incident her teacher decided to acknowledge that Janet had a goal but also refuse to let her use aggressive tactics to achieve the goal.

Example   Janet's teacher held the basket and quietly and firmly told Janet to put the cookie back into it. "It looks like you really want the pink cookie, Janet, but I can't let you just grab it. I'll put the cookie back into the basket so that we can keep passing it around the circle. Your turn is coming."

What happens, though, if Janet is a pampered child who usually gets exactly what she wants? What if the basket gets to her and there is no pink cookie? What should her teacher do if Janet whines, argues, or pouts? The teacher has done exactly the right thing in stopping the instrumental aggression and should simply ignore any further attempts from Janet to continue the aggression. The teacher should ignore any whining, arguing, and pouting and should be matter-of-fact for the rest of snacktime, not cajoling Janet into eating. It becomes Janet's decision whether she wants to eat the color of cookie that is available.

What if the basket comes around to Janet and the pink cookie is still available? What would be an effective strategy for the teacher? Janet, of course, would get the prized cookie, and she should be encouraged by verbally acknowledging her cooperation with the limits.

Example   Janet's teacher said, "I know how hard it was for you to wait, Janet. That's what I call patience!"

This teacher stopped Liona's instrumental aggression by taking the food back and telling Liona, "I can't let you grab the food."

Hostile Aggression

Hostile aggression is person-oriented aggression and is quite different from instrumental aggression. The person who is aggressive perceives a threat to his ego or self-esteem from another person and believes the other person has done something to him on purpose. He may react to this perceived threat with physically or psychologically *hostile* aggression, and this type of aggression often looks like retaliation or revenge to an onlooker. This type of aggression tends to increase with age (Feshbach, 1970; Hartup, 1974; Szegal, 1985).

Example   Two 8-year-olds, Samuel and Theng, worked on their village made of small plastic blocks. Samuel's parents almost constantly criticize their son and frequently call him a "dummy." When Theng offered to help his classmate solve a construction problem Samuel perceived the suggestion as a sign that Theng thought him incompetent (perceived threat to self-esteem). Samuel did nothing then, but later, on the playground, he refused to let Theng play baseball (hostile aggression).

The change in how children express aggression parallels a more general change in their cognitive structure. Preschool children are usually in the second of Piaget stages of cognitive development, the preoperational stage, and one of the major characteristics of this stage is a child's decreased ability to take another person's perspective, a trait called *egocentricity*. A young child is focused on his own needs and wants and may not understand as well as an older person would that someone else has just as much right to choose a pink cookie or to have a turn on a trike.

An older child, in a different Piagetian stage, becomes less egocentric and better able to understand another person's intentions, including mean-spirited intentions to embarrass him. People do, however, make mistakes about the intentions of other people, as Samuel did with Theng's offer of help, but it is a person's perception of reality that matters, even if the perception is a faulty one. Samuel acted on his perception, faulty as it was, and he reacted with hostile aggression.

Accidental Aggression

Accidental aggression is unintentional aggression (Feshbach, 1970) and is common in many early childhood classrooms. It is particularly common in poorly designed, crowded rooms.

Examples   Ethan crashed into Quan's block tower as he zoomed along with his truck. Quan then shoved Ethan out of the way.

Lori and Nan played at the crowded workbench. Nan hit Lori's finger with the hammer and Lori screamed at Nan.

The real problem with accidental aggression is that the injured child often retaliates in an equally aggressive way. Young children may not be able to distinguish between accidental and intentional aggression and do not have the skills needed to deal effectively with anger.

What is a teacher's role with this type of aggression? First, to acknowledge that we adults are responsible for making the classroom as safe as possible, and that we can prevent a lot of this type of aggression through good space management. Second, to be prepared for the inevitable bumping, pushing, or shoving as young children learn how to live and work with others. Third, to help children learn to distinguish between accidental and intentional injury. Children are less likely to retaliate when they understand that the damage was not on purpose.

Example　The teacher said to Quan, "O-o-h. It looks like you're upset, Quan. Use words to tell Ethan that you're angry. No shoving." To Ethan he said, "Drive your truck on the path we set up for trucks, not the block corner."

Sex Differences in Aggression

What do we know about sex differences in aggression during childhood, especially early childhood? A consistent finding from research on sex differences in aggression is that there are clear sex differences in aggression and that these differences are evident during early childhood (Darvill & Cheyne, 1981; Maccoby & Jacklin, 1980; Smith & Green, 1974). These researchers would predict that you will see evidence of these sex differences in a group of 3- to 5-year-olds in the following ways:

1. The boys would show more aggression than the girls.
2. Boys would be both physically and verbally more aggressive than the girls.
3. Older boys would be more likely than older girls to counterattack when physically attacked.
4. There would be more aggressive interactions between pairs of boys than between boy-girl or girl-girl dyads.

The work of Cummings and his associates (1989) supported these findings. In their studies of aggression in 2- and 5-year-old children they noted a sex difference in aggression. Their work also adds to our knowledge by documenting that there were substantial sex differences in the stability of aggression as well. Boys' disposition to be physically aggressive was not only greater than for girls but also more stable; that is, it stayed about the same for boys during the early childhood years.

More important than describing sex differences is an explanation of how the differences might have developed. One explanation can be found by examining how a group socializes boys and girls differently. Our culture has clearly defined attitudes about girls, boys, and aggression, and these attitudes are observable in the different child-rearing tactics used with boys and girls. Parents tend to use more physical punishment with boys than with girls, and boys might adopt these aggressive methods in interaction with others (Block, 1978). Parents may also permit or even encourage aggression in boys and rationalize it by saying "Boys will be boys." Parents also manage the environments of boys and girls differently by choosing different toys for girls and boys. Some "male" toys, such as guns or action figures, are *aggressive cues*, items that seem to elicit aggressive play.

HOW CHILDREN BECOME AGGRESSIVE:
A SYSTEMS/ECOLOGICAL APPROACH

Children are not aggressive when they are born, and not all children become aggressive as they get older. Aggression is a complex social behavior, and this complexity must be reflected in any explanation of aggression that is to be useful to adults helping children cope with aggression. Several socializing forces work together to shape aggression in certain children.

The most complete explanation of how children become aggressive is a *systems* or *ecological approach* (Bronfenbrenner, 1979). Professionals taking this approach acknowledge that a child is embedded in a variety of social systems and believe that these systems work together to shape a child's aggression (Brim, 1975; Bronfenbrenner, 1979; Huesmann, 1988; Parke & Slaby, 1983). A child quite frequently first learns about aggression in his *family system*. Almost equal in importance to a family's influence is *television* in helping children learn aggression. The child's *peer group system* may also teach and reinforce aggression. Families and peer groups are themselves embedded in a larger setting, the *community and culture*, and it is the teachings from these settings that families learn and pass on to their children. This section focuses on how aggression is learned, maintained, and modified in these systems.

Children Learn Aggression in the Family

Families play a critical role in the acquisition, maintenance, and modification of children's aggression (Parke & Slaby, 1983). Some children exist in violent families, and it is here that they receive lessons in how to hurt other people and animals. Some families become violent because members of the system develop aggressive patterns of interacting with one another. Adults in many aggressive family systems deal with anger irresponsibly, are authoritarian and nonsupportive, manage their children's environment poorly, and use ineffective, often harsh, discipline techniques. This section describes how aggressive families teach children to be aggressive.

*Intra*familial Violence

Our society's high level of violence is reflected at the familial level in violent methods of resolving conflict between many adult partners (Straus, Gelles, & Steinmetz, 1980). Violence within a family system is called *intrafamilial violence*. Children in families plagued by intrafamilial violence have many opportunities to observe their parents using aggression when conflicts arise.

There is a lot of *negative affect* between parents in such families. Pederson, Anderson, and Cain (1977) found that the amount of negative affect between husbands and wives was positively related to high levels of negative affect toward children. An atmosphere teeming with negative affect and the acceptance of physical force as a general pattern of family interaction sets the stage for the use of physical force in discipline of children. Parents who use violence to resolve conflicts also tend to use hurtful discipline tactics with their children (Steinmetz, 1977).

Their children, in turn, observe their parents and imitate them by using aggression to resolve their own conflicts (Strauss et al., 1980). Huesmann (1988) argues that aggressive children acquire *aggressive scripts* through observation, scripts that guide behavior early in life. The cumulative result is a network of cognitive scripts for social behavior emphasizing aggressive responding. Once encoded, the scripts (think of them as tapes) for aggressive behavior may be elicited through a general activation of memory or by specific cues to which the child is exposed (war toys, for example). Observing violence does a couple of things. It provides the child with new scripts for calling up in the future, and the newly observed aggression may well trigger the recall of existing aggressive scripts. In addition, a child who practices these scripts is much more likely to recall them in the future.

The Coercive Process in Aggressive Family Systems

Families are a lot like mobiles—they are made up of distinct parts but form a whole; all the parts are connected, yet separate, and each part affects the others. Each member of a family system influences the behavior of all other members. Patterson (1982) observed family interaction patterns and identified a specific *coercive process* used by many families, a process through which members of a family learn, maintain, and increase aggressive behavior. This coercive process involves several steps.

1. *One system member does something aggressive.* Mario pulls his sister's hair.
2. *A second system member is likely to respond in an equally hurtful way.* Mario's sister whirls around and punches Mario in the face.
3. *The aversive interchange continues and escalates in intensity.* Mario responds by pushing his sister and she pushes back. Mario slaps her and she cries.
4. *Other system members are drawn into the process.* Dad hears the children fighting, races to the backyard, grabs and slaps each child, and yells at them to stop the fighting.
5. *One system member eventually withdraws the aversive stimulus and breaks the cycle of aggression for a short time.* Dad retreats to the house, proud of having stopped the fighting. The problem? Dad thinks he succeeded in stopping the aggressive behavior of his children (actually, Mario and his sister's aggressive behavior will probably increase). Dad has been *negatively reinforced* for slapping his children and is highly likely to slap them again in future interactions.
6. *System members reinforced for aggression victimize the same members of the system in future interactions.* Mario continues to aggress against his sister because

she gives in to his demands. Likewise, Dad, reinforced for negative discipline, directs hurtful discipline methods toward both children because he mistakenly believes these tactics to be effective.

Members of families caught up in this coercive process train each other to use aggression. They help each other develop aggressive scripts that will be played back again and again. Dad has a script that says, "Yell, slap, hit when the children fight." He models aggression by slapping. Mario and his sister negatively reinforce Dad for using aggressive discipline by *temporarily stopping their fighting*. Mario has learned how to hurt his sister, and his sister has learned how to be a victim.

The coercive process is more common in certain families because of specific characteristics of the children and because parents in these family systems have ineffective parenting skills. Aggressive children show little self-control, have a reduced responsiveness to threats and reinforcers, are not very responsive to social stimuli, and are noncompliant and impulsive. These characteristics make aggressive children difficult to control (Parke & Slaby, 1983) and partially explains why the coercive process is more evident in some families (Patterson, 1982).

The Caregiving Style of Aggressive Parents Fosters Aggression

Members of aggressive family systems are not very responsive to each other. Recall that parents in the *authoritarian* and the *permissive by default* styles are low in responsiveness. They are neither sensitive to nor supportive of their children, and their caregiving style sets the stage for heightened aggression in children in a number of ways (Feshbach, 1970; Martin, 1975; Parke & Slaby, 1983).

1.   These unresponsive adults often ignore and fail to meet their child's basic psychological needs for protection, love, affection, nurturance, play, and self-esteem. Unmet needs result in frustration, and frustrated, angry children frequently act aggressively if other conditions are present.

2.   Adults low in responsiveness are *in*effective teachers of social behaviors because they model and teach ineffective interactional skills such as irresponsible anger management and aggression. They reward aggressive behavior and fail to teach more appropriate behavior because they don't know how or what to teach. Their children tend to be low in self-control or self-restraint, and children who are not self-controlled are likely to react with aggression under many circumstances.

3.   Adults in aggressive systems tend to use not just one or two negative discipline strategies but a whole cluster of negative discipline tactics, and it is this group of factors that contributes to aggression. From the chapter on negative discipline you already know what these strategies are: using physical discipline, failing to set appropriate limits, inconsistency in discipline, using humor as a weapon, using sarcasm or shame, nattering or nagging, and using hurtful forms

of punishment (Caldwell, 1977; Lefkowitz, Eron, Walder, & Huesmann, 1977; Siegel & Kohn, 1970).

4.   Adults in aggressive systems *indirectly* influence aggression through their management style. This adult managerial role is probably just as important as the adult's direct role because children spend more time interacting with the *inanimate* environment than they do with people (Parke & Slaby, 1983; White, Kaban, Shapiro, & Attonucci, 1976). Parents in aggressive systems provide many cues that elicit aggression—lots of televised violence and toy guns. Other adults consciously avoid providing such cues.

Examples   Tony, 7 years old, is allowed unmonitored access to television and watches much televised violence. He owns several toy guns and frequently plays his brother's video game "Shoot the Rabbit."

David is also 7 years old. His parents monitor how much television he watches. They try to eliminate as much televised aggression as they can, and try to help Dave understand the violence if he does see it. They look for interesting toys that do not serve as cues for aggression (Carlson-Paige & Levin, 1990).

Aggression Develops in a Child's Peer Group

Aggression has its roots in a child's family, but aggression is also learned, maintained, and modified in a child's peer group. Peers influence each other's aggression in several ways (Parke & Slaby, 1983).

Peers Model Aggression

Children learn just as effectively from peer models as they do from other types of models. Hicks (1965) found that the effect of modeling lasted for at least six months after observing the model.

Example   Lonnie, 5 years old, plays with other children who are 6 and 7 years old. He has observed one of these children extort lunch money from one of the girls, has watched his friend Bert twist another child's arm until that child gave up a turn, and has observed yet another push one of the smaller children off a bike.

Peers Reinforce Aggression

Peers also reinforce other children's aggression. Patterson, Littman, and Bricker (1967) studied a child's reactions to being attacked by another child. Some children cried, others withdrew from the attacker, and still others gave in to their attacker.

Example   Sue gave up her turn on the seesaw when Sam pushed her off. Other children, however, did not give in and tried to get adult help. Lew called the teacher and said, "Sam pushed me!"

Sue reinforced Sam's aggression by "giving in." The attacker will continue to aggress on this child, but when a child refuses to give in the attacker seeks out a new victim.

A child's peer group influences the development of aggression.

Peers Teach How to Avoid Being a Victim

Example   Jim is a relatively passive child who has frequently been the victim of Mario's aggression. After being hit several times, pushed out of the way, and having his puzzle dumped, Jim did nothing. One day when Mario pushed Jim out of place at the slide, Jim counterattacked and shoved Mario. The number of attacks against Jim declined, and he realized that he could avoid being a victim by behaving aggressively.

Yes, Jim does need to learn to defend himself, but he also should be taught responsible anger and conflict management. He has learned that aggression is a powerful tool.

Peers Regulate Aggression by Setting Norms

Peer groups influence aggression of members of the group by setting norms about the expression of aggression. Some peer groups, such as gangs, can actually increase aggression through norms that require aggressive behavior for group membership. Other groups might prohibit aggression through its norms. Some children are inappropriately aggressive, thus violating their peer group norms.

Aggressive children lack certain social skills, such as the ability to resolve conflict. Asher and Renshaw (1982) and Bullock (1991) found that aggressive, unpopular children solved conflicts with peers through aggressive means and did not seem to know how to resolve conflict in a positive way.

Television Affects the Development of Aggression

We now have four decades of research showing that children watch a lot of television, that they watch an excessive amount of violence, and that heavy viewing of television violence has major behavioral effects. Along with family and peer group, television should be viewed as one of the major socializers of children's aggression (Kuttschreuter, Wiegman, & Baarda, 1989; Liebert, Spratkin, & Davidson, 1982; NAEYC, 1990). Parke and Slaby (1983) note that any discussion of the development of aggression would be incomplete without an examination of the role of television.

Amount of Television Watched

Almost all American homes (98%) have one television, and over 50% have at least one extra television, the extra set used mainly by children (Nielson Company, 1988). Over 50% of American homes have a VCR, and about 33% have cable programming (Cooper & Mackie, 1986; Stipp & Milavsky, 1988). So, American children have access to an enormous range of programming—regular broadcast stations, hundreds of cable stations, and whatever other video programming is allowed in their homes.

Nobody should be surprised, then, that children watch a lot of television. Television-viewing habits develop in early childhood, and, in spite of large individual differences in how much television children watch (Huston, Rice, Kerkman, & St. Peters, 1990), 2- to 18-year-old children watch television for an average of 28 hours per week (Nielsen Company, 1988). Parents even expose infants (6 months) to an average of 1 hour of television per day (Hollenbeck & Slaby, 1979). Many children spend more time watching television than they do anything else, including exercising, playing, reading, and interacting with friends or family (Huston et al., 1990).

Many parents express concern about the effects of televised violence on their children. In one study parents were as concerned that televised violence may contribute to fear and passivity in their children as they were that television might promote aggressiveness (Ridley-Johnson, Surdy, & O'Laughlin, 1991). Many concerned parents, however, place very few restrictions on children's viewing. They restrict neither the amount of television their children watch nor the content of the programs.

How Is Violence Portrayed on Television?

American television programming shows violence as a common form of social interaction. Gerbner, Gross, Morgan, and Signorielli (1980, 1986) and Gerbner,

Gross, Signorielli, Morgan, and Jackson-Beeck (1979) monitored televised violence over a 13-year period and found that violence was frequently and consistently portrayed on television. Eighty percent of the programs monitored contained violence that occurred at a rate of 7.5 incidents per hour. Children's television contains an especially high level of violence. Ninety-three percent of weekend daytime programs that were designed for children contained violence at a rate of 17.6 incidents per hour (Gerbner et al., 1979, 1980, 1986).

Children see a distorted view of violence on television (Slaby & Quarforth, 1980). Real violence is dirty—people bleed, jaws are broken, people are stabbed, dogs are mutilated, and animals and people suffer and die. Real violence is not funny, but televised violence does not show real violence.

Televised violence is distorted because it depicts shootings, fighting, knifings, and murder as clean, justified, effective, rewarded, and humorous. Television codes forbid showing real violence, so televised violence is clean and devoid of real suffering. Codes also require that programs show that crime does not pay. As a result, "good guys" are allowed to use violence as a way of punishing "bad guys." "Good guys" are just as violent as and break the law just as much as the "bad guys" (Lange, Baker, & Ball, 1969).

Television violence is shown to be effective in attaining goals (Larsen, Gray, & Fortis, 1968). Children's television shows that violence is an effective way to get things and to get things done. They see that "good guys" attain goals by hurting others, and that they are actually rewarded for being violent. Violence is praised and rewarded as often as it is punished (Stein & Friedrich, 1975).

Televised violence is depicted as humorous. Children's television is especially guilty of connecting violence and humor (Parke & Slaby, 1983). Violent cartoons like "Road Runner" are frequently accompanied by laugh tracks. Linking violence and laughter tells children that "violence is funny."

Certain groups are victimized in televised violence. Gerbner et al. (1979) noted that victimization is especially evident in children's programming on weekends. Victims are most frequently men and women in minority roles—old, young, people of color, and women. From this sort of irresponsible programming children learn that groups who have power and status can force their will on less powerful groups or persons.

Children's Understanding of Television Violence

A young child's understanding of televised violence differs from that of an older child (Collins, 1983). Collins, Wellman, Keniston, and Westby (1978), wanting to know what children of different ages would remember about violence on television, showed a program containing violence to children in kindergarten, second, fifth, and eighth grades. Kindergarten and second-grade children remembered either an aggressive act alone or the aggressive act and its consequences. For example, they would remember that a detective successfully extracted information from a victim by threatening to shoot her (aggressive act). Fifth and eighth graders also understood and remembered the motives of an aggressor. Younger children, then, need help in understanding a person's motivation in televised violence.

SPECIAL FOCUS: Television and Children's Aggression

Conclusion #1: Television can and does increase subsequent aggression in children.

This conclusion comes from basic research and reports of professional groups (APA, 1985). Studies using different viewing materials, viewers, viewing circumstances, and different measures of aggression (Funk, 1992; Lefkowitz, Eron, Walder, & Huesmann, 1972; Liebert et al., 1982; Silvern & Williamson, 1987; Singer, 1987; Stein & Friedrich, 1975; Watt & Krull, 1977) highlight the causal link between watching television violence and aggression.

Conclusion #2: Televised violence increases a child's passive acceptance of aggression by others.

Not only do children themselves become more aggressive when they watch televised violence, but they also more readily accept violence by others. Children are most likely to relax their standards if they view violence as effective, justified, reinforced, and commonplace (Eron & Huesmann, 1987). Televised violence, as noted previously, is presented in precisely this fashion. Children are also likely to become apathetic toward another person's violence when their real world matches television's standards for using violence (Singer, 1987).

HELPING CHILDREN COPE EFFECTIVELY WITH AGGRESSION

Strategies described in this section for helping children cope effectively with aggression will focus on helping individual children. If you review the basic processes through which all adults influence children, you will see that we can prevent a lot of aggression or help children decrease aggression through those processes. We can also work with the groups in which a child lives and focus on events in the child's larger community.

Helping Children at an Individual Level

Set and Clearly Communicate Limits Prohibiting Aggression

Create a *non*permissive atmosphere by establishing limits against hurting or disturbing others or damaging toys or equipment and firmly but gently enforcing limits. You will begin to help children see that other people have a right to be safe and secure. You will help them develop values and internal controls about the rights of others.

Example   When Mr. Rivera restated a limit—"Mario, I know that you want to sit in that chair, but I can't just let you push Pete off. I want you to sit in this chair"—he clearly communicated his refusal to tolerate Mario's aggression.

Reduce Exposure to Aggression-Evoking Cues and Aggressive Models

Turner and Goldsmith (1976) wanted to know if children's aggression would increase if toy guns were available. They observed preschool children during free play. In some of the play sessions toy guns were available, but in other sessions the toy guns were replaced by airplanes. Aggression was much more evident when guns were present. Children frequently act aggressively when certain stimuli associated with aggression are available.

Limit the number of models of aggression to which children are exposed. Substitute nonaggressive models (Bandura, 1973; Parke & Slaby, 1983). One of the best ways to do this is to limit the amount of violent television a child watches.

Jeannie's parents limit television watching and encourage her to have fun doing other things.

Another is to carefully screen and select movies, books, pictures, and other media (Graybill, Strawniak, Hunter, & O'Leary, 1987). Another good way is to model cooperative, nonaggressive behavior for children.

Watch Television With Children and Comment on Aggressive Program Content

Example   While John was watching television, his father said, "Why do you think that man punched his neighbor, John? . . . Yes, I think he was mad at him for driving his car over the flowers. That still doesn't make it OK to hit his neighbor. Do you think that they can be friends now?" John's friend Pete watched the same show, but he watched it by himself.

Children who watch televised violence with adults and hear a negative evaluation of the violence, as John did, are less aggressive than children like Pete, who watch televised violence without an adult coviewer (Eron, 1986; Grusec, 1973; Mattern & Lindholm, 1985; Singer, 1987; Singer & Singer, 1985; Slaby & Roedell, 1982). Horton and Zimmer's pamphlet (1990) offers good suggestions on how to teach parents to mediate their children's television watching.

Encourage Children to Be Empathic

Example   "Oh, Susan! You've torn Sarah's painting. I think she's sad because she is crying."

Susan was being encouraged to be *empathic*. Children who are trained to be more empathic (to see things from someone else's perspective) tend to be more sensitive to another's feelings and to be less aggressive (Feshbach & Feshbach, 1982).

Encourage Consequential Thinking

Help children develop a value system that encourages them to treat others with respect and to refrain from hurting others (APA, 1993). One way to help children develop a respectful attitude is to teach them *consequential thinking*, the understanding that a consequence of aggression is that somebody gets hurt. Consequential thinking is one key to changing or preventing aggressive behavior. A good way to encourage consequential thinking is to give gentle but direct instruction in thinking about consequences.

Example   Pam's mother saw Pam hit their puppy when the puppy did not sit on command. "Pam! No hitting. Fluffy is trying to hide. I think you *hurt* her when you hit her."

Pam's mother is arousing Pam's empathy for Fluffy by "feeding back" the puppy's pain. Pam's aggressive behavior is likely to decrease because her mother aroused her empathy, and empathy is incompatible with aggression.

Avoid a common, *but highly unethical*, tactic, that is, to say, "Pam, how would you like it if I hit you?" Adults who use this tactic want children to think consequentially, but their method misses the mark. Young children do not know how the other person felt, so they will not be able to figure it out on their own. Do not expect them to automatically know this unless you say many times when they are young, "That hurt," or "You broke that when you stepped on it," or "It hurts somebody's feelings when you call them names."

A word of caution. Not everyone reacts to pain feedback by becoming less aggressive. For highly aggressive children another person's or animal's pain is merely a signal that the aggression "worked," and these children show little or no sorrow for hurting another person or animal. The person who dragged the dog to death bragged about it, "Yeah, I kept going until he [the dog] stopped squealing!" This person heard and fully understood the suffering he caused, but he did not stop, even when the dog was so obviously hurt.

Teach Behavior Incompatible With Aggression

Give direct instruction about more positive behavior. Show and tell children how to be assertive, to negotiate solutions, to cooperate, and to share. Teach the more positive behavior through modeling and coaching.

Examples   Mr. Rivera used *modeling* to teach about sharing by showing a film-strip to his group of 4-year-olds about two children who had an argument about whose turn it was on the trike. Their teacher helped them negotiate turn-taking.

Rita hit Mario after Mario had grabbed Rita's trike. Mr. Rivera used *coaching* when he verbalized a new way to respond to both children. "Rita, you had the trike first and Mario took it, but I won't let you hit him. *Tell Mario with words* that you are going to finish your ride." "Mario, I want you to tell Rita with words that you would like to ride the trike."

Reinforce Cooperative Behavior

When Mario shared his goggles with another child, Mr. Rivera said, "Thank you for sharing, Mario." Lots of people might think that Mario is an aggressive child, but his teacher has taken Brown and Elliott's (1965) advice and is making an effort to notice and reinforce Mario's cooperative, helpful behavior. Mr. Rivera has noticed that Mario's physical and verbal aggression are very gradually decreasing.

Reinforce Cooperative "Language," Too

In Slaby and Crowley's (1977) study, preschool teachers were instructed to ignore aggressive language ("I'm going to punch you in the nose!") but to pay attention to verbal cooperative statements ("Let's put this puzzle together!"). The teacher was instructed to reinforce a cooperative statement by saying something like, "Jake, I heard you ask Sue if you could use some of the flannel pieces." Slaby and Crowley found that verbal aggression decreased and cooperation increased. This was a real classroom in which the adults found that they could notice and reinforce only a small percentage of cooperative statements, but even this was sufficient to decrease aggression.

Kathryn's and Grace's parents encourage cooperation.

Step Between Children Involved in an Incident, Ignore the Aggressor, and Pay Attention to the Victim

Some children persist in their aggression in spite of very well-developed and well-stated limits.

Example   Mr. Rivera groaned when he saw Mario grab the funnel away from John. He decided to ignore Mario, the aggressor, and attend only to John, the victim. He suggested that John use an assertive way of dealing with Mario's aggression, "John, you were playing with the funnel. Tell Mario it's *your* turn now."

This is effective, first, because there is no reinforcement for the aggression. Mario's teacher ignored him and did not allow his victim to give in to the aggression. Second, the victim learns how to cope with conflict by being assertive. Third, other children observe that aggression is not tolerated, that aggression is not an effective method of interacting with friends, and that it is good to be sympathetic with a victim (Parke & Slaby, 1983; Pinkston, Reese, LeBlanc, & Baer, 1973).

Encourage Responsible Anger Management

Encouraging responsible anger management is one of the most effective methods to prevent or decrease aggression (Novaco, 1978). See chapter 7 for specific strategies for anger management.

Controlling Aggression at the Family Level

Effective control of *intrafamilial* aggression (aggression within the family) focuses on restructuring interaction patterns in aggressive families (Patterson, 1982). Specifically, parents in aggressive families are made aware of the connection between their behavior and their child's aggression. Parents are then taught different, more effective child-rearing techniques (Marion, 1992). Parent education that focuses on positive discipline is recognized as an excellent method for the primary prevention of child abuse.

Controlling Aggression at the Community Level

Families are embedded in communities. Families and communities influence each other, and many people believe that families who are strongly connected to their community are automatically influenced in a positive way. This belief is erroneous because a community's influence on a family can be positive or negative. Consider the negative influence when a community allows battering and abuse of certain groups.

Garbarino (1976) and Garbarino and Crouter (1978) gave clear evidence that child abuse and levels of intrafamilial aggression are largely determined by the availability of community support systems. Aggression within families tends to decrease when families have access to positive support systems. The Wisconsin Children's Trust Fund (1988, 1989, 1990, 1991, 1992) required that grant proposals contain a method for helping families build social support systems.

CASE STUDY ANALYSIS: Aggression

Analyze the case study on aggression (Mrs. Moffett's class) by answering the following questions.

1. Thomas used _____ aggression. I believe this is true because . . .
2. Explain how Mrs. Moffett has taken part in the *coercive process* that is very likely to make the fighting worse, not better.
3. Mrs. Moffett has been *negatively* reinforced for using negative discipline. When did this happen? What was the reinforcer she received? How did this affect her behavior later in the day with the same boys and the same problem?
4. Name at least two different, more effective strategies that the teacher could easily have used:

SUMMARY OF KEY CONCEPTS

1. *Aggression* is behavior that results in injury to a person or animal or damage to or destruction of property. There are various types of aggression, includ-

ing *accidental*, *instrumental*, and *hostile* aggression. As children grow older, hostile aggression tends to increase and instrumental aggression tends to decrease. This shift parallels a more general change in cognitive development. Different socialization practices for boys and girls may explain sex differences in how boys and girls express aggression.

2. Children are embedded in a variety of social systems—family, peer group, and community. Television is also a major socializing element. Children influence and are influenced by each of these systems. The most complete explanation of how aggression develops, then, is a *systems* or *ecological* approach, in which each system's contribution to aggression is acknowledged.

3. Responsible, supportive adults use a number of different methods for preventing or controlling aggression. They work with children on an individual level. An aggressive child often lives in an aggressive family system, and adults who try to help families control aggression teach aggressive families to change aggressive patterns of interaction. Responsible adults also attempt to decrease the amount of televised violence to which children are exposed.

OBSERVE CHILD GUIDANCE IN ACTION
Helping Children Cope With Aggression

Observe an adult working with a group of children under the age of 8. Use the following format to explain how effectively this adult prevents or decreases aggression.

Name: _____

Setting: _____

Approximate age of children: _____

List any aggressive "cues" contained in this setting:

This adult has set limits prohibiting aggression. A specific example is:

When a child was aggressive, this is how the teacher dealt with it:

I believe that this teacher has/has not responsibly dealt with the aggression. My reason:

REFERENCES

American Psychological Association. (1985). *Violence on television*. Washington, DC: APA Board of Ethical and Social Responsibility for Psychology.

American Psychological Association. (1993). *Violence and youth report*. Washington, DC: APA Commission on Violence and Youth.

Asher, S. R., & Renshaw, P. D. (1982). *Social skills and social knowledge of high and low status kindergarten children*. Unpublished manuscript, University of Illinois.

Bandura, A. (1973). *Aggression: A social learning analysis*. New York: Holt.

Berkowitz, L. (1973). Control of aggression. In B. Caldwell & H. Riccuti (Eds.), *Review of child development research*. Chicago: University of Chicago Press.

Block, H. (1978). Another look at sex differentiation in the socialization behaviors of mothers and fathers. In J. Sherman & F. L. Denmark (Eds.), *The future of women: Future directions of research*. New York: Psychological Dimensions.

Brim, O. G. (1975). Macro-structural influences on child development and the need for childhood social indicators. *American Journal of Orthopsychiatry, 45*, 516–524.

Bronfenbrenner, U. (1979). *The ecology of human development*. Cambridge, MA: Harvard University Press.

Brown, P., & Elliot, R. (1965). Control of aggression in a nursery school class. *Journal of Experimental Child Psychology, 2*, 103–107.

Bullock, J. (1991). Supporting the development of socially rejected children. *Early Child Development and Care, 66*, 15–23.

Caldwell, B. M. (1977). Aggression and hostility in young children. *Young Children, 32*, 4–13.

Carlson-Paige, N., & Levin, D. (1990). *Who's calling the shots? How to respond effectively to children's fascination with war toys*. Philadelphia: New Society Publishers.

Collins, W. A. (1983). Social antecedents, cognitive processing, and comprehension of social portrayals on television. In E. T. Higgins, D. N. Ruble, & W. W. Hartup (Eds.), *Social cognition and social development*. Cambridge: Cambridge University Press.

Collins, W. A., Wellman, H., Keniston, A. H., & Westby, S. D. (1978). Age-related aspects of comprehension and inference from a televised dramatic narrative. *Child Development, 49*, 389–399.

Connor, K. (1989). Aggression: Is it in the eye of the beholder? *Play and Culture, 2*(3), 213–217.

Cooper, J., & Mackie, D. (1986). Video games and aggression in children. *Journal of Applied Social Psychology, 16*(8), 726–744.

Cummings, E. M., Iannotti, R. J., & Zahn-Waxler, C. (1989). Aggression between peers in early childhood: Individual continuity and developmental change. *Child Development, 60*(4), 887–895.

Darvill, D., & Cheyne, J. A. (1981). *Sequential analysis of responses to aggression: Age and sex effects*. Paper presented at the Society for Research in Child Development, Boston.

Dawe, H. C. (1934). An analysis of two hundred quarrels of preschool children. *Child Development, 5*, 139–157.

Duhs, L., & Gunton, R. (1988). TV violence and childhood aggression: A curmudgeon's guide. *Australian Psychologist. 23*(2), 183–185.

Eron, L. D. (1986). Interventions to mitigate the psychological effects of media violence on aggressive behavior. *Journal of Social Issues, 42*(3), 155–169.

Eron, L. D., & Huesmann, L. R. (1987). Television as a source of maltreatment of children. *School Psychology Review, 16*(2), 195–202.

Feshbach, N. D., & Feshbach, S. (1982). Empathy training and the regulation of aggression: Potentialities and limitations. *Academic Psychology Bulletin, 4*, 399–413.

Feshbach, S. (1970). Aggression. In P. Mussen (Ed.), *Carmichael's manual of child psychology* (Vol. 2). New York: Wiley.

Funk, J. (1992). Video games: Benign or malignant? *Journal of Applied Developmental Psychology, 12*(1), 63–71.

Garbarino, J. (1976). Some ecological correlates of child abuse: The impact of socioeconomic stress on mothers. *Child Development, 47,* 178–185.

Garbarino, J., & Crouter, A. (1978). Defining the community context for parent-child relations: The correlates of child maltreatment. *Child Development, 49,* 604–616.

Gerbner, G., Gross, L., Morgan, M., & Signorielli, N. (1980). The mainstreaming of America. *Journal of Communication, 30,* 12–29.

Gerbner, G., Gross, L., Morgan, M., & Signorielli, N. (1986). Living with television: The dynamics of the cultivation process. In J. Bryant & D. Zillman (Eds.), *Perspectives on media effects.* Hillsdale, NJ: Erlbaum.

Gerbner, G., Gross, L., Signorielli, N., Morgan, M., & Jackson-Beeck, M. (1979). The demonstration of power: Violence profile No. 10. *Journal of Communication, 29,* 177–196.

Graybill, B., Strawniak, M., Hunter, T., & O'Leary, M. (1987). Effects of playing versus observing violent versus nonviolent video games on children's aggression. *Psychology, 24*(3), 1–8.

Grusec, J. E. (1973). Effects of co-observer evaluations on imitation: A developmental study. *Developmental Psychology, 8,* 141.

Hartup, W. W. (1974). Aggression in childhood: Developmental perspectives. *American Psychologist, 29,* 336–341.

Hicks, D. J. (1965). Imitation and retention of film-mediated aggressive peer and adult models. *Journal of Personality and Social Psychology, 2,* 97–100.

Hollenbeck, A. R., & Slaby, R. G. (1979). Infant visual and vocal responses to television. *Child Development, 50,* 41–45.

Horton, J., & Zimmer, J. (1990). *Media violence and children: A guide for parents.* Washington, DC: NAEYC publication #585.

Huesmann, L. (1988). An information processing model for the development of aggression. *Aggressive Behavior, 14*(1), 13–24.

Huston, A. C., Rice, M. L., Kerkman, D., & St. Peters, M. (1990). Development of television viewing patterns in early childhood: A longitudinal investigation. *Developmental Psychology, 26,* 409–420.

Kuttschreuter, M., Wiegman, O., & Baarda, B. (1989). Aggression, prosocial behaviour and television viewing: A longitudinal study in six countries. *Pedagogische Studien, 66*(10), 377–389.

Lange, D. S., Baker, R. K., & Ball, S. J. (1969). *Mass media and violence: A report to the national commission on the causes and prevention of violence.* Washington, DC: U.S. Government Printing Office.

Larsen, O. N., Gray, L. N., & Fortis, J. G. (1968). Achieving goals through violence on television. In O. N. Larsen (Ed.), *Violence and the mass media.* New York: Harper & Row, 1968.

Lefkowitz, M. M., Eron, L. D., Walder, L. O., & Huesmann, L. R. (1972). Television violence and child aggression: A followup study. In G. A. Comstock & E. A. Rubinstein (Eds.), *Television and social behavior: III. Television and adolescent aggressiveness.* Washington, DC: U.S. GPO.

Lefkowitz, M. M., Eron, L. D., Walder, L. O., & Huesmann, L. R. (1977). *Growing up to be violent: A longitudinal study of the development of aggression*. New York: Pergamon Press, 1977.

Liebert, R. M., Spratkin, J. N., & Davidson, E. S. (1982). *The early window: Effects of television on children and youth* (2nd ed.). New York: Pergamon Press.

Maccoby, E. E., & Jacklin, C. N. (1980). Sex differences in aggression: A rejoinder and reprise. *Child Development, 51*, 964–980.

Marion, M. (1992). Community coordinated family education and support center. Grant proposal. Funded. Madison, WI: Wisconsin Children's Trust Fund.

Martin, B. (1975). Parent-child relations. In F. D. Horowitz (Ed.), *Review of child development research* (Vol. 4). Chicago: University of Chicago Press.

Mattern, K. K., & Lindholm, B. W. (1985). Effect of maternal commentary in reducing aggressive impact of televised violence on preschool children. *Journal of Genetic Psychology, 146*(1), 133–134.

National Association for the Education of Young Children. (1990). NAEYC position statement on media violence in children's lives. *Young Children, 45*, 18–21.

Nielsen Company. (1988). 1988 Nielsen report on television. Northbrook, IL: Author.

Novaco, R. (1978). Anger and coping with stress. In J. Foreyt & D. Rethjen (Eds.), *Cognitive behavior therapy, theory, research and procedures*. New York: Plenum.

Parke, R. D., & Slaby, R. G. (1983). The development of aggression. In P. Mussen (Ed.), *Handbook of child psychology* (Vol. 4). New York: Wiley.

Patterson, B. R., Littman, R. A., & Bricker, W. (1967). Assertive behavior in children: A step toward a theory of aggression. *Monographs of the Society for Research in Child Development, 32* (Serial No. 113).

Patterson, G. R. (1982). *Coercive family processes*. Eugene, OR: Castilia Press.

Pederson, J. A., Anderson, B. J., & Cain, R. L. (1977). *An approach to understanding linkages between the parent-infant and spouse relationships*. Paper presented at the Society for Research in Child Development, New Orleans.

Pinkston, E. M., Reese, N. M., LeBlanc, J. M., & Baer, D. M. (1973). Independent control of a preschool child's aggression and peer interaction by contingent teacher attention. *Journal of Applied Behavior Analysis, 6*, 115–124.

Ridley-Johnson, R., Surdy, T., & O'Laughlin, E. (1991). Parent survey on television violence viewing. *Journal of Developmental and Behavioral Pediatrics, 13*(1), 53–54.

Siegel, A. F., & Kohn, L. G. (1970). Permissiveness, permission, and aggression: The effects of adult presence or absence on aggression in children. In F. Rebelsky & L. Dorman (Eds.), *Child development and behavior*. New York: Alfred A. Knopf.

Silvern, S. B., & Williamson, P. (1987). The effects of video game play on young children's aggression, fantasy, and prosocial behavior. *Journal of Applied Developmental Psychology, 8*(4), 453–462.

Singer, J. L. (1987). Is television bad for children? *Social Science, 71*(2–3), 178–182.

Singer, J. L., & Singer, D. G. (1985). Television-viewing and family communication style as predictors of children's emotional behavior. Special Issue: The feeling child. *Journal of Children in Contemporary Society, 17*(4), 75–91.

Slaby, R., & Crowley, C. G. (1977). Modification of cooperation and aggression through teacher attention to children's speech. *Journal of Experimental Child Psychology, 23*, 442–458.

Slaby, R. G., & Quarfoth, G. R. (1980). Effects of television on the developing child. In B. W. Camp (Ed.), *Advances in behavioral pediatrics* (Vol. 1). Greenwich, CN: JAI Press.

Slaby, R. G., & Roedell, W. C. (1982). The development and regulation of aggression in young children. In J. Worell (Ed.), *Psychological development in the elementary years*. New York: Academic Press.

Smith, P. K., & Green, M. (1974). Aggressive behavior in English nurseries and play-groups: Sex differences and response of adults. *Child Development, 45*, 211–214.

Stein, A. H., & Friedrich, L. K. (1975). Impact of television on children and youth. In E. M. Hetherington (Ed.), *Review of child development research* (Vol. 5). Chicago: University of Chicago Press.

Steinmetz, S. K. (1977). *The cycle of violence: Assertive, aggressive and abusive family interaction*. New York: Praeger.

Stipp, H., & Milavsky, J. R. (1988). U.S. television programming's effects on aggressive behavior of children and adolescents. *Current Psychology: Research and Reviews, 7*, 76–92.

Straus, M. A., Gelles, R., & Steinmetz, S. (1980). *Behind closed doors*. New York: Doubleday.

Szegal, B. (1985). Stages in the development of aggressive behavior in early childhood. *Aggressive Behavior, 11*(4), 315–321.

Turner, C., & Goldsmith, D. (1976). Effects of toy guns and airplanes on children's antisocial free play behavior. *Journal of Experimental Child Psychology, 21*, 303–315.

Watt, J. H., & Krull, R. (1977). An examination of three models of television viewing and aggression. *Human Communication Research, 3*, 99–112.

White, B. L., Kaban, B., Shapiro, B., & Attonucci, J. (1976). Competence and experience. In I. C. Uzgiris & F. Weizmann (Eds.), *The structuring of experience*. New York: Plenum Press.

Wisconsin Children's Trust Fund. (1988, 1989, 1990, 1991, 1992). *Request for proposals*. Madison, WI: Author.

9

Prosocial Behavior: Nurturing the Roots of Concern for Others

Chapter Overview

After reading and studying this chapter, you will be able to

▼   *Define* prosocial behavior.

▼   *Identify, describe, and give an example* of the types of prosocial behaviors studied.

▼   *List* developmental building blocks of concern for others and *explain* their role in prosocial behavior.

▼   *Outline* developmental trends in prosocial behavior and *explain* factors other than age that influence prosocial behavior.

▼   *Explain* the benefits of encouraging prosocial behavior in children.

▼   *Identify, describe, and observe* developmentally appropriate strategies that foster prosocial behavior.

▼   *Apply* your knowledge to problem situations and *analyze* case studies.

"Who raises altruistic children? . . . parents who themselves
are highly concerned about the welfare of others."
(Shaffer, 1993, p. 547)

CASE STUDIES: Prosocial Behavior

Miranda

Three-year-old Miranda lives on a farm with her parents and three older brothers. When Dad takes care of his houseplants, Miranda's regular job is to help by misting the plants needing moisture. After lunch her 16-year-old brother handed her plate to her and said, "Take your plate over to the dishwasher, Miranda . . . Thanks!" She helped her mother feed the barn cats and watched as her mom picked up Puddles, a cat whose leg was cut. Mom said, "O-o-h, come here and let me take care of your cut. Get that cloth for Mommy, Miranda. I'll bet that Puddle's leg hurts, and I think she might be afraid, too. So, we have to tell her it's going to be OK."

Steve

Four-year-old Steve lives with his mom and dad. Within a 2-week time frame this is what he witnessed: Mom and Dad *really* shared the housework. He watched "Mr. Rogers' Neighborhood" when Mr. Rogers talked about working together and showed what it meant. Steve and his dad and uncle made their famous chocolate chip cookies for the day care's bake sale, and Dad helped a neighbor fix the gate on his fence. "Glad to help!" was Dad's reply to the neighbor's thanks. Mom took Steve with her when she showed Humane Society slides on taking good care of pets at the local elementary school and when she took food to the food pantry and quietly said, as they drove away, "There are a lot of people who don't have enough to eat, Steve. It's good to *share* what we have."

John

Seven-year-old John lives with his dad in a single-parent family. "It's time to plan *Project Winterizing,* John," said Dad as they sat down at the table with hot chocolate and a pad of paper. "There are some special things that have to be done in the yard before winter, and I don't have time to do them all by myself. Let's list them . . . I'll do some of the chores, and then I want you to do some, too. We'll get this done a lot more quickly if we work together. We'll go out for pizza for dinner when we finish.

"Let's figure out which things would be done first, second, and third, and then go get the equipment ready that we need. And, I'll show you how to cover the rosebushes so that the cover stays put." They shook hands as they headed off to the garage. "Project Winterizing is under way!"

As an early childhood educator, you will rightly be concerned about encouraging children to be helpful, cooperative, generous, and loving in a world that seems bent on showing quite another set of values—violence, hatred, mean-spiritedness, stinginess, and aggression. Some children, like Miranda, Steve, and John, come from healthy family systems that foster moral development by showing concern for and responding to the needs of family members. But many children come from less healthy family systems in which interactions leave people feeling degraded or demeaned, where adults refuse to respond to the needs of others, and in which compassion is rarely, if ever, demonstrated.

This chapter focuses on the development of *prosocial behavior,* or concern for others, and will target major issues in this area.

UNDERSTANDING PROSOCIAL BEHAVIOR
Defining Prosocial Behavior

Sharing, donating, helping, cooperating, and showing compassion are all examples of *prosocial behavior*, actions intended to relieve another's distress without expecting any external reward (Figure 9.1). There are a number of reasons for cooperating, helping, or donating. One person may cooperate out of fear, or may donate to a charity because everyone at work is expected to. Another person may help someone because she is truly empathic or sad about what has happened to the other. Others may perform some prosocial behaviors occasionally because of self-interest. In this chapter, we will take true prosocial behavior to be based on selfless, not selfish, altruism (Batson & Shaw, 1991).

A child might have been a bystander or might have been the cause of the other's distress and may show concern in either case. Children may show concern when they have witnessed another's distress or may show concern (along with guilt and remorse) for someone that they themselves have hurt. These are all aspects of moral development (Mussen & Eisenberg-Berg, 1977; Radke-Yarrow, Zahn-Waxler, & Chapman, 1983; Zahn-Waxler, Radke-Yarrow, Wagner, & Chapman, 1991).

Figure 9.1
Prosocial behavior

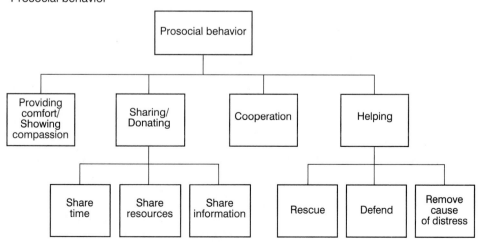

Sharing

Sharing, one form of prosocial behavior, is defined as interchanges in which the original holder grants to another the partial use or possession of a thing (Beauvais, 1982). People can share or donate materials, information, or time.

Examples   Tim shares time at the computer with his friend.

Tim's father works with Habitat for Humanity to build houses for low-income families.

Christina asked Kyle to share some of the water table equipment, and Kyle said, "Here, hold this tube. We'll make the water go through it."

Helping

Helping is another major category of prosocial behavior. Helping includes acts of rescue and defense (Marcus & Leiserson, 1978).

Examples   Seven-year-old David stopped the garden gate just as it was about to close on his sleeping cat's tail. WHEW!

Toby climbed to the top of the climbing structure and cried because he couldn't get down. Brian ran to get the teacher to help. Brian helped Toby by rescuing him.

Cooperation

This is a form of prosocial behavior in which people work together to get a job done, to ensure fair treatment of another, or to help others. A family cooperates when *every*

Cooperating *is one form of prosocial behavior.*

person shares in the responsibility for doing their fair share of the housework and yardwork. Children cooperate when they each decorate a part of a mural.

Providing Comfort or Showing Compassion

Examples   Jake provided comfort and showed compassion when he put a bandage on a doll's leg, explaining, "He hurt his leg when he fell off the wagon."
Jake's family gives $10 to the local food bank each month.

Developmental Building Blocks of Concern for Others

There are some essential capabilities—building blocks—that children must have before it is even possible for them to demonstrate concern for others: (1) specific *cognitive competencies* to experience the other's state; (2) the *emotional competencies* to affectively experience the other's state, that is, to *know how the other feels;* and (3) the *behavioral repertoire* that allows a child to try to help the other (Zahn-Waxler et al., 1992).

Young children do *show compassion and give comfort.*

Cognitive Competencies

A child must have specific cognitive competencies before she can act in a prosocial way (Bohlmeyer, 1989). She should be able to distinguish between herself and others (Amsterdam, 1972; Berthenthal & Fischer, 1978). She has to have begun to use emotion language to describe how others might be feeling and to describe how she herself feels (Bretherton, Fritz, Zahn-Waxler, & Ridgeway, 1986).

She should have the beginnings of representational thought and the ability to use symbols (Bruner, 1972; McCall, 1979; Piaget, 1983) because these abilities underlie the ability to infer how somebody else might be feeling and to understand the other's perspective (Rheingold & Emery, 1986). Every one of these abilities arises during a child's second year of life, so children have the cognitive underpinnings that enable them to *begin* to act prosocially by the time they are toddlers.

Emotional Competencies

To act prosocially, children must also have the emotional capacity to respond to another's needs or distress. Children seem to be biologically prepared for empathy (Hoffman, 1975), and very young infants are responsive to the emotions of others (Sagi & Hoffman, 1976). An infant seems to be able to discriminate between her mother's different emotions and in some cases seems to imitate these emotions (Termine & Izard, 1988).

Very young infants also respond to the affective states of the caregiver; for example, they can respond to the negative arousal of their mother's depression (Cohn, Campbell, Matias, & Hopkins, 1990). All of this means that along with essential cognitive competencies, the emotional competencies enabling a child to know how another might be feeling *begin* to develop very early in life.

Behavioral Repertoire

Children must know how to help or cooperate or be generous or compassionate before they can act that way; that is, they must have a repertoire or collection of behaviors that will enable them to act prosocially. Zahn-Waxler et al. (1992) believe that such behavior patterns in young children may actually have their roots in earlier attachments to their primary attachment figures. Such bonding patterns prepare an infant for later turn-taking, sharing, cooperation, and empathy in social interactions because that is what they as infants experienced with their parents (Trevarthen, 1989). Research has given us some evidence that children demonstrate prosocial behavior patterns in the second year of life (Radke-Yarrow & Zahn-Waxler, 1984; Rheingold, Hay, & West, 1976; Zahn-Waxler & Radke-Yarrow, 1982; Zahn-Waxler et al., 1992).

In the early childhood profession we have refocused recently on *developmentally appropriate practices*. Our concern as early childhood and parent educators is to understand when children acquire cognitive and emotional competencies and a behavioral repertoire, and then to understand how these elements become integrated to form organized patterns of responding in a kind, generous, and compassionate way. Having one or two of these capabilities is not enough; it is the overlap of *all three* that enables a child to act in a prosocial way (Figure 9.2). Understanding this important part of child development will assist you in guiding children effectively.

Developmental Trends

Child development research tells us, then, that children bring a range of cognitive, emotional, and behavioral competencies to their relationships with others within the first two years of life. The research clearly delineates developmental trends in prosocial behavior but also shows that there are, at every developmental level, factors other than age that influence a child's willingness to act prosocially.

Infancy and Toddlerhood

An older view of children under age 3 painted a picture of an egocentric and socially unskilled person who was incapable of responding to anyone else's distress (Freud, 1958; Piaget, 1965), but more recent work portrays even very young children as empathic and with the beginnings of moral sensibilities (Hoffman, 1975).

There is evidence that prosocial behaviors (helping, sharing, comforting) *emerge* between the first and second years of life, increase with age, and are more varied in form as children grow older (Hay, 1979; Radke-Yarrow & Zahn-Waxler, 1984; Rheingold, 1979; Rheingold et al., 1976; Stanjek, 1978; Zahn-Waxler & Radke-Yarrow, 1982; Zahn-Waxler et al., 1992). Zahn-Waxler et al. (1992) also show that a child's willingness and ability to repair damage she has caused, or *reparative behaviors*, increase with age.

Figure 9.2
The *overlap* of three competencies enables young children to act in a kind, generous, compassionate way.

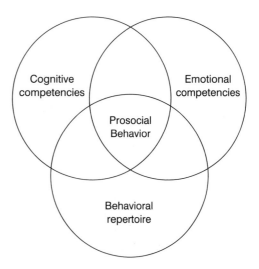

Prosocial behaviors (helping, sharing, comforting) **emerge** *between a child's first and second birthdays.*

A 1986 study by Dunn and Munn shows that the relationship between 2-year-olds and an older sibling is not necessarily fraught with rivalry but can be one in which young children develop their powers of cooperation, sharing, and comforting. This observational study found that cooperation was frequently shown by the 2-year-olds whose older brother or sister had previously been cooperative (effect of modeling). The 2-year-olds were also capable of sharing, helping, and comforting but did not act this way very often. In another study, Caplan (1991) found that toddlers (2-year-olds) were capable of resolving conflicts by sharing but that they shared more often when toys were somewhat scarce than when there was an overabundance.

Early Childhood Years: Age 3 to 8

Children in this age range are better able to act prosocially (Eisenberg-Berg & Lennon, 1980) because their cognitive and emotional skills are even better than they were during infancy and toddlerhood. Lewis (1989), for example, shows us that children have typically learned *emotional scripts* by age 5 or 6. These scripts tell the child how someone might be feeling and what an appropriate course of action would be.

Many studies have documented increases in cooperation, sharing, donating, rescuing, and comforting during early childhood (Bryan, 1975; Marcus, Telleen, & Roke, 1979; Murphy, 1937; Radke-Yarrow & Zahn-Waxler, 1976; Rosenhan, 1972; Sawin, 1980; Yarrow, Scott, & Waxler, 1973). In many cases, though, the rate of prosocial behavior was low (Beauvais, 1982; Caplan & Hay, 1989), show-ing that a child will not automatically act prosocially just because she is capable of doing so.

Several factors may affect a child's willingness to act prosocially, two of them being a child's self-concept (Cauley & Tyler, 1989) and a child's relationships (Hartup & Sancilio, 1986; Radke-Yarrow, Richters, & Wilson, 1988). Cauley and Tyler (1989) found a significant correlation between self-concept and cooperative behavior in 4- and 5-year-olds. Costin and Jones's work (1992) highlights the importance of how the type of relationship between a child and someone else affects the child's level of prosocial behavior. Their work with 4- to 6½-year-olds shows children more likely to report sympathy when a *friend, rather than an acquaintance,* was in trouble, and were also more likely to propose a helpful inter-vention with a friend.

Caplan and Hay (1989) found low rates of responding by nursery school chil-dren to distressed peers, and they emphasize how important it is to examine the *context* or setting in which children operate. These children expressed the belief that they are not supposed to help when adults are present. Thus, they were able to help but did not do so because they thought that they should not.

Middle Childhood and Adolescence

Cognitive skills continue to undergo changes, making older children and adoles-cents even better able to understand the concepts of helping or comforting (Naparstek, 1990), to take somebody else's perspective (Buckley, Siegel, & Ness, 1979), and to behave in helpful ways (Miller, 1991; Rubin & Schneider, 1973). But, Radke-Yarrow et al. (1983) believe it unwise to say that there is an automatic increase in all kinds of prosocial behavior.

Necessary and sufficient?   Acquiring more sophisticated cognitive skills is *nec-essary* before someone can be helpful or cooperative. This is why older children tend to be more prosocial than younger children. But, becoming more sophisti-cated cognitively, by itself, is not a *sufficient* condition for becoming prosocial. The ability to think at a higher level does not guarantee that an older child will act prosocially.

Some older children are actually less willing to rescue other people or to cooperate (Madsen, 1971). Older children, adolescents, and adults can be exceedingly cruel because a cognitively sophisticated person can figure out how to hurt somebody just as well as how to help somebody. Children are neglected and abused, for example, by adolescents or adults, people with the cognitive capacity to understand that children need loving interactions. In spite of this cog-nitive ability, many adolescents and adults either commit outright acts of violence or refuse to give children what they need.

Example   Fourteen-year-old Cathy has good cognitive skills and can take other people's perspective fairly well. She fully understood that her friend Car-olyn needed help with geometry, but said, "I know what you need, Carolyn, but you're not going to get it from me."

Cathy's emerging cognitive skills and perspective-taking ability do not guarantee that she will treat others with respect. Whether a person becomes cooperative or helpful depends on many other factors, which will be discussed in the next section.

The Importance of Encouraging Prosocial Behavior

It is often easy to be helpful, and there are few risks in some small acts of generosity. Much of the research carried out thus far has tested only small donations and small acts of helping, and has rightfully not placed children in situations involving great risk or sacrifice (Radke-Yarrow et al., 1983). Some prosocial behavior, however, does involve great risk (e.g., rescuing someone from a mugger) and a lot of personal investment (e.g., parenting).

Just as there are risks associated with prosocial behavior, there are also benefits. Interestingly, the benefits go to the person who acts prosocially, the recipient of the altruism, and the system in which the prosocial behavior takes place (Marcus & Leiserson, 1978). Personal benefits include the feeling of competence, the belief that *I am capable of helping* that develops from helping someone. The desire for competence is a strong motivational factor (White, 1959). Children who act prosocially also tend to receive help from other children and adults (Marcus, 1977). A child who never gives help willingly to classmates will probably receive little assistance in return.

Encouraging prosocial behavior has two positive side effects on the systems in which children live. First, the work of the system is shared when all members do their share. As members of family and classroom systems, children have an obligation to share in the work of the system, whether the work involves farm or ranch chores, shoveling snow, setting tables, washing paint cups, or putting away trikes. Second, when children are encouraged to be cooperative and helpful the general atmosphere of the home, classroom, or other setting is more friendly, pleasant, and relaxing (Edwards, 1992; Kreidler, 1984).

DEVELOPMENTALLY APPROPRIATE STRATEGIES FOR FOSTERING PROSOCIAL BEHAVIOR

Prosocial behavior develops largely because of the relationships children experience. Authori*tative* adults make it possible for kindness, compassion, cooperation, and generosity to flower by understanding the developmental level of the children they teach, by helping children understand how others feel (develop emotional scripts), and by showing children how to help or cooperate. The adults use practical and developmentally appropriate strategies to foster prosocial behavior.

Model Prosocial Behavior

Modeling prosocial behavior is a powerful way to encourage it in children (Bryan, 1975; Bryan & Walbek, 1970; Marcus & Leiserson, 1978; Mussen & Eisenberg-Berg, 1977; Rushton, 1975). But, children do not imitate all models.

Several factors determine whether a child will imitate any model. Children are more likely to imitate a *powerful* model (Bryan, 1975; Mussen & Eisenberg-Berg, 1977; Rushton, 1975, 1976)—a person who controls resources—and children usually perceive parents and teachers as powerful because caregivers do control resources. They are also more likely to imitate a *nurturant and supportive* model, one who is highly responsive to their needs but who also makes expectations known.

Children are more likely to imitate a *consistent* model, that is, a model who "practices what she preaches." For example, a family who only talks about generosity or volunteering but never actually gives or volunteers is likely to have children who are far less likely to be generous (Bryan & Walbek, 1970). In terms of compassionate, generous, helpful behavior, the research shows that *what a child sees is what the child does*.

Children are more likely to imitate models who *give without grumbling*, who are quietly and effectively generous, cooperative, and helpful, and who are genuinely pleased to be able to help someone else, and who don't seem to expect anything in return (Midlarsky & Bryan, 1972; Yarrow et al., 1973). If a child is able to vicariously experience the same good feeling as the model, the possibility that the child will also act prosocially is increased.

Sean's dad is helping a neighbor fix his car. Sean is likely to imitate his dad, who is a powerful, nurturant, supportive model and who helps others without grumbling.

Honig and Wittmer (1991) advise that teachers and parents provide models of prosocial behavior by arranging regular viewing of prosocial media and video games. Programs whose messages are about cooperation, helping, and compassion promote these behaviors in children (Friedrich & Stein, 1975). A major study analyzing 190 other studies found that prosocial programming does have powerful effects on children's prosocial behavior (Hearold, 1986).

CASE STUDY ANALYSIS:　Modeling Prosocial Behavior

Analyze the case study on Steve at the opening of this chapter by completing these sentences.

1. I think a good example of how Steve's models were *consistent* (i.e., practiced what they preached) was when . . .

2. Steve had a model of an adult who was genuinely pleased about having been able to help when . . .

3. Steve's parents seem to be nurturant and supportive models. The things that lead me to believe this are . . .

4. Based on what we know about the effect of certain types of models on children's prosocial behavior, make a brief statement about how likely it is that Steve will act prosocially.

Help Children Develop Emotional Scripts

A growing body of research on emotions reveals that young children are able to identify another person's distressed state and the situation that produced the distress (Fabes, Eisenberg, McCormick, & Wilson, 1988; Michalson & Lewis, 1985). How children understand the emotional states of others seems to be organized in a knowledge structure in the form of *emotional scripts* learned by the age of 5 to 6 years (Russell, 1989). These scripts include information about the appropriate emotion for the child and the emotion or affective state of another person or animal in specific situations (Lewis, 1989). Children learn emotional scripts as they interact with parents, siblings, teachers, and others, as they watch television, and as they have books read to them.

Example　Derek is an overweight 4-year-old. At snacktime Adam snickered when Derek took one of the snacks, "Hey, Derek. You're so fat! You don't even need to eat." The teacher took Adam aside and said, "Adam, it hurts somebody's feelings when you make fun of them. I think that Derek probably feels bad because you called him fat. In this classroom I will not allow you to make fun of others."

Adam's teacher is helping him develop an emotional script by helping him understand how Derek probably felt in this particular situation. Reading stories about sharing was found to be another excellent way to help children learn emotional scripts. This strategy increased children's willingness to share and their ability to take another person's perspective (Trepanier & Romatowski, 1981). The experimental group had nine children's books focusing on sharing read to them at a rate of three per week. They discussed sharing, its relationship to the feelings of the characters, and the causes of the feelings.

State Expectations for Prosocial Behavior and Accept Children's Help When Offered

Children learn to be prosocial in families and classrooms when adults ask them to cooperate, help, share, or give comfort or by actually accepting a child's offer of help or cooperation (Child Development Project, 1988, 1991; Schenk & Grusec, 1987).

Examples   The teacher said to two 4-year-olds, "Louie and Portia, Mrs. Dunn is going to need some help taking the trikes and wagons out of the shed. I want both of you to go with her and help her."

The next day Louie approached Mrs. Dunn when she was in the shed getting trikes out, "Can I help you again today, Mrs. Dunn?" Mrs. Dunn replied, "That would be wonderful, Louie. Sure!"

Adults, as socializing agents, have the responsibility to help children learn *norms of social responsibility*. One of these norms deals with prosocial behavior. The norm tells children that helping or cooperating with others is expected (Bryan, 1975), and each of these adults has actually told the children that they are expected to work together, to cooperate, or to help someone else. It is difficult, if not impossible, for children to learn this norm of socially responsible behavior without adult guidance.

Communicate your expectations that children are an important part of a family or classroom system by assigning age-appropriate responsibilities to them. Authori*tative* adults, high in demandingness and responsiveness, assign household chores and tasks. This might have accounted for Baumrind's (1971) finding that children in these families were the most cooperative when observed at school. Rheingold (1982) discovered, however, that some parents were often reluctant to accept their child's offer of help even though the child offered to help fairly often. The parents seemed to prefer to do the task at hand by themselves rather than guide the child through the process.

Responsibilities should be assigned to children based on their developmental ability. A 3- to 4-year-old child can certainly mist plants, feed or water pets, clean out her own locker at school, place toys back in the spot where they belong, help set and clean tables for meals, hang up her own clothes, and take good care of books, games, and other materials. Older children should be expected to regularly help with yardwork and housework. They can carry out trash, rake leaves, shovel snow, make centerpieces for a dinner table (it is pleasant to be assigned a creative task occasionally), help plan menus, cook simple meals under supervision, wash dishes, write things on the shopping list, and wash the car. Children who grow up on farms and ranches are regularly assigned chores that are real contributions to the functioning of the unit.

CASE STUDY ANALYSIS: Developing Emotional Scripts and Stating Expectations

Decide how well Miranda's family (case study at chapter opening) is helping her develop emotional scripts and whether they make expectations clear about prosocial behavior.

1. Point out the times when Miranda was given some responsibility for specific *chores*, such as household tasks.

2. Miranda is learning emotional scripts. How has her mother helped her understand the emotional state of another?

Summary: Based on data in the case study, I predict that the likelihood of Miranda's developing prosocial behavior and concern for others is very good/good/can't tell/not so good/almost nil. Be prepared to defend your opinion with observable data.

Use Positive Discipline

Adults who use positive discipline have an authori*tative* style of caregiving. Two traits that characterize this style are high demandingness and high responsiveness. For several reasons, this style of caregiving tends to foster cooperation, helpfulness, compassion, and generosity.

1. *Adults who use positive discipline clearly communicate their expectations about helping, sharing, and cooperating.* Because these parents or teachers make their expectations of the child's cooperation clear, they are more likely to get that cooperation than adults who threaten punishment if the child does not help.

2. *Adults who use positive discipline encourage children to take someone else's perspective,* and children are more likely to be cooperative, helpful or compassionate if they understand another's perspective.

Examples   The teacher watched 3-year-old Cheryl take the Raggedy Andy doll from another child. "No, Cheryl. Mary wants to play with the doll, too, and she had it first."

A teacher said to his group of 4-year-olds when they made too much noise near the gerbils' house, "Whoa! You're making so much noise that the gerbils look really afraid. Play more quietly when you're around the gerbils."

A word of caution. Emotionally vulnerable, depressed caregivers in one study overemphasized their child's responsibility for others' problems, leading children to believe that they had created problems for which they were not responsible at all (Zahn-Waxler, Kochanska, Krupnick, & McKnew, 1990). So, while children need to learn that they are responsible for their own behavior, they should not be held responsible for things beyond their control.

3. *Adults who use positive discipline give suggestions on how to help, cooperate, or share*. Stating expectations is an excellent strategy, but adults can be even more helpful if they also give specific suggestions on how to help or cooperate with someone. This means that adults have to do some skill development by telling or showing children specifically how they can help or cooperate with someone.

Example   Mrs. Lombardi said to Vinnie, "Here, Vinnie. I'm going to hold this tricycle steady, and your job is to squirt just a little oil right here, on the spots where the wheels join the trike body. We'll fix that squeak together."

4. *Adults who use positive discipline tell children what TO do*. They try to avoid telling children what not to do. Some adults have a *pro*scriptive value orientation, frequently telling children what *not* to do, such as "Don't throw the towel on the floor," "Don't hold your fork like that," "Don't wiggle around," and "Don't pick your nose!" Adults who use positive discipline and whose style is authori*tative* have a *pre*scriptive value orientation, preferring to tell children what *to* do, such as "Hang the towel on the rack," "Hold your fork like this, Jane," "Stand still so that I can brush your hair," and "Tonya, use this tissue to clean your nose." Children whose parents have a prescriptive value orientation tend to be more prosocial than children whose parents have a proscriptive orientation (Cain, 1987; Olejnik & McKinney, 1973).

CASE STUDY ANALYSIS: Positive Discipline

Examine Dad's behavior with John (case study at beginning of chapter) to determine whether he has an authori*tative* style of parenting, one that is likely to encourage John to develop prosocial behavior.

1. When and how clearly did John's father communicate his expectation that John would share in the yardwork?

2. When did Dad encourage John to understand the adult's point of view about the yardwork?

3. When did Dad give specific suggestions on how John could help?

4. John's dad has a *pre*scriptive value orientation. He demonstrated this when he . . .

Summary: Based on my responses to these questions, I predict that the probability that John will develop concern for others is very good/good/no opinion/not so good/almost nil. Be prepared to defend your opinion with observable data.

Effect of Authoritarian/Permissive Discipline on Prosocial Behavior

Neither permissive nor authoritarian adults foster prosocial behavior. A *permissive* adult, low in demandingness, frequently fails to tell the child that she is expected to help or cooperate. Some permissive parents might actually have expectations that their child will help or cooperate but not know how to effectively communicate their expectations. These permissive adults also lack skills for getting their children to comply and simply give up and stop expecting cooperation.

An autho*ritarian* adult does not show or encourage empathy or perspective-taking, communicates unreasonable expectations, and is not responsive to a child. As a result, children from authoritarian systems tend not to be very cooperative, helpful, or compassionate unless the child is trying to avoid an adult's anger or unless there is *something in it* for the child.

Example   When Joe forgot to rake leaves, his father slapped him and said, "That will teach you not to forget your work," playing on Joe's fear of physical punishment to get chores done. Even though Joe might do the chores, he will do them grudgingly and not because he sees the need to share his family's work.

Verbally Label and Discuss Prosocial Behavior

All of the following examples come from the same early childhood classroom with 4-year-old children.

Examples   The teacher said to the children who made applesauce, "We all worked together to make the applesauce, and it's going to be a good snack for the rest of the group."

The aide said to two children after cleanup, "You did a fine job of cooperating. You put all the blocks on the shelf and cleared the space for group time."

The teacher showed a short segment of "Mr. Rogers' Neighborhood" and then led a discussion: "It was kind of Mr. Rogers' visitor to help him build the shelves. How could we tell that his friend wanted to help? How could you tell that his friend was happy about helping? What did Mr. Rogers say that made you think he was grateful for the help?

In each case the adults made an effort to *verbally label* prosocial behavior, and the teacher actually planned a *discussion* of the television episode on helping as a part of her lesson plan. There are a number of ways to teach children about cooperation and helpfulness, and *talking about prosocial behavior* is an excellent but often neglected technique (Honig & Wittmer, 1991).

We acknowledge the need to help children learn to label lots of things, such as, "You picked up the *red square*" or "This animal is called a *Timber wolf.*" We consider this a part of direct instruction, one of our basic responsibilities as teachers and one of the processes through which we influence children. We should not hesitate to also label acts of kindness and compassion as a way to teach children about these traits.

Certain types of verbal labeling are more effective than others in fostering prosocial behavior. Statements that would be considered mere preaching, such as

"It is good to give," were far less effective in encouraging prosocial behavior than statements focusing on how cooperative behavior affects others (Grusec, 1991). Our examples showed adults noting how acts of kindness or cooperation affected others ("It's going to be a good snack for the rest of the group," "You . . . cleared the space for group time"). Grusec (1991) called this *empathy training*, instruction for children in how their behavior affected other people or animals.

Practice Prosocial Behavior

Suppose that Luka *learns* how to help and cooperate by observing models and by hearing the behaviors labeled. Does that mean that he will automatically *perform* the prosocial behavior? No, but chances that he will actually perform cooperative, helpful acts that he has seen modeled increase when his parents and teachers set up opportunities for him to *practice the desired behavior* (Child Development Project, 1988, 1991; Friedrich & Stein, 1975; Orlick, 1981; Rogow, 1991; Solomon, 1988; Staub, 1971). Orlick's (1981) work with preschool children demonstrated that children taught to play cooperative games were later more cooperative in

---

PROBLEM FOR YOU TO SOLVE: Help These Children Verbally Label or Discuss This Prosocial Behavior

For each situation generate at least one statement or question that focuses the children's attention on the prosocial nature of the activity. In your statement emphasize how the cooperation, helpfulness, sharing, or compassion affects someone else.

Situation: During group time the teacher showed a newspaper photo of rescue workers cleaning oil from the bodies of ducks after an oil spill.

I would say this to emphasize prosocial behavior:

Situation: Working in pairs, children planted a green bean plant in a small vegetable garden outside their school.

I would say this to emphasize prosocial behavior:

Situation: The children drew pictures and dictated a message to the brother of one of the children, a marine who had been sent to Somalia.

I would say this to emphasize prosocial behavior:

Situation: Shannon, working with white play dough, decided to make pink by mixing in some red dough but found that all the red dough was in use. She asked Eli for some, and Eli said "OK" and broke off a chunk for her.

I would say this to emphasize prosocial behavior:

other settings. In addition, the cooperative game training resulted in increased generosity. Rogow's (1991) work suggested a variety of ways for teachers to facilitate the practice of prosocial behavior of children with a variety of handicapping conditions.

Teachers and parents can do a variety of things to ensure that children have an opportunity to practice prosocial behavior. Plan specific activities focusing on concepts of *cooperation, helpfulness, generosity,* and *compassion*. Plan these activities just as you would math, science, language arts, and social studies activities. Write a lesson plan, for example, the objective of which is for children to practice cooperation.

Reinforce Prosocial Behavior

Probably one of the most obvious methods of promoting prosocial behavior in young children is to encourage or reinforce them for their generous or cooperative acts (Schenk & Grusec, 1987; Smith, Gelfand, Hartmann, & Partlow, 1979).

Examples   "You put all of your dirty clothes in the hamper, Jim, just as you agreed to do. That's great!" said Mom as she smiled at him and placed his favorite sticker on the chart for that day.

"You two did a fine job of putting the sand toys away. You followed my suggestions about where to place each toy," noted the aide as she held the hands of both children.

"Each of you had a second helping because Rudy took my suggestion and broke his second cookie so that he could share it with Christina and George!" The teacher clapped her hands softly, "Good thinking, Rudy." (Rudy, by the way, basked in the *warm glow of success*.)

In each case a supportive, author*itative* adult used either social reinforcement (smiles, verbal praise), more tangible rewards (favorite stickers), or a combination of the two. Effective *praise* is a form of social reinforcement. The praise in each example was specific and descriptive; that is, it was informative to the child. It was appreciative but did not evaluate a child's character. The praise was given almost immediately after the act of prosocial behavior and was sincere. It was used to recognize successful completion of an agreed-upon task (putting clothes in hamper, breaking a cookie). It was *not* used to manipulate. The praise was also accompanied by appropriate physical contact or nonverbal communication.

Why Reinforcers and Encouragement Increase Desired Behaviors

There are two views on why reinforcers seem to increase desired behaviors. One view is that a positive reinforcer is usually perceived as pleasant and that a child will be quite likely to repeat behaviors that are reinforced or will behave that way more frequently (Rudy will share more frequently) because of the pleasant consequences of the reinforcer.

Another cogent view is offered by Shaffer (1993), who argues that rewards given for successes or successful completion of designated portions of activities

SPECIAL FOCUS: Practicing Prosocial Behavior

Activity: Game: Tug of Peace (Kreidler, 1984)
Children are in a circle. Lay a rope in a circle inside the children's circle. Objective: for all children to raise themselves to a standing position by pulling on the rope. Briefly discuss how they worked together.

Activity: Using Puppets
Do this short puppet story about helping or cooperation. One puppet, Sam, has trouble placing paper on an easel.

> Amanda: "Hey, Sam. What's the matter?"
> Sam: "I can't reach the clip for the paper."
> Amanda: "Maybe I can reach it." (She clips the paper onto the easel.) "There, it's done."
> Sam: "Thanks for helping."

Place the puppets in a learning center after this demonstration. Encourage children to practice what they observed. Encourage them to take both roles—helper and the one helped—so that each has a chance to practice helping.

Activity: Circle Game: Sharing (adapted from Smith, 1982)
This is a good game to play when children are learning each other's names. It emphasizes kindness and generosity. Children sit in a circle. An adult holds a bowl of nutritious cookies. The adult takes one cookie out of the bowl and says, "I want to be *friendly* to Jim," and gives the cookie to Jim (the child to her left). Then it's Jim's turn to be friendly to the person sitting to his left by sharing a cookie with that person.

Activity: Game: Cooperative Musical Chairs (Kreidler, 1984)
Place chairs in a circle. Children slowly circle the chairs to music. When the music stops, children scramble for a seat. Then one chair is taken away. Objective: for every child to get a seat every time the music stops. Tell the children that they may *share* a seat with someone. Contrast this version with the version in which the objective is to shut others out of a turn. (Caution: don't take more than half the chairs away. Permit only two children to share one chair.)

Activity: Making Pudding (small-group activity)
Children work in pairs. Give one child in the pair a plastic container with a lid containing enough dry instant pudding mix for two children, a spoon, and an empty paper cup. Give the other child a measuring cup with just enough milk to mix pudding for two children, a spoon, and an empty paper cup. Emphasize *working together* and *cooperating* by noting the need to share resources if they want to make and eat pudding.

serve an important *informational* function. This means that the rewards allow children to attribute their positive outcomes to their own competence in the activity because of the information conveyed in the praise. They begin to understand that they do indeed have some control over the outcomes of certain situations (Rudy gets information, for example, about his competence in problem-solving that led to sharing). Achieving a sense of control is viewed as a problem that people have to solve throughout their lives (Wong, 1992). Shaffer believes that it is this sense of control over the environment and a feeling personal competence that increases the chances of a child's repetition of reinforced behavior.

Help children by remembering this about reinforcers: What children like about praise or stickers is not that they get them but that they have the power to do something, that they are competent enough to get the sticker or praise.

Smith et al. (1979) found that both tangible rewards (stickers) and social rewards (verbal praise, smiles) increase the likelihood that children will help someone else. The social rewards, however, seem to foster different reasons for helping in some children. In Smith's study, children who received a penny (tangible reward) each time they shared said that they shared to get the reward, while children who received verbal praise said they shared because they were concerned about the welfare of the other child.

How Frequently Should Adults Use Reinforcement?

How often do adults actually reinforce prosocial behavior? One study found that 4- and 5-year-olds in a preschool received positive feedback for spontaneous prosocial behavior only about 30% of the time (Eisenberg, Cameron, Tryon, & Dodez, 1981). In contrast, Grusec (1982) found that 4-year-olds with nonworking mothers were reinforced for prosocial behavior about 80% of the time. Grusec (1991) found that young children were as likely to receive praise and social approval as they were to receive no response at all.

Bryan (1975) suggests reinforcing a group of children for prosocial behavior whenever possible. He notes that group-administered rewards are consistently more effective in fostering cooperation and friendliness and in decreasing competitive behavior than are rewards given to individuals. There are several ways in which adults can recognize the efforts of a group of children for prosocial behavior.

Examples   Mrs. Thomas made a special fruit salad for the whole kindergarten after all the children cooperated on the "litter patrol" on the playground. "You all worked together so well, and the playground looks terrific. Let's all celebrate!"

All the children in Mrs. Thomas's school held a carnival and then donated the money they made to the Humane Society to sponsor a cage for an entire year. The principal gathered the entire group together in the cafeteria and read a letter of thanks from the director of the Humane Society. It said, "Your *generous donation* will pay for food and care for cats in this cage for one year."

A student teacher sang a short song with the children at group time about how each child had acted prosocially during the morning's activities (to the tune of *Mary Had a Little Lamb*):

Bill and Jim cleaned the gerbil house,
the gerbil house, the gerbil house
Bill and Jim cleaned the gerbil house
when they came to school.

Anne Marie put away her trike,
put away her trike, put away her trike
Anne Marie put away her trike
when she came to school.

Then the student teacher said, "I saw Antonio and Anna sharing the flannelboard pieces. And, I saw Olivia help Steven separate his orange sections at snack time. Let's sing about that."

This student did not just pull this activity "out of the air." She *planned* it. She had written a lesson plan for it, and to carry it off well she had to carefully observe how each child showed prosocial behavior during the self-selected activity period.

Reinforce Cooperation, Not Competition

Make sure that you are actually rewarding cooperation and not competition. Some teachers form groups, for example, and pit one group against the others (e.g., at cleanup, for reading the largest number of picture books, for bringing in the most for a food drive). Although group members do have to work together, their goal in these examples is to *beat* another group, and they may easily lose sight of their real goal—to gather food for a food drive, to read, or to work together to clean up. And, even though all the children take part in the work or read books, only one group *wins*.

SUMMARY OF KEY CONCEPTS

1. *Prosocial behavior* includes a variety of behaviors—sharing, donating, helping, cooperating, giving comfort, and showing compassion.

2. Adults who want to guide children in a developmentally appropriate way understand that there are *developmental building blocks* of concern for others. These are specific developmental abilities that a child must possess before she can demonstrate concern for others.

3. Research shows that prosocial behaviors emerge between the first and second years of life, increase with age, and are more varied in form as children grow older. However, the research also demonstrates that there are factors besides chronological age at every developmental level that influence a child's willingness to act prosocially.

4. Both immediate and long-range benefits accrue when prosocial behavior is valued and encouraged. These advantages are experienced by the individual child, by the group with whom the child lives or works, and ultimately by the society in which the child exists.

5. Authori*tative* adults set the stage for the development of prosocial behavior by using several practical and developmentally appropriate strategies, including modeling, helping children develop *emotional scripts*, stating expectations for prosocial behavior, accepting children's help when offered, using positive discipline, verbally labeling and discussing prosocial behavior, and practicing and reinforcing prosocial behavior.

OBSERVE CHILD GUIDANCE IN ACTION
These Adults Encourage Prosocial Behavior

Observe at least three episodes in an early childhood classroom. Look for specific strategies from this chapter that the teachers, aides, or parents use to encourage prosocial behavior. Use the following format.

Name: _____

Setting: _____

Approximate age of children: _____

This is what I observed (describe actions. Write direct quotes. If appropriate, describe material/equipment):

This is an example of: modeling, stating expectations, using positive discipline, verbally labeling or discussing prosocial behavior, encouraging children to practice helpfulness/cooperation, or reinforcing prosocial behavior

Summary: Briefly summarize how the adults in this setting foster prosocial behavior. Use the data you have collected to make your judgment and concentrate on what they are doing especially well.

RESOURCES FOR SPECIFIC ACTIVITIES

Honig, A., & Wittmer, D. (1991). *Helping children become more prosocial: Tips for teachers.* Available from ERIC Document Reproduction Service. Contains numerous examples of cooperative games and activities.

Kreidler, W. (1984). *Creative conflict resolution.* Evanston, IL: Scott, Foresman. Also contains lots of good examples of cooperative games and activities.

Ragow, S. (1991). The dynamics of play: Including children with special needs in mainstreamed early childhood programs. *International Journal of Early Childhood, 23*(2), 50–57. Suggests several ways for teachers to encourage participation of children with a variety of special needs in prosocial play activities.

Schmitz, D. The design and implementation of 40 manipulative tasks to develop cooperation in a kindergarten class at Palmer School. ERIC Document Reproduction Service.

Smith, C. A. (1982). *Promoting the social development of young children: Strategies and activities.* Palo Alto, CA: Mayfield Publishing Co. Provides a sound theoretical framework for over 100 strategies and activities. An excellent addition to your professional library.

Spivack, G., & Shure, M. (1989). Interpersonal cognitive problem solving (ICPS): A competence-building primary prevention program. *Prevention in Human Services, 6*(2), 161–178. Description of ICPS, a competence-building program for preschool, kindergarten, and first-grade children. Concise outline of the ICPS program based on the kindergarten/first grade script. Describes problem-solving skills training using a lesson from a program script.

REFERENCES

Amsterdam, B. (1972). Mirror self-image reactions before age two. *Developmental Psychology, 5*(4), 297–305.

Batson, C. D., & Shaw, L. L. (1991). Evidence for altruism: Toward a pluralism of prosocial motives. *Psychological Inquiry, 2*(2), 107–122.

Baumrind, D. (1971). Current patterns of parental authority. *Developmental Psychology Monograph, 4*(1, Pt. 2).

Beauvais, C. (1982, April). *Sharing in preschool: A naturalistic observation.* Paper presented at the Annual Meeting of the Western Psychological Association, Sacramento, CA.

Berthenthal, B. I., & Fischer, K. W. (1978). The development of self-recognition in the infant. *Developmental Psychology, 14*, 44–50.

Bohlmeyer, E. (1989, April). *Age differences in sharing as a function of children's ability to estimate time and motivational instructions.* Paper presented at the Biennial Meeting of the Society for Research in Child Development, Kansas City, MO.

Bretherton, I., Fritz, J., Zahn-Waxler, C., & Ridgeway, D. (1986). The acquisition and development of emotion language: A functionalist perspective. *Child Development, 57*, 529–548.

Bryan, J. H. (1975). Children's cooperation and helping behaviors. In E. M. Hetherington (Ed.), *Review of child development research* (Vol. 5). Chicago: University of Chicago Press.

Bryan, J. H., & Walbek, N. H. (1970). Preaching and practicing generosity: Children's actions and reactions. *Child Development, 41*, 329–353.

Bruner, J. (1972). The nature and uses of immaturity. *American Psychologist, 27*, 1–22.

Buckley, N., Siegel, L. S., & Ness, S. (1979). Egocentrism, empathy, and altruistic behavior in young children. *Developmental Psychology, 15*, 329–330.

Cain, S. H. (1987). *The relationship of role-taking, temperament, and parent behaviors to prosocial behaviors in children.* Unpublished master's thesis, Wake Forest University, Winston-Salem, NC.

Caplan, M. (1991). Conflict and its resolution in small groups of one- and two-year-olds. *Child Development, 62*(6), 1513–1524.

Caplan, M. Z., & Hay, D. F. (1989). Preschoolers' responses to peers' distress and beliefs about bystander intervention. *Journal of Child Psychology and Psychiatry, 30*(2), 231–242.

Cauley, K., & Tyler, B. (1989). The relationship of self-concept to prosocial behavior in children. *Early Childhood Research Quarterly, 4*(1), 51–60.

Child Development Project: Description of Program. (1988). Report. Palo Alto, CA: Hewlett Foundation.

Child Development Project: Summary of Findings to Date. (1991). Palo Alto, CA: Hewlett Foundation.

Cohn, J. F., Campbell, S. B., Matias, R., & Hopkins, J. (1990). Face-to-face interactions of postpartum depressed and nondepressed mother-infant pairs at 2 months. *Developmental Psychology, 26*, 15–23.

Costin, S. E., & Jones, D. C. (1992). Friendship as a facilitator of emotional responsiveness and prosocial interventions among young children. *Developmental Psychology, 28*(5), 941–947.

Dunn, J., & Munn, P. (1986). Siblings and the development of prosocial behaviour. *International Journal of Behavioral Development, 9*(3), 265–284.

Edwards, C. (1992). Creating safe places for conflict resolution to happen: Beginnings. *Child Care Information Exchange, 84,* 43–45.

Eisenberg, N., Cameron, E., Tryon, K., & Dodez, R. (1981). Socialization of prosocial behavior in the preschool classroom. *Developmental Psychology, 17,* 773–782.

Eisenberg-Berg, N., & Lennon, R. (1980). Altruism and the assessment of empathy in the preschool years. *Child Development, 51,* 552–557.

Fabes, R. A., Eisenberg, N., McCormick, S. E., & Wilson, M. S. (1988). Preschooler's attributions of the situational determinants of others' naturally occurring emotions. *Developmental Psychology, 24,* 376–385.

Freud, S. (1958). *Civilization and its discontents.* New York: Doubleday (originally published in 1930).

Friedrich, L. K., & Stein, A. H. (1975). Prosocial television and young children: The effects of verbal labeling and role-playing on learning and behavior. *Child Development, 46,* 27–38.

Grusec, J. (1982). The socialization of altruism. In N. Eisenberg (Ed.), *The development of prosocial behavior.* New York: Academic Press.

Grusec, J. (1991). Socializing concern for others in the home. *Developmental Psychology, 27*(2), 336–342.

Hartup, W. W., & Sancilio, M. F. (1986). Children's friendships. In E. Schopler & G. B. Mesibov (Eds.), *Social behavior in autism.* New York: Plenum.

Hay, D. F. (1979). Cooperative interactions and sharing between very young children and their parents. *Developmental Psychology, 15,* 647–653.

Hearold, S. (1986). A synthesis of 1043 effects of television on social behavior. In G. A. Comstock (Ed.), *Public communications and behavior* (Vol. 1). New York: Academic Press.

Hoffman, M. L. (1975). Developmental synthesis of affect and cognition and its interplay for altruistic motivation. *Developmental Psychology, 11,* 607–622.

Honig, A., & Wittmer, D. (1991). *Helping children become more prosocial: Tips for teachers.* Available from ERIC Document Reproduction Service.

Kreidler, W. (1984). *Creative conflict resolution.* Evanston, IL: Scott, Foresman.

Lewis, M. (1989). Cultural differences in children's knowledge of emotional scripts. In C. Saarni & P. L. Harris (Eds.), *Children's understanding of emotion.* Cambridge, England: Cambridge University Press.

Madsen, M. C. (1971). Developmental and cross-cultural differences in the cooperative and competitive behavior of young children. *Journal of Cross-Cultural Psychology, 2,* 365–371.

Marcus, R. F. (1977, March). *A naturalistic study of reciprocity in the helping behavior of young children.* Paper presented at the biennial meeting of the Society for Research in Child Development, New Orleans.

Marcus, R. F., & Leiserson, M. (1978). Encouraging helping behavior. *Young Children*, *33*(6), 24–34.

Marcus, R. F., Telleen, S., & Roke, E. J. (1979). Relation between cooperation and empathy in young children. *Developmental Psychology*, *15*, 346–347.

McCall, R. B. (1979). Qualitative transitions in behavioral development in the first two years. In M. H. Bornstein & W. Kessen (Eds.), *Psychological development in infancy*. Hillsdale, NJ: Erlbaum.

Michalson, L., & Lewis, M. (1985). What do children know about emotions and when do they know it? In M. Lewis & C. Saarni (Eds.), *The socialization of emotions*. New York: Plenum.

Midlarsky, E., & Bryan, J. H. (1972). Affect expressions and children's imitative altruism. *Journal of Experimental Research in Personality*, *6*, 195–203.

Miller, D. (1991). Do adolescents help and share? *Adolescence*, *26*, 449–456.

Murphy, L. B. (1937). *Social behavior and child personality*. New York: Columbia University Press.

Mussen, P. H., & Eisenberg-Berg, N. (1977). *Caring, sharing and helping*. San Francisco: W. H. Freeman.

Naparstek, N. (1990). Children's conceptions of prosocial behavior. *Child Study Journal*, *20*(4), 207–220.

Olejnik, A. B., & McKinney, J. P. (1973). Parental value orientation and generosity in children. *Developmental Psychology*, *8*, 311.

Orlick, T. D. (1981). Positive socialization via cooperative games. *Developmental Psychology*, *17*, 426–429.

Piaget, J. (1965). *The moral judgment of the child*. New York: Norton.

Piaget, J. (1983). Piaget's theory. In P. Mussen (Ed.), *Handbook of child psychology* (Vol. 3). New York: Wiley.

Radke-Yarrow, M., Richters, J., & Wilson, W. E. (1988). Child development in a network of relationships. In R. A. Hinde & J. Stevenson-Hinde (Eds.), *Relationships within families*. Oxford, England: Clarendon Press.

Radke-Yarrow, M., & Zahn-Waxler, C. (1976). Dimensions and correlations of prosocial behavior in young children. *Child Development*, *47*, 118–125.

Radke-Yarrow, M., & Zahn-Waxler, C. (1984). Roots, motives, and patterning in children's prosocial behavior. In E. Staub, D. Bar-Tal, J. Karylowski, & A. Raykowski (Eds.), *The development and maintenance of prosocial behavior: International perspectives on positive morality*. New York: Plenum.

Radke-Yarrow, M., Zahn-Waxler, C., & Chapman, M. (1983). Children's prosocial dispositions and behavior. In P. Mussen (Ed.), *Handbook of child psychology* (Vol. 4). New York: Wiley.

Rheingold, H. L. (1979, March). *Helping by two-year-old children*. Paper presented at the meeting of the Society for Research in Child Development, San Francisco.

Rheingold, H. L. (1982). Little children's participation in the work of adults, a nascent prosocial behavior. *Child Development*, *53*, 114–125.

Rheingold, H. L., & Emery, G. N. (1986). The nurturant acts of very young children. In D. Olweus, J. Block, & M. Radke-Yarrow (Eds.), *The development of anti- and prosocial behavior*. San Diego, CA: Academic Press.

Rheingold, H. L., Hay, D. F., & West, M. J. (1976). Sharing in the second year of life. *Child Development*, *47*, 1148–1158.

Rogow, S. (1991). The dynamics of play: Including children with special needs in mainstreamed early childhood programs. *International Journal of Early Childhood*, *23*(2), 50–57.

Rosenhan, D. L. (1972). Prosocial behavior of children. In W. W. Hartup (Ed.), *The young child: Reviews of research* (Vol. 2). Washington, DC: NAEYC.

Rubin, K. H., & Schneider, F. W. (1973). The relationship between moral judgment, egocentrism, and altruistic behavior. *Child Development*, *44*, 661–665.

Rushton, J. P. (1975). Generosity in children: Immediate and long-term effects of modeling, preaching, and moral judgment. *Journal of Personality and Social Psychology*, *31*, 459–466.

Rushton, J. P. (1976). Socialization and the altruistic behavior of children. *Psychological Bulletin*, *83*, 898–913.

Russell, J. A. (1989). Culture, scripts, and children's understanding of emotion. In C. Saarni & P. L. Harris (Eds.), *Children's understanding of emotion*. Cambridge, England: Cambridge University Press.

Sagi, A., & Hoffman, M. L. (1976). Empathic distress in the newborn. *Developmental Psychology*, *12*, 175–176.

Sawin, D. B. (1980). *A field study of children's reactions to distress in their peers.* Unpublished manuscript, University of Texas at Austin.

Schenk, V., & Grusec, J. (1987). A comparison of prosocial behavior of children with and without day care experience. *Merrill-Palmer Quarterly*, *33*(2), 231–240.

Shaffer, D. (1993). *Developmental psychology* (3rd ed.). Pacific Grove, CA: Brooks/Cole.

Smith, C. L., Gelfand, D. M., Hartmann, D. P., & Partlow, M. P. (1979). Children's causal attributions regarding help giving. *Child Development*, *50*, 203–210.

Solomon, D. (1988). Enhancing children's prosocial behavior in the classroom. *American Educational Research Journal*, *25*(4), 527–554.

Stanjek, K. (1978). Uberreichen von Gaben: Funktion und Entwicklung in den ersten Lebensjahren. *Zeitschrift for Entwicklungspsychologie und Padagogische Psychologie*, *10*, 103–113.

Staub, E. (1971). The use of role playing and induction in children's learning of helping and sharing behavior. *Child Development*, *42*, 805–816.

Termine, N. T., & Izard, C. E. (1988). Infants' responses to their mothers' expressions of joy and sadness. *Developmental Psychology*, *24*, 223–229.

Trepanier, M., & Romatowski, J. (1981, April). *Classroom use of selected children's books to facilitate prosocial development in young children.* Paper presented at the annual meeting of the American Educational Research Association, Los Angeles.

Trevarthen, C. (1989). Origins and directions for the concept of infant intersubjectivity. *Society for Research in Child Development*, newsletter, pp. 1–4.

White, R. W. (1959). Motivation reconsidered: The concept of competence. *Psychological Review*, *66*, 297–323.

Wong, P. T. (1992). Control is a double-edged sword. *Canadian Journal of Behavioural Science*, *24*(2), 143–146.

Yarrow, M. R., Scott, P. M., & Waxler, C. Z. (1973). Learning concern for others. *Developmental Psychology*, *8*, 240–260.

Zahn-Waxler, C., Kochanska, G., Krupnick, J., & McKnew, D. (1990). Patterns of guilt in children of depressed and well mothers. *Developmental Psychology*, *26*, 51–59.

Zahn-Waxler, C., & Radke-Yarrow, M. (1982). The development of altruism: Alternative research strategies. In N. Eisenberg (Ed.), *The development of prosocial behavior*. San Diego, CA: Academic Press.

Zahn-Waxler, C., Radke-Yarrow, M., Wagner, E., & Chapman, M. (1992). Development of concern for others. *Developmental Psychology*, *28*(1), 126–136.

Part Three

Developing a
Personal/Eclectic Approach
to Child Guidance

What will *you* do when a child in your class curses? Put him in time-out? Ignore the cursing? Figure out what he seems to be getting by cursing? Think about whose problem the cursing is? Deliver an "I-message"? Set limits on cursing? As you can see, you have lots of choices, and the mark of a professional is the ability to make active, conscious decisions and to be able to articulate reasons for those choices. You do not have to be trapped into using the first "trick" that comes to mind. You can reject certain strategies, too, if they do not fit with your personal set of values and principles or with what you believe about child development.

Chapter 10. Theories and Their Strategies: Roadmaps to a Personal Approach to Child Guidance. This chapter describes three different theories of child guidance—Rogerian, Adlerian, and social learning. Each of these models is a roadmap for making decisions about how to handle different dilemmas, and each offers specific child guidance strategies that are consistent with the basic beliefs in the theory. For example, social learning theorists believe in using feedback and reinforcement, so the specific strategy *effective praise* comes out of this model. You will read about the basic beliefs of each theory and then examine specific, concrete child guidance strategies that come from the theory. You will have a chance to practice using the strategies as you analyze case studies and solve problems. You will also probably find yourself saying, "Hmmm, I like that strategy," or "That strategy is *not* for me!" When you do, you are on the road to . . .

Chapter 11. The Decision-Making Model of Child Guidance: A Personal/Eclectic Approach. This chapter will help you use the positive strategies that were presented throughout this book in developing guidance plans for children. The decision-making model is an active one in which you will use strategies from *all* theories to make conscious, self-responsible decisions about how best to help individual children. You will practice this personal/eclectic approach through case studies and by developing a guidance plan.

10

Theories and Their Strategies: Roadmaps to a Personal Approach to Child Guidance

Chapter Overview

After reading and studying this chapter, you will be able to

▼ *Define* terms associated with the Adlerian, Rogerian, and social learning models.

▼ *List* and *explain* the major principles of the three models.

▼ *Explain* how a responsible, autho*ritative* adult could choose any of the three models.

▼ *List, give examples of, and describe* some of the major strategies used in each model.

▼ *Explain* how each model views the use of punishment.

▼ *Name* the form of punishment under which time-out is classified, *explain* the function of time-out, *explain* why time-out does not teach anything, and *explain* why time-out should be used only rarely, if at all.

"A theory of child development can be likened to a lens . . .
[It] filters out certain facts and gives a pattern to those it lets in."

(Thomas, 1992, p. 4)

CHILD GUIDANCE STRATEGIES MUST BE DEVELOPMENTALLY APPROPRIATE FOR ADULTS, TOO

Early childhood professionals have focused recently on the concept of developmentally appropriate practice for children. It is just as important that we focus on developmentally appropriate practice for adults (Vartuli & Fyfe, 1993) because teachers use positive strategies with children only when they understand and willingly accept them (Wahler, 1980).

Whether adults realize it or not, they accept or reject strategies because of their basic theory about how children grow and develop. The recent debate in the early childhood profession about time-out has come about because professionals who reject one theory of child development also tend to reject the strategies (e.g., time-out) that have evolved out of that view.

In this chapter you will study three models of child guidance—Rogerian, Adlerian, and social learning. You will meet three responsible teachers, each of whom uses developmentally appropriate activities and who has a very nicely set up room. All three teach in the same school. Mrs. Morgan explains behavior from a Rogerian perspective and chooses guidance strategies primarily from that model. Mrs. Yang explains behavior from the Adlerian perspective and chooses guidance strategies primarily from that model. Mr. Tomski explains behavior from a social learning perspective and chooses guidance strategies primarily from that model.

All three teachers have an authori*tative* style: they are high in both demandingness and responsiveness. Each is warm and nurturant and has created a safe and secure classroom environment. Each is adept at setting good limits. Each is an excellent observer of children's behavior, and each firmly believes that adults in a child's world have an impact on how a child behaves—not *total* responsibility, but an impact. Each is articulate about the strategies they use, and they understand why they reject other strategies. These teachers are effective because the positive guidance strategies they choose match their basic explanation of development and behavior.

ROGERIAN THEORY AND CHILD GUIDANCE

CASE STUDY: Mrs. Morgan's Classroom

Charles

"Teacher, Jim and Sam won't let me play in the water. I want to play with the boats!" Mrs. Morgan turned around to face Charles and stooped so that she could be closer and said, "You want to play with the boats, and Jim and Sam told you to go away." Charles said, "Yeah, they told me 'Go away, splasher.'" She nodded, saying, "They called you a splasher and told you to go away." Charles started to cry. Mrs. Morgan took both his hands in hers and said, "You really seem to be feeling sad about this, Charles." Gulping air, he said, "I want . . . to play . . . with the boys."

Grouptime

Mrs. Morgan has noticed that despite reasonable, clearly stated limits for cleanup time, some children almost always leave block accessories (small figures of people, animals, and transportation toys) on the floor or on the shelves in a heap. She has already delivered an I-message, but that did not solve the problem. She does not believe in using punishment, but she realizes that she must do something to resolve this conflict because she gets angry every time she looks at the jumbled pile of accessories.

Carl Rogers: Originator of the Rogerian Model

Rogerian theory was formulated by Carl Rogers, who was born in 1902 in Chicago. Rogers studied to be a minister, but eventually he became an educational psychologist and worked in both clinical and academic settings. He counseled children and their parents at the Child Study Department of the Society for the Prevention of Cruelty to Children in Rochester, New York. Rogers was also a teacher. It was during the period from 1940 to 1963 that he developed and disseminated his views on counseling and therapy (Rogers, 1961).

Rogerian Concepts

The Rogerian model is based on beliefs about the nature of the self, and adults who use Rogerian-based child guidance strategies believe that children have an active awareness of the *self*. They believe that a child develops a *self-concept*, which is a set of ideas about the self, and it is this self-concept that helps a child make sense of and operate effectively in a world of constant change.

Adults who are guided by Rogerian principles believe that children have the *capacity for self-direction* and that they can become increasingly able to control their own actions. These adults also believe that *a child's perception of his experience is private*, personal, and highly subjective because the events in a child's life have meaning as they are perceived by that child and not as perceived by anyone else.

Rogerians believe that humans have a tendency to develop all of their abilities, to *actualize* or realize their full potential. The ultimate goal for a human, in the Rogerian framework, is to become a *fully functioning person*, a person who is *open to experience* and aware of all his feelings—including the unpleasant ones like anger or jealousy. Fully functioning people do not feel shame for having unpleasant feelings.

Fully functioning people also tend to *live fully in each moment* because they perceive things accurately. Such children tend to be much less defensive in dealing with new people, experiences, and problems. Fully functioning people think for themselves and trust their ability to make decisions. They do not need other people to tell them how to act, because they have the ability to accurately appraise situations and they trust themselves to develop good solutions to problems (Rogers, 1957).

Rogerians believe that children move in the direction of becoming fully functioning people when they receive *positive regard*—that is, support, acceptance, and approval—from others. Children begin to regard themselves as positive when they receive and internalize positive regard from important people in their lives. Children who do not receive unconditional positive regard from important adults may spend lots of time and energy trying to attain the elusive adult approval and may not have enough time or energy to work on becoming a fully functioning person (Rogers, 1961).

Applying Rogerian Concepts to Child Guidance

Mrs. Morgan, the teacher in the case study at the beginning of this section, is an early childhood teacher who understands the Rogerian concepts and has created a classroom atmosphere in which Rogers (1957) would maintain that it will be quite possible for the children to move in the direction of becoming fully functioning persons.

Mrs. Morgan has a warm and nurturant (not permissive) relationship with her children, and they seem to feel safe in her classroom. She has a great deal of respect for each child but is still open to all of her feelings about individual children. She does not deny these feelings but accepts them as real. Mrs. Morgan is genuine, congruent, and integrated.

One of the things she has learned in workshops that teach how to apply Rogerian principles is to accept the existence of all kinds of feelings in children, not just the friendly, cooperative feelings. She understands a child's fear, rage, or jealousy but does not become entrapped in those feelings and does not allow children to hurt others when they are angry. She has also worked on learning specific strategies for clearly communicating what she understands about a child's feelings and is also able to make a child feel understood (Coletta, 1977; Thomas, 1992).

Mrs. Morgan wants the children to be able to make good decisions. She believes that she can best help them by refusing to tell them how to solve problems that they themselves should be solving. Mrs. Morgan does not believe she has to play a role or that she has to be a perfect teacher. She simply tries to put her beliefs and her understanding of the Rogerian model into practice when she has to deal with typical classroom issues.

Guidance Strategies Used in a Rogerian-Based Program

Parent Effectiveness Training, widely known as PET, is a program of child guidance based on Rogerian theory. It was begun in 1962 by Thomas Gordon, who had been trained as a Rogerian therapist. In his clinical work with children and their families, Gordon found that many adults experiencing interpersonal problems with children were simply uninformed about more effective interpersonal skills. Gordon's objective in starting the PET program was to teach adults some of the skills used by professional Rogerian counselors. In PET, adults learn some of the skills that Rogers considered necessary and sufficient to effect a positive personality change. Gordon has also instituted a program of Teacher Effectiveness Training (TET), which incorporates most of the PET skills.

The fundamental Rogerian principle is that people *can* change their methods of interacting with others, and this principle is the backbone of both PET and TET. Gordon helps adults change ways of interacting by teaching the basics of what goes on in all relationships between two people and by teaching specific new interactional skills (Gordon, 1970, 1974, 1978). This section presents a sampling of the skills taught in the PET course, including problem ownership, active listening, I-messages, and the no-lose method of conflict resolution.

Problem Ownership

The principle of problem ownership is a central concept in the PET model. Gordon believes that many adults tend to try to solve a child's problems for him rather than encouraging the child to solve his own problems.

When the adult owns the problem.   Problems or issues arise in all relationships. Adults find some child behavior irritating because a child is interfering with the adult's rights—for example, the child is being noisy when the parent is reading, or the child leaves his bike in the driveway. In these cases the adult "owns the problem."

Defusing this adult-owned problem requires that an adult use specific child guidance strategies that focus on self-responsible, nonaccusatory communication skills, skills that tell a child: "I have a problem, and I need your help." These skills also help adults learn how to encourage a child to modify his behavior out of respect for the adult's needs. You will read about one of these communication skills, sending *I-messages*, later in this chapter.

When a child owns the problem.   Children own problems, too, when their needs are thwarted, as when an infant cannot reach a toy, a toddler cannot fit puzzle pieces together, a 4-year-old is afraid of an injection, or a kindergartner is embarrassed when somebody calls him a name. These are problems the child experiences, separate and independent from an adult's life. Therefore, the child owns the problem.

We can best help a child who owns a problem by using specific communication skills that send the following message: "You seem to have a problem. Do you need my help?" Active listening is the PET/TET communication skill you will read about in this section.

When there is no problem.   Some behaviors are not a problem. They represent what adults strive for in guiding children: the times when things seem to be going well. The goal in the PET program is to teach adults the skills that will help them enlarge the area of no problems.

SPECIAL FOCUS: How to Listen Actively

▼   Listen carefully.

▼   Do not interrupt.

▼   Try to understand what the message means.

▼   Listen for what the child is feeling.

▼   Suspend judgment.

▼   Avoid preaching, giving advice, or trying to persuade the child to feel something else.

▼   Merely feed back your perception of the child's feelings.

Active Listening

Example   Six-year-old Mark said, "I don't want to play cards with Grandpa. He makes fun of me."

Mark *owns* this problem. Active listening would be the strategy that an adult trained in the Rogerian framework would use to encourage Mark to solve the problem by himself. Active listening is a strategy used by professional counselors and taught to adults who take the PET or TET courses. Mark needs to know that his teacher recognizes his feelings, and active listening is an excellent way for his teacher to convey that understanding.

What will Mark's teacher accomplish if she chooses to listen actively to him? By listening closely, carefully, and accurately she will discover his message. Listening without judging will communicate her recognition and acceptance of Mark and his feelings. She will also communicate trust in Mark's ability to work through his own problem and to find a solution by himself.

Think about the last time you had a problem and confided in someone who really listened. They did not deny your problem or your feelings. They did not judge you. They did not offer you a quick solution, but they listened well and understood and accepted your feelings. You can show the same courtesy to children by listening actively. The special focus box summarizes things to remember about active listening.

CASE STUDY ANALYSIS: How Well Has Mrs. Morgan Used Active Listening?

Decide how well Mrs. Morgan (case study) has used active listening by using the guidelines from the special focus box to answer the following questions.

1.   How could you tell that Mrs. Morgan listened carefully as Charles spoke?

2.   When did Mrs. Morgan show that she was trying to understand his message?

3.   Which statement showed that Mrs. Morgan listened for what Charles was feeling?

4.   How well did Mrs. Morgan avoid preaching and trying to persuade Charles to feel differently?

5.   Which statement showed that Mrs. Morgan was merely trying to feed back her perception of Charles's feelings?

Teachers are *mandated reporters of child abuse* according to their state's statutes on child abuse and neglect, and it is therefore essential that we know how to act appropriately when we suspect child abuse or neglect. These children might make indirect allusions to problems at home, and we will help them best when we listen actively without judging or acting shocked.

Example   Joyce and her teacher were playing a board game while Joyce waited for her dad to pick her up.

Teacher: "I like playing games. Do you, Joyce?"

Joyce: "Uh-huh. Uncle Charlie likes games, too."

Ms. Antolini is listening actively to Grace because it is Grace who has a problem.

| Teacher: | "Uncle Charlie likes to play games?" |
| Joyce: | "He likes one game the best. We play when he babysits." |

(By this time the teacher was worried. She knew about the indicators of sexual abuse, and it was beginning to look as if Joyce was trying to tell her something.)

| Teacher: | "There's one game that he really likes?" |
| Joyce: | "Yeah. But he told me that it's a secret game and I shouldn't tell anybody else that we play it." |

This teacher has listened and responded well to frightening information. She has not closed the conversation down or denied the child's feelings. She has not preached, she has not acted shocked—she has listened actively. And, she will follow her state's law on the reporting of this information.

Sending I-Messages

Gordon (1970, 1974, 1978) believes that every member of the guidance system, adult as well as child, has a right to have his needs met. Children occasionally do things that interfere with the satisfaction of an adult's legitimate needs (e.g., an adult cannot get work done because of interruptions from a child, an adult must replant flowers run over by a child on a trike, or an adult has to clean paint brushes not cleaned by a child).

Sending an *I-message* is the communication strategy an adult should use when the adult, not the child, owns the problem and when a child has done something that is usually perceived as annoying, frustrating, or anger-arousing by the adult. I-messages should be simple statements of facts and should not accuse the child of creating the adult's feeling (Gordon, 1970). (See chapter 3 for a case study problem solving on using I-messages.)

No-Lose Method of Conflict Resolution

Rogerians believe that conflict between adults and children is inevitable and should not be denied. They believe that conflict is not necessarily bad, and that there are times in any relationship when conflict arises simply because the needs of the people in the relationship do not match. Gordon teaches an approach to responsible conflict resolution called the *no-lose method of conflict resolution*. He also advises that we avoid the following two ineffective methods for resolving conflict (Gordon, 1970; Mead, 1976).

1. *I win, you lose.* Some adults see a conflict as a battle in which there has to be a winner and a loser. With this ineffective technique for trying to resolve conflict, the adult wins and the child loses. An adult who uses this method quite often resorts to using authori*tarian* strategies to win. Rogerians are adamantly opposed to resolving conflicts through this method.

2. *You win, I lose.* This is also an ineffective way to try to resolve conflict: the child wins and the adult loses. It is frequently used by adults who are permissive, who do not feel confident in following through with limits, and who do not know how to do problem solving. The adult usually feels discouraged—even angry—after such an episode and often ends up doing the task for which a child has responsibility.

To counter the idea that there has to be a winner and a loser when conflict arises, Gordon (1970) proposed a third, more responsible method of resolving the inevitable conflicts in a relationship. He called this the *no-lose* method of conflict resolution. One of the main goals of this approach is to teach adults to avoid the use of power so that nobody wins or loses and so that everybody gets their needs met. This method involves decision making by adult and child to achieve a mutually agreeable solution to a problem without resorting to the use of power. Children are more likely to carry out the solution to a conflict or problem if they have played a role in reaching the solution (Gordon, 1976).

Adults who use the no-lose method acknowledge that the child's needs are important and communicate trust in the child's ability to carry out decisions. Using this method, therefore, requires that adults truly accept the child's feelings and needs as valid and important. Adults who use this method must also be adept at active listening and sending I-messages.

SPECIAL FOCUS: Resolve Conflicts With the "No-Lose" Method

This method involves simple problem solving and negotiation in which both parties participate. The steps in this process are:

1. *Identify and define the conflict.* Avoid using accusatory statements. "We have a problem . . ."
2. *Invite children to participate in fixing the problem.*
3. *Generate possible solutions as a group.* Accept a variety of solutions. Do not evaluate solutions during this brainstorming phase.
4. *Examine each idea for its merits and drawbacks.* Decide which one to try. Thank everybody for brainstorming.
5. *Work out ways of implementing the solution.*
6. *Follow up to evaluate how well the solution worked.* If the solution worked, thank the group for their help in cooperating to solve the problem. If the solution did not work, ask the group to try to figure out why and to fine-tune the solution or to try another solution.

CASE STUDY PROBLEM SOLVING: Conflict Resolution

Demonstrate how the conflict over block accessory cleanup in Mrs. Morgan's classroom would be solved by using all three methods of conflict resolution. Work with another person and develop a short role-play based on each of the three methods.

Role-Play #1: I win, you lose. Develop a short vignette that illustrates at least one specific strategy used by an adult who believed in using this method to solve the issue of proper storage of block accessories.

Role-Play #2: You win, I lose. Again, develop a short vignette illustrating a specific strategy used by an adult who believed in using this method to resolve the same issue.

Role-Play #3: No-lose method. Demonstrate how Mrs. Morgan would use each step in negotiating a solution to this problem using the no-lose method.

ADLERIAN THEORY AND CHILD GUIDANCE

CASE STUDY: Mrs. Yang's Classroom

Greg

Mrs. Yang said, "Greg's Mom told me that Greg was a *problem eater*, and now I know what she means. He hardly ever tries the snack, and I have to coax him to eat what we have for lunch. I decided to use the *try-a-bite* strategy and told him he'd have to stay at the lunch table until he tried a bite of everything. He ate so slowly that I thought I'd scream. What am I supposed to do?"

Kee

Mrs. Yang said, "You know, I've really had it with Kee at naptime. He goes to his cot but won't stay there! It's just one thing after another—drink, the bathroom, get his teddy bear, sing him a song, tapping another child, getting up. I tell him to stay on the cot, but then I hear him whining that he needs me. He disturbs the other children, and I don't know what to do."

Adlerian theorists have a unique perspective on how the personality develops (Adler, 1964). Their view of the adult-child relationship is different from that of a behaviorist or a Rogerian. An Adlerian has specific ideas on why these children acted as they did, as well as on the role of the adult in child guidance.

Alfred Adler: Originator of the Adlerian Model

Alfred Adler was the founder of individual psychology. His life paralleled that of Sigmund Freud in many ways. Both were from Vienna, and Adler was born in

1870, only a few years after Freud. They both attended medical school and developed an interest in psychiatry, but they held divergent views on how the personality develops. Freud maintained that each person is primarily a biological being, while Adler believed that each person is primarily a social being. Freud believed that personalities are shaped by biological needs, but Adler maintained that personalities are shaped by individual social environments and interactions. And while Freud believed that people are driven by unconscious forces that cannot be controlled, Adler maintained that people actively and consciously direct and create their own growth (DiCaprio, 1974).

The Adlerian approach is used by many adults as a major guide in their interactions with children. These adults accept the basic concepts of Adler's theory and have learned specific positive child guidance strategies based on these concepts. Adlerians do *not* believe in using punishment. They believe in figuring out what a child is getting out of a misbehavior and then changing their own reaction to the misbehavior to try to help a child make some changes. By offering *safe, natural, and logical consequences*, they allow children to learn from their behavior (see chapter 3 for a more detailed discussion of logical consequences).

Adlerian Concepts

Each Person Has an Individual Style of Striving for Psychological Strength

Adler believed that humans, with their long period of utter dependency, realize that they lack the physical strength of many other species and because of this tend to develop feelings of psychological inferiority and helplessness (Mead, 1976). Adler believed that people try to overcome a sense of inferiority with feelings of psychological strength.

Each person develops a characteristic individual style of striving for the goal, that is, a core set of ideas about how to understand, predict, and have some control over his experiences. This *life-style* affects how a child deals with problems encountered in daily life. A child's characteristic style of dealing with the world and his place in it is established by the age of 4 or 5 (Dinkmeyer & McKay, 1988; Dreikurs, 1958; Schultz, 1976).

Humans Develop Different Levels of Social Interest

Social interest refers to a sense of being a vital part of the group, realizing one's role in a group's functioning. Adlerians believe that humans are primarily social beings and that achieving feelings of psychological strength is best done through cooperation with others (Adler, 1964). Consequently, a person with a high degree of social interest is willing to cooperate with other group members and contributes to the functioning of the group. A person with little social interest tends to do things that benefit the self but not necessarily other group members.

Self-Esteem Influences Social Interest

Adlerians believe that a child who develops positive self-esteem (feelings of competence and self-worth) during childhood will develop a strong sense of social interest and will strive to cooperate with others, while a child who develops negative self-esteem will have a low level of social interest (Mead, 1976). In short, a child who likes and respects himself and is confident about his abilities is likely to become a person who will respect, work well with, and help others, while a child who is given little respect or who is treated as incompetent is likely to become a person who shows little respect for others and who refuses to cooperate with and help other group members.

Family Systems Influence Social Interest

Every child is born with the capacity to cooperate, but Adlerians believe that cooperation must be nurtured by a child's environment. Parents, other caregivers, and teachers influence a child's level of social interest and cooperation because they create the atmosphere in which the child exists, an atmosphere in which cooperation with and respect for others can be valued, modeled, and encouraged. It can be a place in which hurting others is prohibited through reasonable, firmly enforced limits on behavior.

Accuracy of Personal Perceptions Affects Social Interest

Adlerians believe that children play a large role in their development, that their interpretation or perception of their experiences is important. And, children go about fitting into a group by following their own interpretation of the rules for group membership (DiCaprio, 1974; Dreikurs, 1958; Mead, 1976).

Some children are able to achieve a sense of belonging to their group by cooperating and making useful contributions. They make accurate interpretations of the rules of group membership. Other children have a pattern of misbehavior and noncooperation because they interpret their world inaccurately. These children have a faulty perception of how to fit into the group and use ineffective approaches to gain a place in it.

Goals of Misbehavior: Attention, Power, Revenge, and Inadequacy

The case studies (Kee and Greg) at the beginning of this section show typical adult-child interactions that occur when a child has a faulty perception of how to fit into a group. Children like Greg and Kee have a faulty perception or mistaken goal on how to be a group member and seek group membership through one of the following approaches (Dreikurs, 1958):

▼   By striving for undue attention from others

▼   By seeking power over others

▼   By hurting others through revenge

▼   By displaying inadequacy or incompetence

Some children make accurate interpretations about how to be a member of the group.

Striving for Undue Attention

The child's faulty perception.   Everyone, including a child, has a need for and a right to attention. Some children, however, make demands for undue attention from adults, indicating that they have the mistaken belief that they are important only when they are the center of attention. Getting the attention of others, then, is their mistaken goal.

What the child does.   Attention seekers accomplish their mistaken goal by keeping adults busy. The child becomes skillful at using different attention-getting techniques. Some attention seekers are active mischief makers, in trouble all the time, but others are passive and get attention through laziness and demanding that things be done for them.

How the adult feels and usually reacts.   Adults usually feel annoyed when children demand undue attention and tend to give in to the child's demands, but this reinforces both the attention-getting behavior and the child's faulty perception of how to become a member of the group (Mead, 1976). Other adults reinforce attention-seeking behavior by scolding the child.

A better approach.   Adlerians believe in helping a child discover that he can be a valuable group member without having to be the center of attention. Here are specific steps to take when you are confronted with attention-seeking behavior; the basic ingredient is changing how you react to demands for undue attention (Mead, 1976).

1. *Ignore the impulse to give in to the attention-seeking behavior.*

2. *Acknowledge the child's request but let him know that he can complete the task.* Leave the area if necessary so that he can finish the job.

3. *Give the child attention when behavior is more appropriate.*

4. *Encourage the child to take the perspective of others* by telling him their perspective and by helping him learn to cooperate.

Example   Just when Mrs. Yang received an emergency phone call from a child's parent, Kelly demanded her attention: "I found the book." Mrs. Yang said, "I'm talking to Jon's mom about something important. Read by yourself for now and I'll read to you later." Later, she stopped by the reading corner, "Thanks for helping me by waiting, Kelly. Let's read that book."

Struggling for Power

The child's faulty perception.   Some children think that they are important only when they demonstrate power over others. Their faulty perception is that their personal value comes from being in charge and showing others that they are the boss. For such a child a loss of power to an adult is the same as a loss of personal value.

What the child does.   The child develops several techniques for involving adults in a power struggle and for gaining control over them. These children might have tantrums, be very disobedient, or, with older children, be very argumentative. Some power seekers are active and rebellious. Others are passive, striving for power through stubbornness, forgetfulness, and laziness.

How the adult feels and usually reacts.   Adults often feel threatened or angry when confronted with a power-seeking child. Some adults feel that their authority has been challenged, and their first impulse is to fight back and remind the child that the adult is in power. Adlerians believe that some children are so skillful at the power game that adults do not even realize they are in a power struggle. Some adults resort to punitive, hurtful strategies in trying to reestablish authority and overpower the child.

Adults who allow themselves to be drawn into a power struggle with a child reinforce a child's power-seeking behavior. They do nothing to help power-seeking children clarify their faulty perception but instead reinforce the child's faulty perception of how to become a group member. Mrs. Yang made this mistake with Amy.

Example   Mrs. Yang said to Amy, "You can have two more turns, and then I want you to park your trike." (Amy took several more turns, got off the trike, and ran over to the slide.) Mrs. Yang said, "Amy, it's time to come in. Please park your trike." (Amy got on the tricycle and rode it to the shed. She got off but did not put the trike inside. Instead, she walked toward the classroom. Mrs. Yang glared at her.) Mrs. Yang said, "Amy for the last time, get over to the shed and put your trike inside." Amy replied, "No!" Mrs. Yang said, "We'll see about that." Amy has controlled and manipulated her teacher, engaging her in a power struggle.

A better approach.   Whether a child continues to play the power game depends largely on how important adults react. Children like Amy need adults to guide them toward more positive ways of becoming group members; they do not need adults as sparring partners. Adlerians maintain that adults who change their ways of reacting to a defiant child have the best chance of actually helping that child. The following are their suggestions (Dinkmeyer & McKay, 1988; Mead, 1976):

1. *Resist the first impulse to fight back.*
2. *Decide to respond differently.* You do not have to be drawn into a power struggle. You can choose to respond differently.
3. *Decline the child's invitation to argue or fight.* This will surprise a child, particularly if you have previously been locked in power struggles with him. A useful technique is to label the interaction as a power struggle.

Example   Mrs. Yang says, "It looks to me like you feel like fighting with me about the trike. I don't feel like fighting, so I'm going inside to watch the movie. You may watch it, too, when you put your trike away." (She refuses to fight back and communicates her intention to Amy.)

Getting Revenge

The child's faulty perception.   These children feel hurt, and their goal is to get even by hurting others. Like all children, they need recognition, but these children get it in quite a negative way.

Example   Mrs. Yang said, "Tom, when you talk during naptime you wake the others. I want you to be quiet and read this book when you wake up" (a reasonable request). Tom said nothing but ripped three pages out of the book.

What the child does.   These children expend a lot of energy convincing people that they are not likable. The child works hard at getting even with those he perceives as having hurt him. The revenge may be active, in which the child is easily recognizable as a troublemaker, or the revenge may be passive. The passively vengeful child is quietly defiant.

How the adult feels and usually reacts.   An adult who has been attacked by a child usually feels hurt and either backs away from the child or retaliates against the hurtful behavior. The typical adult reaction does not help a child bent on revenge. Retaliating or backing away reinforces both the child's hurtful behavior and his faulty perception: that he is a bad, unlikable person of little value who has to hurt others to be a part of the group.

A better approach.   Do the unexpected and resist the first impulse to retaliate, give sermons, or back away. A child who seeks revenge has poor self-esteem and needs your help. Adlerians believe that you can best help this child by fostering positive self-esteem because he will value others enough to refrain from hurting them only when he feels valued.

Example   Mrs. Yang decided to concentrate on Tom's acceptable behavior instead of focusing on his errors: "You've stayed on your cot, Tom. Thanks. But I see that you're ready to be awake. You may read a book quietly or help me mix play dough. Which would you rather do?"

Displaying Inadequacy or Incompetence

The child's faulty perception.   These children feel completely discouraged and think they cannot do anything well. They believe they have nothing to contribute to the group, so they do not even try. They want to be left alone.

What the child does.   These children let others know how inadequate they perceive themselves to be with the hope of discouraging others from expecting much from them. They quietly work out a deal with adults in which the adult leaves the child alone and does not ask much of the child, just as the child asks very little of the adult. These children tend to act in an incompetent way.

How the adult feels and usually reacts.   Adults are usually puzzled and frustrated when they interact with an intelligent child who has given up and acts like he cannot do anything. Adults are often at a loss to help such a child. Their first impulse is often to highlight the child's errors, but this results in further discouraging the child. Many adults then perform the task for the child, which reinforces the child's faulty perception that he can be a group member only by demonstrating incompetence.

A better approach.   Rely on knowledge of child development. For example, if a healthy 4-year-old should be able to zip his own coat, refrain from performing the task for him. Most important, learn how to encourage children who mistakenly believe that they have to demonstrate incompetence. Your role is to light the fire of self-confidence in the child so that he can solve problems and carry out tasks on his own.

Example   "I think you can zip your own coat. Put this part of the zipper into this part . . . Good . . . Now catch that little tab and pull it up. That's it . . . Z-Z-Z-ZIP!"

CASE STUDY ANALYSIS: Identify "Mistaken Goals"

Decide how Mrs. Yang felt about Greg's and Kee's behavior and what each child's "mistaken goal" was. Finally, decide on a different way for Mrs. Yang to help each child get his needs met in a more acceptable way.

Greg

I think that Mrs. Yang felt _____ about having to coax Greg to eat.

Greg's mistaken goal was _____.

An Adlerian would advise Mrs. Yang to use the following approach instead of coaxing:

Kee

I think Mrs. Yang felt _____ about Kee's naptime behavior.

Kee's mistaken goal was _____.

An Adlerian would advise Mrs. Yang to use the following approach with Kee at naptime:

SOCIAL LEARNING THEORY AND CHILD GUIDANCE

CASE STUDY: Mr. Tomski's Classroom

Background

Mr. Tomski teaches a group of 4- and 5-year-olds, many of whom are fans of the Ninja turtles. He was worried about the turtles becoming aggressive, but he wanted to allow the superhero play to continue—within limits.

What He Did

Mr. Tomski showed a short segment of a Ninja tape, the segment clearly demonstrating how the turtles helped somebody without fighting. The class discussed the concept of helping, and Mr. Tomski noted that the Ninjas do not always fight. The next day, when turtle activity began, the teacher stepped in saying, "Remember our Ninja film yesterday, and how the turtles helped that man? Well, there's somebody over in the block corner who needs help. Let's go see if we can help. No fighting, though."

Reinforcement

As the turtles solved the problem with the teacher's guidance, Mr. Tomski said, "I like the way you thought about how to help the man fix his flat tire." When the play episode was over, Mr. Tomski showed the turtles the Ninja "chart," on which he pasted a turtle sticker under that day's name, explaining, "Every day the Ninjas will have to think about how to solve a tough problem. And, every day that the turtles *play together without fighting* they get a turtle sticker. As soon as the turtles get *two stickers* [printed on chart] you can trade them in for one of our special snacks. Which one will it be? . . . Turtle toast it is!" (Turtle toast is a much-loved invention of the class that they whip up at snacktime only on special occasions.) Mr. Tomski *drew a picture of the toast* on the chart.

Making Progress

For each day that the "turtles" cooperated, Mr. Tomski put a sticker on their chart and also verbally encouraged their accomplishment. The group traded in the completed chart for their favorite snack. When they reverted to fighting one day, Mr. Tomski simply did not put a sticker on the chart. He did *not* take a sticker away.

Fading out the Chart

On the next week's chart the Ninjas had to solve three days' dilemmas before getting a sticker, but Mr. Tomski still praised their nonviolent problem solving each day. This time the group chose a turtle helper badge as their reward. At the end of two weeks Mr. Tomski noted with relief that the Ninjas were still very active turtles but that the fighting had decreased dramatically. He stopped using the chart but continued to verbally encourage cooperative play.

Albert Bandura and the Social Learning Model

A major social learning theorist is Albert Bandura, who was born in 1925, and this section focuses on Bandura's view of social learning theory (Bandura, 1977; Bandura & Walters, 1963). Social learning theory is one branch of general learning theory. It emphasizes *social* variables that determine a child's behavior (Thomas, 1992).

Social learning theory combines three things: elements of cognition, principles of behavior modification, and an emphasis on social influences on development. A social learning theorist like Bandura does believe in many of the principles of behaviorism, but he has also expanded behavioral theory to help teachers understand the important role of imitation in child development. He has helped us understand that children are not just machines responding to stimuli. Social learning theorists believe that children are active in their own development, that they are affected by their environment but that they also contribute to producing their environment (Thomas, 1992).

Social Learning Principles Applied to Child Guidance

Principle No. 1: Social Learning Theorists Do Not Emphasize Stages of Development

Developmental theorists like Jean Piaget (1952, 1970, 1983) view development as a series of phases, or stages, each stage being qualitatively different from the ones before and after. In learning theory, however, development is not viewed as a series of stages but rather as a gradual accumulation of knowledge (Thomas, 1992).

Principle No. 2: Development Occurs Through Learning From the Environment

The major belief common to all branches of behavioral or learning theory is that human behavior is learned (Cairns, 1983; Fogel, 1984; Langer, 1969). All learning theorists believe that a child's behavior is gradually shaped as he interacts with his environment. For example, learning theorists believe that a child who treats dogs humanely has learned this behavior.

Principle No. 3: Most of a Child's Learning Occurs Through the Process of Modeling

Social learning theorists believe that learning takes place in and cannot be separated from a child's social setting. Social learning theorists demonstrated over 30 years ago that children could learn new behavior by observing another person perform the behavior (Bandura & Walters, 1963). A child who treats animals humanely, the social learning theorists would insist, has learned this behavior by imitating his model's actions and words about how to treat animals.

Children learn from a variety of models: a real person who is physically present; real persons on television, movies, or videos; cartoon characters; graphic representations of human figures in video games; models in books; or audio models (Maccoby & Martin, 1983; Stevenson, 1983; Thomas, 1992). Children become increasingly accurate in their ability to imitate a model as they grow older.

In the process of modeling, the actual content that is demonstrated for the child depends on the child's social environment. All children learn simple things like vegetable preference, facial expressions, and table manners through observation. More complex social behaviors are also taught through modeling, with some social environments modeling behaviors like respectful treatment of others and assertiveness while other social environments model behaviors like aggression and selfishness.

Children are not just machines, automatically imitating every behavior that they observe. What accounts for a child's selectivity in who or what they imitate? Children imitate models who possess certain characteristics: they are powerful, more skillful than the child, have a lot of prestige, and are nurturant (Maccoby & Martin, 1983). The model's behavior may be positive (e.g., an ad in which an admired athlete says not to smoke or take drugs) or negative (e.g., an older brother who is a gang member).

An explanation of why children do not imitate all of their models is that children actually build a *prototype* of behavior after observing several models (Perry & Bussey, 1979). They observe a large number of models performing a certain type of behavior and then construct a prototype or composite of the behavior of the group. Then, when a child observes another model of the same type of behavior he will imitate the model's behavior only if it matches his construction of what the behavior should be. Thus, social learning theorists believe that children are active in their development and not just passive recipients of every stimulus in their world.

Example   Joseph has observed lots of males in real life and on film and has constructed a prototype of how males act with babies: they hold them and smile, and they seem to like playing with them. Joseph imitated these models of male behavior with his infant sister. He then observed a friend's father refuse to change his infant's diaper or to feed the baby. The new model's behavior with infants did not fit Joseph's construction of "how males act with babies," and he did not imitate this model.

There are a variety of cognitive factors that determine whether a child will learn something after observing a behavior.

1. *Attentional factor:* A child must be able to discriminate and interpret the event before he can learn from it.

2. *Retentional factor:* A child must also be able to retain information about (remember) the event.

3. *Reproductive factor:* A child must be able to reenact the event.

4. *Motivational factor:* A child must want to learn the material even if he can discriminate, interpret, remember, and reproduce it (Bandura, 1969; Cairns, 1983; White, 1970).

Even though social learning theorists do not emphasize stages of development, they do acknowledge that a child's level of development plays a part in learning from models: for example, whether his perceptual skills are sophisticated enough to enable him to pay attention to; whether his memory is well enough developed to enable him to remember; and whether his motor skills are good enough to enable him to reproduce something he has observed.

Principle No. 4: Children Learn Complex Behaviors in Big Chunks Rather Than in Tiny Steps

Some learning theorists believe that children learn things in tiny steps with each step reinforced. But social learning theorists believe that children learn complex behaviors in big chunks (Thomas, 1992).

Example   After a unit called "Showing Kindness to Animals," Nick acted out in the dramatic play area outdoors the entire set of behaviors demonstrated or described by his teacher or by visitors or through videos.

Principle No. 5: Behavior Can Be Changed if a Child's Social Environment Is Changed

Social learning theorists believe that the most effective way to change (modify) a child's behavior is to alter the child's environment. Because they believe so strongly in the effect of the social environment, they place great emphasis on changing the social environment. In practice this means that people in the child's social environment might need to change how they respond to his behavior (Mead, 1976; Thomas, 1992).

Principle No. 6: Children Do Not Need to Be Reinforced to Learn a Behavior

Example   Sam observed the Ninja turtles fight in a way that he had never fought. Sam learned (acquired) the new behavior simply by observing the model. He did not need to be reinforced to learn how to fight like the Ninjas; he only had to watch them and remember what he observed.

Principle No. 7: Reinforcement Gives Children Information on the Consequences of That Behavior for the Person Who Modeled It

Example   Then Sam listened to and observed that the other moviegoers cheered for the Ninjas when they fought. Sam thought to himself, "Hmmm. The people liked how the Ninjas fight."

How has reinforcement operated in Sam's observational learning? First, he learned how to fight like the Ninjas by simply observing them. Then reinforcement entered the picture. Whether he actually imitated (reproduced) the behavior depended on how he looked at the consequences of that activity for the models. Social learning theorists would predict that Sam is highly likely to imitate the Ninja fighting because he heard and watched the cheering (positive consequences) for the Ninjas (Bandura, 1977). Reinforcement, then, is feedback and is a basic process through which adults influence children.

Types of Positive Reinforcement: Effective Praise and Token Systems

There are different forms of positive reinforcement, and Mr. Tomski (case study) believes in using them. He has made an effort to learn to use them ethically and effectively. The two forms he uses that are emphasized here are positive verbal reinforcement (praise) and token systems.

Effective Praise

Effective praise is specific, descriptive, and appreciative but is not "gushy or mushy."   When you praise, notice and then describe specifically what it was that a child did. Describe what you saw, heard, tasted, or touched. Relate the praise directly to the event. Avoid making judgments about what the child did and avoid making comments about the child's character, but let the child know that you appreciate what he has done.

Example   Mr. Tomski walked over to the block area just after cleanup and said, "Thanks for putting away all the small blocks. You put each one in its own spot on the shelf, right behind the outline for the block." (He had set a limit on where to place blocks, communicated the limit clearly, and has now noticed and encouraged their willingness to accept the limit.)

Effective praise is given as soon as possible after the event.   Praise is most effective when it is delivered as soon as possible after a child performs a desired behavior and requires that you concentrate and make an effort to watch for, notice, and then immediately give feedback. There is a good reason for reinforcing as quickly as possible. Reinforcers give children information about the consequences of their behavior. Children make more accurate connections between their behavior and your feedback if the two happen close together.

Example   Immediately after closing the storybook, Mr. Tomski leaned forward and said, "Everybody could hear the story today because the whole class listened so carefully and sat so quietly."

This teacher's praise is specific and is given immediately after an event: "Good for you, Janie! You zipped your parka by yourself and put up your hood."

Effective praise is sincere and rewards effort and small steps.   If you choose to use praise, use honest and sincere praise. Your firmly grounded set of values and ethical standards and your respect for children will forbid you from giving insincere, phony, or perfunctory praise. When you think feedback would be helpful for a child, try to find something in a situation that you can praise sincerely and honestly.

You can foster persistence in children when you give feedback about a child's effort to complete difficult tasks. Children need to know that *they* control the effort that they put into a task, and you can help them increase their effort by giving feedback, specifically about effort (Dweck, 1975; Dweck & Elliott, 1981).

Example   Mr. Tomski watched Rick, who has a reputation for not being able to stay on task, work for 25 minutes with a small tray of wet sand. Rick's concentration was evident when he was not distracted by the noise in the dramatic play area. Rick drew in the sand with his finger and a small stick and then pressed designs into the sand with a variety of objects set out for that purpose. Mr. Tomski has been working on helping Rick concentrate, and this is what he praised, quietly and quickly, without fanfare: "You've worked with the sand tray for almost the whole work period, Rick. That's what I call *concentration*."

Praise is even more effective when given along with appropriate physical contact or other nonverbal communication.   Increase the impact of your verbal feedback by combining it with appropriate physical contact or other appropriate forms of nonverbal communication, such as nodding your head or smiling.

Pitfalls to Avoid: Ineffective Praise

There are a several things that make praise or any type of reward ineffective. Authoritative adults make an effort to avoid the following forms of ineffective praise.

Avoid combining praise with some form of negative comment.   Note the praise as well as the negative comment in the following example. Why do you think that this form of praise is so ineffective?

Example   Teacher to a kindergartner: "I'm glad to see that you've washed your hands. Maybe you can remember to do it again tomorrow."

Avoid praising only perfection.   Some adults praise only perfection, but this is one way to decrease the effectiveness of praise. Instead of noticing and praising a child's effort to do something helpful, some adults attend only to some part of the job the child is not doing.

Example   Teacher to 5-year-old who is washing paintbrushes at the sink, "Kerry! You forgot to wipe the easel."

Avoid praising only completion of a difficult task.   Children should be encouraged as they successfully complete each step in a difficult task.

Example   A day-care aide says nothing to a 3-year-old who is working with a difficult puzzle. She fails to praise the child's effort to match colors or to finally fit two pieces together. Later that day the aide noticed the same child again having trouble with the puzzle. She said, "Here. Let me do that for you."

Do not overdo praise.   Children seem to adapt to a particular level of praise (Maccoby & Martin, 1983). An adult who uses praise indiscriminately will find it necessary to use even more because the child receiving such lavish praise becomes accustomed to it. Rewards (like candy) that are given too frequently lose their reward value. Children come to expect to receive the reward, and if it is not offered they might think they are being punished. Many adults have been trapped into constantly having to escalate the value of treats so that children still view the treat as a reward. What often started out as a legitimate reward (e.g., a trip to their favorite restaurant for practicing a musical instrument) can become, in an adult's eyes, a bribe.

Do not give praise if it is not necessary.   It is possible for rewards to backfire and negatively affect a child's motivation. Children who are spontaneously interested in an activity but are then rewarded for performing the activity may lose interest in the activity because they perceive the adult's reward as an attempt at control (Lepper & Green, 1979). The child's decreased interest is actually resistance to external control (Maccoby & Martin, 1983).

Example   Molly really liked sweeping the sand off the trikeway. She made designs with the broom, imitated the scrape-scrape sound of the sand on sidewalk, and watched sand slide into the sandpit. Mr. Tomski started to praise her work, and she stopped her sweeping.

Do not confuse rewards with bribes.   Reinforcers and bribes are not the same thing. Here is an example of a bribe.

Examples   Julie whines when her mother is talking on the phone. Mother stops and says, "I'll give you some candy if you stop bothering me." Julie stops whining, and mother gives her the candy.

Julie's mother also gives bribes before a behavior occurs. She gave Julie a dime so that Julie would place her toys on the shelves in the family room.

Effective reinforcers are aimed at giving accurate information about the consequences of a behavior and are used to increase the chances that a child will imitate a behavior that she has witnessed. Julie's Mom, on the other hand, has done nothing to teach more acceptable behavior. She has reinforced Julie's obnoxious behavior (whining) by giving a bribe of candy and will very likely have to continue to bribe Julie to keep her quiet.

All children need feedback.   Some children deserve praise and encouragement but seem unable to accept it. How can you help a child who deserves praise but rejects it when it is given? A child who rejects praise may not feel comfortable receiving it because he has negative self-esteem and may feel unworthy of the praise. Such a child may not have received much praise in the past. It is important for you not to argue with the child about whether he deserves praise—just deliver the praise in a positive, matter-of-fact way. Ignore the child's rejecting behavior about the praise. Do not argue. Continue to praise appropriate behavior.

Tokens: Nonsocial, or Tangible, Positive Reinforcers

Praise is a positive social reinforcer. Another class of positive reinforcers is called nonsocial or tangible reinforcers. Some authoritative adults make a deliberate attempt to modify a child's environment and therefore to help a child modify his behavior by using tangible rewards, or tokens, as positive reinforcement.

A token is an object, so the term *tangible* is applied. Some examples are a sticker, a smiley face, a star, a check, a plastic chip. An adult who decides to use a token system targets a specific behavior that he wants to see more of (e.g., cooperation), and a child earns a token for demonstrating that behavior.

Responsible, ethical adults realize that tokens are a means to an end, not an end in themselves. Tokens are merely a way to remind adults to give a child feedback for his efforts to behave appropriately. Responsible adults realize that tokens are a gimmick, that the tokens must be combined with appropriate social reinforcement and that the tokens must be used ethically. They realize that effectively carrying out a token system requires concentration and special effort from adults.

PROBLEM FOR YOU TO SOLVE: Using Effective Praise

Examine each of these situations. Write exactly what you would say to praise effectively. (Reminders: Praise specific behaviors. Describe what you see or hear. Describe appropriate nonverbal communication. Be sincere and honest. Praise effort. Praise small steps. Praise in a low-key, matter-of-fact way.) Then say why your praise is effective.

Situation. Lucy loves to fingerpaint. Today she painted with three colors, piling on color until her paper was saturated. The paper dried with the colors blended into one another, making a muddy green-brown. She shows it to you proudly. Even though you do not personally like the outcome of her effort, you try to find something in this situation that you can honestly praise: her delight in the feel of the paint as she smoothed it onto the paper? the fact that she covered every inch of paper? her concentration?

I would say this for effective praise:
This praise is effective because . . .

Situation. John hung his sweater in his cubby this morning. He also placed his painting there. You've tried for about a week to encourage him to abide by the limit of keeping personal possessions in cubbies and he has finally done so.

I would say this for effective praise:
This praise is effective because . . .

Situation. J.T. is a child in your class. He usually gets a lot of attention for things he should not do, and it is easy to disregard his efforts at cooperation. Yesterday, however, you observed him at the woodworking table. He had been there about 15 minutes when Lauren walked up to the table. She couldn't work because she didn't have goggles. J.T. said, "Here Lauren. See if my goggles fit you. I'm done here."

I would say this for effective praise:
This praise is effective because . . .

CASE STUDY ANALYSIS: Mr. Tomski's Use of Tokens

There are several things to remember for effective use of a token system. Decide how Mr. Tomski (case study) met the criteria for effectively using a token system by answering the following questions.

1. *Reward often.* Considering the age of the children, explain why Mr. Tomski rewarded the new behavior often enough.

2. *Reward small steps.* What was Mr. Tomski's overall goal for the children? How did he encourage/reinforce their small steps toward the bigger goal?

3. *Combine the token with a social reward* (smile, praise, encouragement). Mr. Tomski uses tokens to remind *himself* to use social reinforcers. When did he combine tokens and social reinforcers?

4. *Keep a record of tokens.* How did Mr. Tomski's chart define the desired behavior? How did his chart specify the number of tokens that had to be earned? Explain when his chart defined how the tokens were to be spent.

5. *Ask the child what he would like to work for.* The item or activity used as the reinforcer (the thing for which the chart is traded) must be highly desirable to the child and is best if chosen by the child within certain limits. When did Mr. Tomski do this?

6. *Spend tokens by letting the children exchange their tokens for the reward fairly often.* How well did Mr. Tomski do on this criterion?

7. *Do not take away tokens as fines for undesirable behavior.* What did the teacher do about a turtle sticker when the children made a mistake and fought?

8. *Gradually fade out the use of tokens as the child shows willingness to use the behavior, but continue to give social reinforcers periodically.* One way to do this is to increase the time period between tokens until the child no longer gets a token. How did Mr. Tomski do this?

Extinction: Withdrawing a Reinforcer

A behavior can decrease if it is no longer followed by reinforcement.

Example   Two-year-old Josh had begun to have temper tantrums when his parents put him to bed at night. They reinforced the tantrums by going to his room when he screamed and by staying with him, often spending an hour in his room until he went to sleep. When they realized that they had reinforced Josh's tantrums, they decided to *extinguish* the tantrums by withdrawing the reinforcement. Here are the steps they followed:

1. They made bedtime pleasant by singing a song and reading a favorite story to Josh.

2. They told Josh that after the story was done they would leave the room, close the door, and not come back.

3. The first time they carried out their plan Josh screamed and had his usual tantrum for 30 minutes, but Mom and Dad did not go back to his room.

4. Each night for the rest of the week Josh whimpered when his parents left the room, but each night his protest lasted for a shorter length of time. On the eighth night of the extinction program Josh's parents were pleased that their son went to bed happily after his story. He no longer had a tantrum.

Note that there was no punishment. Josh's parents did not do anything to Josh; they merely withdrew the reinforcer they had previously given, and by so doing they extinguished Josh's behavior that they had previously reinforced (Birnbauer, 1978; Thomas, 1992). (See chapter 3 for a longer discussion of this strategy.)

Teaching and Strengthening More Appropriate Behavior

Example   Four-year-old Linda screeched whenever she was frustrated, and Mr. Tomski had reinforced the screeching by occasionally paying attention to Linda when she screeched. He decided that he should stop paying attention to her screeching by using extinction. The school psychologist advised that he combine extinction with another procedure, strengthening a more appropriate behavior, which makes extinction even more effective.

In addition to ignoring demands made with a screech, the teacher was instructed to teach and strengthen a behavior that is incompatible with screeching, one that cannot be done at the same time as screeching. Asking for things in a normal voice is incompatible with screeching. The teacher told Linda that he would listen to requests made in a normal voice but not to requests made with a screech. Then he demonstrated normal voice. Then Mr. Tomski positively reinforced Linda's effort to use a normal voice and withdrew reinforcement for screeching. (See chapter 3 for a more detailed discussion of this strategy.)

Social Learning Theory's View of Punishment

Punishment is a procedure for weakening or eliminating behavior. It is one of the most widely used (and misunderstood) of all the strategies for influencing children (Richards & Siegel, 1978). Learning theorists are *not opposed* to using punishment to try to change a child's behavior. But, responsible authoritative adults who believe in the social learning model *refuse to use hurtful punishment.*

There are several forms of punishment. Some forms of punishment hurt children and are *never* used by responsible, authoritative adults. But social learning theorists do approve of using other forms of punishment that do not seem to have negative side effects. I will present here a brief summary of the different forms of punishment. (You may also want to reread the section on negative discipline in chapter 2.)

Punishment by Hurt

Punishment by hurt is degrading and is *never* used by ethical professionals.

Examples   Mary swore, and her mom slapped her.

Danny reached across the table for the butter. Dad grabbed his wrist and shoved him back into his chair.

Danny's dog raced to the fence to bark at the neighbor, and Dad threw a tennis ball and hit the dog on the head.

Eighteen-month-old Ron bit his brother, and Ron's dad bit Ron.

Mary's, Danny's, and Ron's parents have used *punishment by hurt* to try to weaken behaviors that irritated them (swearing, reaching across the table, barking, biting). They did something to the child (and to the animal). They applied an aversive, hurtful stimulus (slapping, grabbing, shoving, biting, and throwing the ball) after the undesirable behavior. As you know, there are many ways to punish by hurting, both physically and psychologically (ridicule, sarcasm), and all are unethical and irresponsible.

Hurtful punishment is firmly embedded in the repertoire of many parents and teachers because it *seems* to work quickly and decrease obnoxious behavior. A person does not have to be very creative to use hurtful punishment. As you have learned, hurtful punishment has a negative effect on a child's development and on adult-child relationships. There are many positive, and ultimately more effective, ways to guide children.

Punishment by Loss: Time-Out and Response Cost

Punishment by loss is also a procedure for weakening a behavior, but it is quite different from hurtful punishment. An adult who uses punishment by loss pays careful attention to the reinforcement a child receives for a behavior. The adult then removes or reduces the reinforcement. But the adult does not hurt the child; the child merely loses the positive reinforcement or has to wait a bit longer to receive the reinforcement.

Time-Out.   Professionals in early childhood education are quite concerned about the misuse of *time-out* as a disciplinary practice. (Time-out involves removing a child from a place where he is reinforced for a behavior to a place where the reinforcers are no longer available.) *Time-out, if carried out as specified, is, officially, punishment.* Specifically, time-out is a punishment by loss (Shaffer, 1989). There is so much controversy about time-out in the early childhood profession because it does not match many people's basic beliefs of why children behave as they do. Time-out is also controversial because so many others either do not understand how to use it, overuse it, use it incorrectly, or confuse it with other strategies, and do not understand that *time-out is a form of punishment*.

Time-out should be used rarely—even if one believes that it is an acceptable strategy—and only after a person understands how to carry it out well. Time-out should not be used with all children, and it must be supplemented with the teaching of more appropriate behavior. By itself, time-out does not teach. Some adults use it far more often than is warranted and do not teach more appropriate behavior.

Do not confuse time-out/punishment with the more positive strategy of cooling off or of withdrawing from a situation for a short time and then going back to solve a problem. Time-out is *punishment by loss*. The intention in time-out is to take away the reinforcement you have given a child. (Review chapter 3 for suggestions on how to teach children to take themselves out of situations when necessary.)

Response cost.   *Response cost* is another method of punishment by loss. In this method, the person controlling the reinforcement decreases the amount of reinforcement awarded. Not getting points for not attending class, having to pay a library fine, being penalized 15 yards in a football game, and not getting a sticker on a chart are all are examples of response cost (Wagonseller, Burnett, Slazberg, & Burnett, 1977).

These punishments by loss are most effective only under certain circumstances.

1. Each of these methods requires that a child have a storehouse of reinforcements before reinforcement can be decreased.
2. These methods are forms of punishment and are used only to weaken a behavior. Punishment, if used at all, should not be overused.
3. They weaken a behavior but do not teach anything more appropriate, so they are effective only when they are combined with methods that teach more-acceptable behavior, such as modeling, coaching, instructing, or reinforcing.

Other Branches of Behaviorism

The social learning model has evolved from a long line of learning models. It rejects the extreme form of environmentalism of the earlier forms and has given us new information on how to understand the concept of giving feedback/reinforcement and how to use it to help children make wise decisions about their behavior. Ethical, authoritative adults choosing strategies based on the social learning model refuse to use punishment by hurt and use punishment by loss only rarely.

Watson: Classical Conditioning

John Watson (1878–1957) was one of the first experimental child psychologists. He believed that techniques used with animals could also be used with humans, and he carried out a series of experimental studies with newborn babies (Cairns, 1983). Watson's research group wanted to demonstrate that a child's emotions and personality were shaped by the environment through classical conditioning. You have probably read about the Watson and Raynor (1920) study of aversive conditioning with Albert, a 9-month-old infant. The study is usually used to illustrate how children can learn responses like fear through classical conditioning. Watson's work generated many other research studies, but his "Little Albert" study has been heavily criticized (Harris, 1983).

All behaviorists believe that the environment has a large impact on development, but Watson's view was one of extreme environmentalism. He believed, for example, that rearing children was simply a matter of conditioning "habits" (Watson, 1928, 1958).

Skinner: Operant Conditioning

B. F. Skinner, who carried on the work initiated by Watson, believed in a radical form of behaviorism. Since his major concern was with modifying (changing) behavior, he was not concerned about thoughts or feelings. Skinner is perhaps best known for his reliance on the principles of operant conditioning to change behavior (Skinner, 1953).

Stevenson (1983) notes that Skinner carried reinforcement theory to an extreme. Much of Skinner's time was spent studying the contingencies between a child's response and reinforcement that would either weaken a behavior or make it stronger. He wanted to know which type of schedule for giving reinforcement would most effectively weaken, strengthen, or maintain a given response. He believed that an organism's behavior remained stable if the proper schedule of reinforcement was used but that new behavior would result from withholding reinforcement or reinforcing different responses.

Skinner's early work on operant conditioning was with caged rats, but the principles of reinforcement derived from this work were eventually applied to children and adults. Bijou and Baer (1961), for example, analyzed child development and behavior in a Skinnerian framework. They, like Skinner, did not consider a child's motives or feelings.

Skinner and his followers formulated general principles of behavioral change and showed how to apply these relatively simple principles to a variety of behavioral problems. The process is called behavior modification, and the *reinforcement approach to behavior modification* is probably the best known of several approaches to behavior modification. This approach involves assessing the problem, choosing target behavior, determining the reinforcer, specifying short-term behavioral goals, monitoring constantly, and allowing adequate rehearsal.

Professionals have been using behavior modification for several decades. Mary Cover Jones (1924a, 1924b) used conditioning to reduce fear in children, and children with enuresis (bed-wetting) were treated successfully with conditioning procedures (Mowrer & Mowrer, 1938). Behavior modification has been extremely popular in the last 20 years and has been widely used in schools, hospitals, and other institutions (Franklin & Biber, 1977; Redd & Sleater, 1978; Stevenson, 1983).

SUMMARY OF KEY CONCEPTS

1. Adults choose or reject child guidance strategies because of their basic beliefs about how children grow and develop. This chapter presented three models of child guidance—the *Rogerian, Adlerian,* and *social learning* models. It introduced three teachers—all responsible and author*itative*—each of whom used a different model to explain children's behavior and therefore chose different (but all positive) child guidance strategies based on his or her model.

2. The concept of self is central in the Rogerian model. Rogerians also believe that people are capable of conscious perception of experience, that perception of experience is private and subjective, that people have the capacity to develop to their fullest potential, and that humans have a need for positive regard from others.

3. Rogerian theorists maintain that it is possible for adults to help children become more fully functioning persons by demonstrating acceptance of the child through the communication strategies of *active listening, delivering I-messages,* and the *no-lose method of conflict resolution.* A core concept in this model is the principle of problem ownership.

4. The Adlerian model assumes that *all behavior or misbehavior has a purpose, or goal,* and that because people are primarily social beings their main goal is to belong to their social group. Adlerians also believe that each individual has a personal style of striving to reach this goal. Children whose self-perception is accurate tend to have a goal of cooperation. Other children have inaccurate perceptions about how to be accepted in their group and display these mistaken goals by seeking group membership in inappropriate ways.

5. Adults using the Adlerian model believe that they are most helpful when they encourage a child to develop more accurate perceptions of himself and how to fit in with his group and when they resist their first impulse to simply react to the child's misbehavior.

6. Adults following the social learning model believe that a child's behavior occurs in and cannot be separated from his social environment. This model emphasizes that most of a child's learning happens through the process of modeling but that whether a child imitates a model depends on several factors. The social learning model believes that a child's behavior will have a better chance of changing if the child's social environment is changed, thus requiring that adults in the child's environment change the way they deal with the child's behavior.

7. Responsible, authoritative adults who believe in the social learning model use a variety of positive strategies. They emphasize teaching appropriate behavior, noticing and reinforcing the desired behavior, targeting inappropriate behavior, and then decreasing reinforcement for the inappropriate behavior. Ethical adults who believe in the social learning model *never* use hurtful punishment.

OBSERVE CHILD GUIDANCE IN ACTION
Identify the Guidance Strategy Used by an Adult

+ Constructivist

Observe at least three episodes of adult-child interaction using the format below. Name the strategy and match it with one of the three models presented in this chapter. For example, if an adult says, "Josh, I think that *you* can hold your own glass," then that adult is *encouraging* a child who might be demonstrating inadequacy, an Adlerian concept. An adult who says, "You ate every one of those green beans," is using praise, a social learning concept.

Name: _____

Setting: _____

Approximate age of child: _____

Describe the situation. Be precise. Write as precisely as possible (use direct quotes if possible) what the adult says to the child or child to adult.

I think this adult has used the strategy known as _____. Justify your response.

This strategy fits within the _____ model.

REFERENCES

Adler, A. (1964). *Social interest*. New York: Capricorn Books.

Bandura, A. (1969). *Principles of behavior modification*. New York: Holt, Rinehart & Winston.

Bandura, A. (1977). *Social learning theory*. Englewood Cliffs, NJ: Prentice-Hall.

Bandura, A., & Walters, R. H. (1963). *Social learning and personality development*. New York: Holt, Rinehart & Winston.

Bijou, S. W., & Baer, D. M. (1961). *Child development: A systematic and empirical theory* (Vol. 1). New York: Appleton-Century-Crofts.

Birnbauer, J. S. (1978). Some guides to designing behavioral programs. In D. Marholin (Ed.), *Child behavior therapy*. New York: Gardner Press.

Cairns, R. B. (1983). The emergence of developmental psychology. In P. Mussen (Ed.), *Handbook of child psychology* (Vol. 1). New York: Wiley.

Coletta, A. J. (1977). *Working together: A guide to parent involvement*. Atlanta: Humanics.

DiCaprio, N. S. (1974). *Personality theories: Guides to living*. Philadelphia: W. B. Saunders.

Dinkmeyer. B., & McKay, G. D. (1988). *Systematic training for effective parenting*. Circle Pines, MN: American Guidance Service.

Dreikurs, R. (1958). *The challenge of parenthood*. New York: Hawthorne Books.

Dweck, C. S. (1975). The role of expectations and attribution in the alleviation of learned helplessness. *Journal of Personality and Social Psychology, 31,* 674–685.

Dweck, C. S., & Elliott, E. S. (1981). *A model of achievement motivation, a theory of its origins, and a framework for motivational development*. Unpublished manuscript, Harvard University.

Fogel, A. (1984). *Infancy*. St. Paul: West Publishing.

Franklin, M. B., & Biber, B. (1977). Psychological perspectives and early childhood education: Some relations between theory and practice. In L. G. Katz (Ed.), *Current topics in early childhood education* (Vol. 1). Norwood, NJ: Ablex.

Gordon, T. (1970). *P.E.T.: Parent effectiveness training*. New York: Peter H. Wyden.

Gordon, T. (1974). *T.E.T.: Teacher effectiveness training*. New York: David McKay.

Gordon, T. (1978). *P.E.T. in action*. Toronto: Bantam. (Published by Wyden in 1976.)

Harris, P. L. (1983). Infant cognition. In P. Mussen (Ed.), *Handbook of child psychology* (Vol. 2). New York: Wiley.

Jones, M. C. (1924a). The elimination of children's fears. *Journal of Experimental Psychology, 7,* 382–390.

Jones, M. C. (1924b). A laboratory study of fear: The case of Peter. *Pedagogical Seminary, 31,* 308–315.

Langer, J. (1969). *Theories of development*. New York: Holt, Rinehart & Winston.

Lepper, M. R., & Green, D. (Eds.). (1979). *The hidden costs of reward: New perspectives on the psychology of human motivation*. Hillsdale, NJ: Erlbaum.

Maccoby, E. E., & Martin, J. A. (1983). Socialization in the context of the family: Parent-child interaction. In P. Mussen (Ed.), *Handbook of child psychology* (Vol. 4). New York: Wiley.

Mead, D. E. (1976). *Six approaches to child rearing*. Provo, UT: Brigham Young University Press.

Mowrer, O. H., & Mowrer, W. N. (1938). Enuresis: A method for its study and treatment. *American Journal of Orthopsychiatry, 8*, 436–459.

Perry, D. G., & Bussey, K. (1979). The social learning theory of sex differences: Imitation is alive and well. *Journal of Personality and Social Psychology, 37*, 1699–1712.

Piaget, J. (1952). *The origins of intelligence in children*. New York: International Universities Press.

Piaget, J. (1970). Piaget's theory. In P. Mussen (Ed.), *Carmichael's manual of child psychology* (Vol. 1). New York: Wiley.

Piaget, J. (1983). Piaget's theory. In P. Mussen (Ed.), *Handbook of child psychology* (Vol. 1). New York: Wiley.

Redd, W. H., & Sleater, W. S. (1978). The theoretical foundations of behavior modification. In D. Marholin (Ed.), *Child behavior therapy*. New York: Gardner.

Richards, C. S., & Siegel, L. J. (1978). Behavioral treatment of anxiety states. In D. Marholin (Ed.), *Child behavior therapy*. New York: Gardner.

Rogers, C. (1957). The necessary and sufficient conditions of therapeutic personality change. *Journal of Consulting Psychology, 21*, 95–103.

Rogers, C. (1961). *On becoming a person*. Boston: Houghton-Mifflin.

Schultz, D. (1976). *Theories of personality*. Monterey, CA: Brooks/Cole.

Shaffer, D. (1989). *Developmental psychology*. Pacific Grove, CA: Brooks/Cole.

Skinner, B. F. (1953). *Science and human behavior*. New York: Macmillan.

Stevenson, H. (1983). How children learn: The quest for a theory. In P. Mussen (Ed.), *Handbook of child psychology* (Vol. 1). New York: Wiley.

Thomas, R. (1992). *Comparing theories of child development* (3rd ed.). Belmont, CA: Wadsworth.

Vartuli, S., & Fyfe, B. (1993). Teachers need developmentally appropriate practice too. *Young Children, 48*(4), 36–42.

Wagonseller, B., Burnett, M., Slazberg, M., & Burnett, J. (1977). *The art of parenting*. Champaign, IL: Research Press.

Wahler, R. (1980). The insular mother: Her problems in parent-child treatment. *Journal of Applied Behavior Analysis*, 13, 207–219.

Watson, J. B. (1928). *Psychological care of the infant and child*. New York: Norton.

Watson, J. B. (1958). *Behaviorism* (rev. ed.). Chicago: University of Chicago Press.

Watson, J. B., & Raynor, R. (1920). Conditioned emotional reactions. *Journal of Experimental Psychology, 3*, 1–4.

White, S. H. (1970). Learning theory tradition and child psychology. In P. Mussen (Ed.), *Carmichael's manual of child psychology* (Vol. 1). New York: Wiley.

11

The Decision-Making Model of Child Guidance:
A Personal/Eclectic Approach

Chapter Overview

After reading this chapter, you will be able to

▼ *Explain* what the decision-making model to child guidance is and identify the building blocks of the decision-making model.

▼ *Analyze* a case study to determine how well a teacher has used the decision-making model.

▼ *Summarize* the benefits of using the decision-making model for both adults and for children.

▼ *Apply* your knowledge of the decision-making model by writing a guidance plan intended to solve specific discipline dilemmas.

"To solve a problem, one must first pay attention to the right kinds of information."

(D. Shaffer)

CASE STUDY: Mr. Alvarez Meets With the Student Teachers

No Blaming, Please

Mr. Alvarez is Gary's teacher and is the cooperating teacher for student teachers Cecelia, Hector, and Janet. They are having an end-of-the-day discussion about the day's events.

Mr. Alvarez said, "OK . . . So you all noticed that Gary curses."

"I suggest time-out for Gary," responded Cecelia.

"His father uses the word a lot," added Hector.

"You're *blaming* Gary, and that won't help him," said Mr. Alvarez. "This is a problem, so let's do some *decision making* and make a *guidance plan*."

What Is the Problem?

Mr. Alvarez said, "First of all, he's 4 years old. To Gary, *!#! is just another word, and he's imitating his dad. I don't want to tell him that his dad is bad for using that word, but I want him to know that I don't want him to use it here. Do you think he knows that this word is not permitted here?"

"Hmmm, probably not," responded Hector. "Are you talking about setting limits?"

"Yes," said Mr. Alvarez.

Who Owns the Problem?

Mr. Alvarez said, "I also want you to think about who really has a problem here—Gary or us?"

"Gary, of course!" said Cecelia. "No . . . wait . . . the P.E.T. people say *I'm the one with the problem* because when he curses *I* get upset. So, *we* have a problem?"

"Correct," said Mr. Alvarez. "We're all tangibly affected, but let's help Gary find a different way to say what he feels."

Writing a Guidance Plan

Mr. Alvarez showed the student teachers their list of guidance strategies and said, "Look at this list of strategies. Do you all agree with Hector's suggestion to state limits on cursing? OK, that's our first item. Now, what do you think Gary gets from us when he curses?"

"Our attention!" said Janet. "We all laugh!"

Mr. Alvarez said, "Attention for *inappropriate* behavior."

Janet responded, "So, start giving attention for appropriate behavior" (she looks at her list).

"Use the Adlerian approach to give him attention for appropriate behavior," said Mr. Alvarez.

Cecelia added, "We could give him a different word he could use and encourage him when he uses it."

"Good. Item number two in the plan. What do we all do when he tests the limit?" asked Mr. Alvarez.

What About Punishment?

"Sounds like you don't want to use time-out," said Hector.

"Right," said Mr. Alvarez. "I just don't like using punishment, and anyway, limit setting and noticing the more acceptable word will work in the long run."

Cecelia said, "I've got it! Since we have the problem, let's tell Gary to go into your office whenever he wants to say that word, but not to say it here . . . no attention from us . . . that's not time-out, is it?"

Mr. Alvarez responded, "That is a great idea, Cecelia! Item number three on our guidance plan for the cursing. Let's review the plan. We'll evaluate it in two days at the next staff meeting. I like how we made this decision."

THE DECISION-MAKING MODEL OF CHILD GUIDANCE

This is a textbook about working with real children in the real and complex world in which they live. There are some issues that every one of us faces as a teacher, regardless of where we teach, such as cursing. But, other issues arise out of specific circumstances and challenge us as we guide the children affected—children for whom English is a second language, abused infants or toddlers, children whose neighborhoods ring with the noise of gunfire, neglected children, children from permissive homes, children whose parents model anger, aggression, and lack of empathy.

The focus in this chapter is on the decision-making model, a personal/eclectic approach to child guidance. I want to help you understand that you can use the positive strategies described throughout this book to help you make positive, developmentally appropriate guidance plans for children. A guidance plan based on clear thinking and good decision making will help you solve a variety of discipline dilemmas.

When you have your own classroom, you will be energized (exhausted on occasion!) by the often confusing, sometimes exasperating, wildly wonderful differences that make each of your children truly a unique person. You will meet a new group of individuals every year that you teach—children, yes, but individuals first.

Each infant to 8-year-old individual has a basic style or temperament and a rich personal history of interactions that have taught her how to *be* in this large world. They all come from different families, each with its own scripts and rules, its own communication style, its own cultural history, its own view of how children should behave, and its own style of discipline. Some of these children will have parents who feel secure, who understand children and children's needs, who know how to communicate legitimate rules and limits, who know how to help children live within limits, and who know how to demonstrate their love and respect to that child.

Some of your children will have parents whose own needs for nurturance were never met and who cannot, as adults, meet their child's needs for nurturance and security. These parents do not understand how infants and children develop, are angry, and do not know how or refuse to take their child's perspective. They lack empathy for their children. These parents have very poor and ineffective child guidance skills; for example, they do not know how to set limits effectively or how to help children accept limits. These parents do not know how to demonstrate the love that they feel for their child.

It is precisely because the children for whom you care are individuals that you should consider adopting as flexible as possible an approach to guiding children. The decision-making model is an individualized, personal model that allows you to determine the course of action most beneficial for a specific child in specific circumstances. The decision-making model allows you to combine your knowledge and personal strengths to deal more effectively with issues facing individual children.

You will meet a new group of individuals every year you teach—children, yes, but individuals first. We are most effective when we adopt a personal, developmentally appropriate style of child guidance.

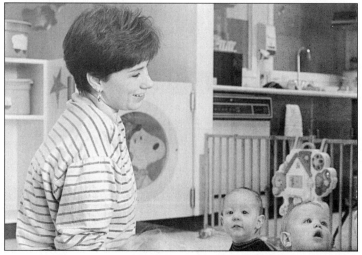

FOUNDATIONS OF THE DECISION-MAKING MODEL
Respect for Children and Knowledge of Child and Family Development

The two most important and strongest building blocks in the foundation of the decision-making model of child guidance are your respect for children and your knowledge of child and family development. Understanding what children are like at different ages and then understanding the impact of that child's family on her development and behavior will help you clarify your expectations of certain children.

> ***Examples***   Is it reasonable to expect a 6-month-old infant to obey?
> How empathic can you expect an abused toddler to be?
> How likely is it that a 4-year-old whose dad curses will say the same words?
> How difficult is it for 3-year-old children to wait in line for the next activity?
> Will an aggressive preschool child *outgrow* his aggression by the time he is 7 or 8 years old?

An Interactionist Approach

Another building block in this foundation is understanding that both you and a child are quite active partners in the *dance of interaction*, but that your adult part in the dance differs from the child's. You have a realistic perspective on the balance of responsibility in an interaction between you and a child, and you understand that adults have a much greater responsibility to recognize signals that children of different ages send. An infant cries or smiles to make contact with you (her part), but it is up to you to tune in to the smile or cry and then meet the baby's needs (your part). A young child curses in an attempt to be recognized. Irritating? Yes. But it is up to you to recognize the attention seeking as a cry for recognition and a signal that you can be most helpful by resisting the urge to punish and by figuring out a more positive way to respond.

Other Factors

This foundation also includes your commitment to effective indirect guidance—management of the physical environment, the time schedule, and the curriculum. Still another building block is your commitment to positive authoritative (respectful) discipline, that is, to set and communicate reasonable limits while remaining highly responsive to children. Your commitment includes a willingness to actively make decisions about what you will do when confronted with a discipline dilemma or problem.

STEPS IN THE DECISION-MAKING MODEL

1. *Stay focused on solving a problem, not on blaming a child.*
2. *Zero in on the child's developmental level.* Ask yourself how the child's age might be affecting her behavior.

3. *Examine the contribution of the child's family or caregiving system to this behavior,* not to place blame but to get an accurate picture of the origin of the behavior.

4. *Clearly identify the problem and decide who owns it.*

5. *Match the problem with developmentally appropriate strategy.* Consult your list of guidance strategies in the appendix and in chapter 3.

6. *Say why this strategy is appropriate for this child at this time.*

7. *Use the strategy and evaluate the solution.*

CASE STUDY ANALYSIS: The Decision-Making Model in Action

Decide how well Mr. Alvarez used the steps in the decision-making model by completing the following sentences.

1. He encouraged the student teachers to focus on the cursing as a problem to be solved and to stop blaming Gary when he said . . .

2. The group focused on Gary's developmental level when they . . .

3. The group identified the real problem as . . .

4. Then they identified who really owned the problem when . . .

5. Mr. Alvarez encouraged his students to adopt *developmentally appropriate strategies* when he . . .

Summary: How well has Mr. Alvarez used the decision-making model of child guidance?

The Decision-Making Model Is an Active Approach

The decision-making model of child guidance is an active model. Mr. Alvarez made an active, conscious, self-responsible decision about how best to help Gary. He did not just use the first strategy that popped into his head. He deliberately walked the student teachers through the step-by-step process of choosing a strategy. He has encouraged them to recognize their responsibility for choosing the adult behavior most likely to help Gary at this time, that is, to choose individually appropriate strategies. Choosing our adult behavior also means consciously rejecting certain strategies that do *not* fit our personal philosophy of guidance, as Mr. Alvarez rejected time-out.

The Decision-Making Model Is a Personal/Eclectic Approach

The fact that Mr. Alvarez has chosen strategies from different approaches indicates that he has an eclectic approach in decision making. An eclectic approach to decision making does *not* mean that you "go with the flow" or do "whatever works." On the contrary, an eclectic approach means that you understand different theoretical approaches, not just one. You know how to use a number of different strategies (Mr. Alvarez knows quite well how to use time-out) because you realize that each approach does offer appropriate strategies. A professional who relies on an eclectic approach also realizes that no single approach is sufficient in all cases. Another thing that you do when you use the eclectic approach is justify your choices, not defensively, but in a logical fashion.

Like a skillful, well-equipped carpenter, a well-equipped teacher searches for and chooses the most appropriate tools available to the profession. A large pool of positive strategies will give you a great deal of flexibility in making good decisions about developmentally appropriate guidance. The decision-making model's eclectic approach will enable you to

▼ use active listening when necessary (a Rogerian concept)

▼ use a token system on occasion, ignore certain behaviors when appropriate, and use effective praise (all social learning concepts)

▼ use encouragement and logical consequences when desired (an Adlerian concept)

The purpose of the rest of this chapter is to help you practice using the decision-making model of child guidance.

PRACTICING THE DECISION-MAKING MODEL
Decision-Making Issue No. 1: "Outdoor Cleanup Time"

Situation. It's time for your classroom of 5-year-olds to go inside for story, and you notice that Levi and Dave have left the trucks out on the path again instead of putting them in the spot designated for trucks. You and the staff have stated the limits clearly and positively, and the designated parking spots are easily accessible—you have managed the physical environment very well. Levi's parents are permissive-by-choice and do not set limits. Dave follows Levi's lead.

Learning the Decision-Making Model

Go through the first several steps in the decision-making model. Think of this as a problem to be solved: clearly identify the problem and decide who really owns it, you or the boys. Then work on matching the problem with a developmentally appropriate strategy, avoiding punishment.

1. *You have set the limit. Explain why restating the limit is individually appropriate,* especially for Levi, who has never had to follow limits, and for Dave, who follows Levi's lead.

2. *Explain how you could use the Adlerian strategy of logical consequences* to help the boys make better decisions about cleaning up. State the specific words

you would use to present the choices to them and then to acknowledge and accept their choices. Avoid turning this experience into punishment by reviewing how to do logical consequences in chapter 3 and the appendix.

3. *Explain how you could also use an I-message* (Rogerian approach) to help Levi and Dave understand your position. Write the I-message, including all three elements (again, see the appendix).

4. *Explain how you could use the social learning approach's strategy called effective praise* to encourage the boys when they do cooperate. Write out the exact statements that you would use.

5. *Explain how you could use the social learning approach's strategy called a token system to help you follow through with the limit.* Review information on token systems in chapter 10 and the appendix. Keep it simple, but be specific and draw the chart that you would use. Write the script that you might follow when you first tell the boys about the system. Be prepared to role-play the explanation.

6. *Explain why punishment (time-out, response cost) is not an appropriate choice* in this case. Explain why *ignoring* this problem is also not appropriate in this case.

Writing Your Guidance Plan

List the strategies that you think fit in best with your developing philosophy of guidance:

1. Restate the limit (this one *is* necessary but probably is not sufficient by itself to change things). I would say this to restate the limit:

2. From my perspective, the most effective other strategy would be . . .

3. This strategy is age-appropriate because . . .

4. I deliberately chose not to use _____ (name the rejected strategy) because . . .

Decision-Making Issue No. 2: "Teacher, He Won't Share!"

Situation. It is individual choice time in your classroom of 3-year-olds. The room is set up well, and your curriculum is developmentally appropriate. The art table has a basket containing pieces of red and blue paper ready to be pasted onto recycled cardboard for a red/blue collage at each of four spots, each spot with a chair. You have placed a glob of paste on paper and set it between two places at the table, the paste to be shared by two children (you are working on helping the children learn to share). Blake, the first to settle into this activity, was soon joined by Jordan, who sat next to Blake (they were to share the paste). Soon you hear Jordan's complaint, "Teacher, Blake won't *share*!"

Learning the Decision-Making Model

Again, go through the first several steps in the decision-making model. Think of this as a problem to be solved; clearly identify the problem and decide which boy really owns it. Then work on matching the problem with a developmentally appropriate strategy, avoiding punishment.

1. *Avoid blaming Blake. Focus on problem solving.* Explain how Blake's age affects his ability to share.

2. *Explain why Jordan owns this problem*, from the Rogerian perspective. *Explain how you could use the Rogerian strategy of active listening* to help Jordan recognize that he has a problem. Then, help him again by teaching him how to tell Blake what he wants. (From the Rogerian perspective, your role is not to solve Jordan's problem but to teach him how he can solve it.)

3. Think about how you have set limits on the use of the paste. You placed the paste between the two children's spots at the table, a good indirect strategy. *Now, verbally state your expectation about sharing the paste as each child settles in to do a collage.* Write what you would say, and make your explanation brief.

4. Suppose that Blake gets to the collage table first and you state that the paste is to be shared by two children. He is joined by Jordan. *Explain how you could use the social learning strategy of using a signal or a cue* to remind Blake about sharing.

5. Suppose that you have effectively helped both boys deal with this problem. *Explain how you could notice and then let the boys know that you appreciate their willingness to share.* Write the verbal statement of encouragement (social learning advocates call it *effective praise*).

6. *Explain why punishment (time-out, response cost) is not the appropriate choice* in this case. Explain why ignoring this problem is also inappropriate.

Writing Your Guidance Plan

List the strategies that you think fit in best with your developing philosophy of guidance. Briefly explain your choices.

1.
2.
3.
4.

Self-Test: Making Your Own Guidance Plan

Use the *Problem for You to Solve* box and make a guidance plan for the following problems. Focus on guiding and avoid punishing.

PROBLEM FOR YOU TO SOLVE: Self-Test

1. The problem to be solved is . . .
2. The person who really *owns* this problem is _____. Explain your choice.
3. The age of the children involved is _____. Their age might be a factor in this problem because . . .
4. Other factors that might also be affecting their behavior (e.g., family history, attention-getting) are . . .
5. Consult the list of guidance strategies and match this problem with a developmentally appropriate strategy or strategies.

Strategy	*Appropriate Because*
▼	
▼	
▼	

▼   Five-year-olds in a multi-age grouping getting younger children to do inappropriate things (e.g., swearing, throwing things)

▼   Three- to five-year-olds pushing other children while having to wait for an activity (e.g., going outdoors)

▼   Children from 2½ to 5 years old who spit at other children

▼   A 4-year-old whose family consistently uses physical discipline (hitting, pinching) who hits the teacher when the teacher tries to use even a positive strategy like restating a limit

▼   A 7-year-old who tattles

WHAT THE DECISION-MAKING MODEL MEANS FOR CHILDREN

Adults who adopt the authori*tative* style of caregiving realize that a big part of their job is to create a safe and secure emotional climate for children. They realize that it is not their job to mold children but to be self-responsible and to set the stage for a child to develop certain behaviors. When you actively make decisions about guidance plans, you will have set the stage for lots of good things to happen.

By using the decision-making model of child guidance you can help children

▼ feel safe and secure

▼ develop positive self-esteem and a strong moral compass

▼ honor and respect themselves and others

▼ develop healthy self-control

▼ understand and deal effectively with a variety of feelings: anger, sadness, love, jealousy

▼ walk a mile in another person's shoes—or an animal's tracks—to be empathic

▼ be cooperative, helpful, and generous

▼ learn when to be assertive

▼ become self-responsible

▼ become a competent partner in the dance of interaction

SUMMARY OF KEY CONCEPTS

1. Developmentally appropriate *child guidance plans* grow out of a conscious, active decision-making process about the strategies most likely to best help a specific child at a specific time.

2. Each child for whom you care is an individual with a rich personal history that has taught her how to *be* in this world. Each child's family system has set the stage for the behavior that you will see in your classroom.

3. Because children are individuals, you will best help them by using as individualized, *personal*, and positive an approach to child guidance as possible. An *eclectic approach* enables you to identify the appropriate strategies in all approaches and then to choose those strategies that match your philosophy and the needs of a specific child.

4. Develop your personal, individualized eclectic approach to child guidance by combining your personal knowledge and strengths with the needs of a particular child. Then use the steps in the decision-making model and the list of positive discipline strategies to develop a child guidance plan with which you can make active, clearly thought out, logical decisions about how to best help a child.

Appendix

Review of Major Positive Discipline Strategies

Refer to this Appendix when making decisions about developmentally appropriate guidance plans. Positive strategies are listed in outline form along with suggestions of things to remember and to avoid when using the strategy. The following strategies are described:

▼ Limit setting

▼ Identifying problem ownership

▼ Teaching more appropriate behavior

▼ Giving signals or cues for appropriate behavior

▼ Teaching new behavior that is self-rewarding

▼ Identifying mistaken goals and using encouragement

▼ Using effective praise

▼ Using tokens

▼ Ignoring behavior when it is appropriate to do so (Extinction)

▼ Redirecting young children's behavior: Diversion/distraction

▼ Redirecting older children's behavior: Substitution

▼ Active listening

▼ Using I-messages

▼ Using logical consequences

▼ Resolving conflict through problem solving

▼ Managing strong emotions responsibly

▼ Withdrawing from certain situations

▼ Helping children preserve their dignity and save face

You will find a discussion of each of these strategies in either chapter 3 or chapter 10. The numbers in parentheses next to the name of a strategy refer to the chapter to which you may refer for more discussion of the strategy.

LIMIT SETTING (chapter 3)

Purpose of the strategy: State expectations for desired behavior. Clarify boundaries or limits on behavior.

Appropriate limits: Never arbitrary, limits focus on important things and are developmentally appropriate.

Effective limit setting:

1. Focus child's attention, use appropriate nonverbal cues.

2. Speak naturally and slowly enough so that child hears limit, use concrete words and short sentences, tell child what *to* do, use suggestions, give choices when possible.

3. Give very few suggestions at a time.

4. Allow child enough time to process information and complete the task.

5. Effectively repeat limit if necessary.

6. Give short, simple reasons for limit (before stating limit, after stating limit, or after child complies).

Things to avoid in setting limits:

1. Avoid abstract words or phrases.

2. Avoid emphasizing what *not* to do.

3. Avoid ordering or commanding.

4. Don't give choices when child should not have choice.

5. Avoid giving *chain of limits*.

6. Avoid rapid repetition of limits.

7. Avoid playing *why game* with children.

IDENTIFYING PROBLEM OWNERSHIP (chapter 10)

Purpose of the strategy: Determine whether a problem is *owned* by an adult or by a child so that appropriate follow-up can be used.

When an adult owns a problem: Use strategies focusing on self-responsible, nonaccusatory skills (e.g., I-messages).

When a child owns a problem: The child's needs are the ones thwarted. Deal with child-owned problems by using active listening.

TEACHING MORE APPROPRIATE BEHAVIOR (chapter 3 for major description, chapter 10 for follow-up)

Purpose of the strategy: Teach appropriate behaviors and deemphasize inappropriate behaviors. Means that adults must pinpoint behavior considered appropriate.

Method used: Several methods can be used. With young children modeling is effective (i.e., demonstrate desired behavior, such as handwashing, table manners, social skills like introducing oneself, using words instead of hitting to express anger).

Steps in teaching more appropriate behavior:

1. Identify inappropriate behavior (e.g., whining).

2. Think about a behavior that is more appropriate (e.g., asking for things in a normal voice).

3. Model more appropriate behavior (e.g., model a *normal* voice for child. Demonstrate normal voice yourself, use a segment of a show like Sesame Street, use a puppet, read a story. Tell her that this is the way to make requests, not with a whine).

GIVING SIGNALS OR CUES FOR APPROPRIATE BEHAVIOR (chapter 3)

Purpose of the strategy: To help children remember to use the appropriate behavior.

Steps in giving signals or cues:

1. Identify behavior for which you will use a signal or cue (e.g., asking for something in a normal voice).
2. Figure out what would be a logical signal for new behavior (e.g., quiet verbal reminder, "normal voice, please," hand signal).
3. Observe child for when appropriate behavior should be used (e.g., asking to join other children).
4. Give signal just before new behavior should occur and not after child has forgotten (e.g., just before child asks for something).

SUPPORTING CHILDREN IN USING MORE APPROPRIATE BEHAVIOR: TEACHING NEW BEHAVIOR THAT IS SELF-REWARDING (chapter 3)

Purpose of the strategy: To avoid using external reinforcement.

Steps in teaching self-rewarding behavior:

1. Identify inappropriate behavior (e.g., not washing hands after toileting).
2. Identify more appropriate behavior (e.g., handwashing after toileting).
3. If possible, think about setting up the situation so that it is attractive enough for child to continue without further reinforcement (e.g., using a soap that smells wonderful or that turns colors when used for scrubbing hands).

SUPPORTING CHILDREN IN USING MORE APPROPRIATE BEHAVIOR: IDENTIFYING MISTAKEN GOALS AND USING ENCOURAGEMENT (chapter 10)

Purpose of the strategy: Identify child's faulty perception of how to fit into a group. Be aware of what a child does to accomplish mistaken goal (seek undue attention, power, revenge, or demonstrate inadequacy). Explain how adult usually feels and reacts. Outline a better way to deal with child who has any of the four mistaken goals.

Steps in changing how you react to demands for undue attention:

1. Ignore the impulse to give in to the attention-seeking behavior.
2. Acknowledge the child's request, but let her know that she can complete the task. Leave the area if necessary so that she can finish the job.
3. Give the child attention at times when her behavior is more appropriate.
4. Encourage a child to take the perspective of others by telling her their perspective and by helping her learn to cooperate.

Steps in changing how you react to a child who seeks power:

1. Resist the impulse to fight back.
2. Decide to respond differently. You do not have to be drawn into a power struggle. You can choose to respond differently.
3. Decline the child's invitation to argue or fight. This will surprise a child, particularly if you have previously been locked in power struggles with her. A useful technique is to label the interaction as a power struggle.

Steps in changing how you react to a child who seeks revenge:

1. Resist impulse to retaliate or give sermons.
2. Focus on helping this child change her view of herself from a person who she thinks is not valued to the view that she is a good, worthwhile person (i.e., encourage development of self-esteem, the missing ingredient).

Steps in changing how you react to a child who demonstrates inadequacy:

1. Focus on what a normal child of this age should be able to do (e.g., should a 3-year-old be able to put on her own coat?).
2. Refrain from performing the age-appropriate task for her.
3. Encourage child who mistakenly believes she has to act like she is incompetent (e.g., tell her that she can carry out the task, demonstrate how she can do it, encourage her to try).

SUPPORTING CHILDREN IN USING MORE APPROPRIATE BEHAVIOR: USING EFFECTIVE PRAISE (chapter 10)

Purpose of the strategy: A form of positive reinforcement. Gives give information on the consequences of a behavior for the person who modeled or performed it.

Elements of effective praise:

1. Notice and describe specifically what it was a child did. Relate verbal praise directly to behavior. Convey your appreciation but avoid making judgments about child's character.
2. Give praise as soon as possible after child performs a behavior.
3. Be sincere and honest. Try to find something in a situation that you *can* praise sincerely.
4. Encourage child for her effort and small steps.

5. Combine praise with appropriate forms of nonverbal communication (e.g., nod of head, smile, pat on back).

Avoid these things when using praise:

1. Do not combine praise with a negative comment.
2. Do not praise only perfection.
3. Do not focus on what child is *not* doing.
4. Avoid praising only completion of a multistep task.
5. Do not overdo praise or use it indiscriminately.
6. Do not give praise if it is not necessary.
7. Do not confuse praise or other rewards with bribes.

SUPPORTING CHILDREN IN USING MORE APPROPRIATE BEHAVIOR: USING TOKENS (chapter 10)

Purpose of the strategy: To modify a child's environment by giving feedback for effort so that a child may more easily modify her behavior. A social learning concept. Child accumulates nonsocial, tangible reinforcers—sticker, smiley face, star, checkmark—for appropriate behavior and trades in evidence of accumulated tokens for reward.

Things to remember about using tokens effectively:

1. Give a token often.
2. Give tokens for small steps toward a bigger goal.
3. Combine tokens with social reinforcers (smile, praise).
4. Keep a record of tokens. Chart should define desired behavior, specify number of tokens to be earned to get reward, define how tokens are to be spent.
5. Ask child what she considers to be a reward; reward should be desirable to child; best if chosen by child, within certain limits.
6. Let child exchange tokens for reward fairly often.
7. Do not take away tokens as fines for "backsliding."
8. Gradually *fade out* use of tokens as child shows willingness to use appropriate behavior, but continue to give periodic social reinforcers.

IGNORING BEHAVIOR WHEN IT IS APPROPRIATE TO DO SO (chapter 3; also called Extinction [chapter 10])

Purpose of the strategy: Eliminate payoff for inappropriate behavior (i.e., stop attending to and reinforcing inappropriate behavior). Goal is to weaken inappropriate behavior by changing the way an adult reacts to the behavior.

*Do **not** ignore these behaviors:*

1. Behavior that endangers anyone, including the child herself.

2. Behavior that damages or destroys property or that could potentially damage or destroy property.

3. Treating someone rudely, embarrassing another person, being intrusive, or causing an *undue* disturbance.

Guidelines for ignoring behavior:

1. Pinpoint behavior to be ignored.

2. Tell child you will no longer pay attention when child acts in this way.

3. Be prepared. It takes time to effectively use the ignore strategy (e.g., be prepared for a bigger and better whine before it decreases).

4. Decide to thoroughly ignore the behavior—don't mutter to yourself under your breath; don't make eye contact; don't communicate with the child verbally or with gestures.

5. Teach and encourage more acceptable behavior along with the *ignore* strategy.

✓ REDIRECTING CHILDREN'S BEHAVIOR: DIVERTING AND DISTRACTING THE YOUNGEST CHILDREN (chapter 3)

Purpose of the strategy: To distract a very young child from a forbidden or dangerous activity and then involve the child in a different activity.

Things to keep in mind:

1. Responsible caregivers understand that they perform most of an infant's or a young toddler's ego functions.

2. Avoid a power struggle when stopping dangerous behavior.

3. Be prepared to act quickly when working with infants and toddlers. This requires constant supervision and observation even in a *babyproofed* area.

Steps in using diversion and distraction:

1. Identify for yourself the things that you do not want a baby or toddler to do because the activity is dangerous (e.g., playing with an electrical outlet, even if it is covered).

2. Tell infant or toddler not to do whatever it is that is dangerous (e.g., "No playing with the outlet, Sara").

3. *Immediately* do something different to distract infant or toddler from forbidden activity (e.g., roll ball to Sara the instant you tell her not to play with the outlet).

REDIRECTING CHILDREN'S BEHAVIOR: MAKING SUBSTITUTIONS WHEN DEALING WITH OLDER CHILDREN (chapter 3)

Purpose of the strategy: Form of redirection in which an adult shows a somewhat older child (over age 2 to 2½) how to perform the same activity or type of activity but in a more acceptable, safer way.

Steps in using substitutions:

1. Specify activity needing a substitution (e.g., outdoors, zigzagging through sandbox when others are playing there).

2. Develop substitution, a similar activity, or same activity done more safely (e.g., zigzagging through set of tires laid flat on ground).

3. Present substitution to child (e.g., "Looks like you want to do an obstacle course, but not in the sandbox. Try zigging and zagging through these tires").

4. Be prepared for a testing of your substitution. Resist getting drawn into a fight or power struggle. Respond to testing with positive discipline: continue to make the substitution calmly and with good will (e.g., if two children run back through the sandbox, say "Tom and Jim, the obstacle course is the set of tires, not the sandbox").

ACTIVE LISTENING (chapter 10 for main description; 3 for brief description)

Purpose of the strategy: Careful, accurate listening to feelings of child. Conveys adult's recognition and acceptance of child and child's feelings. Communicates adult's trust in child's ability to work through her own problem.

Things to remember about active listening:

1. Listen carefully.
2. Do not interrupt.
3. Try to understand what the message means.
4. Listen for what the child is feeling.
5. Suspend judgment.
6. Avoid preaching, giving advice or trying to persuade the child to feel differently.
7. Merely feed back your perception of the child's feelings.

USING I-MESSAGES (chapter 3)

Purpose of the strategy: Give information; communicate feelings in respectful way; give child chance to change behavior (a Rogerian concept).

Steps in constructing a good I-message:

1. Name exact behavior causing the problem. Give observable data about child's behavior—what you see, hear, touch, smell, taste (e.g., "Adam, I see that the puzzles you used are still on the table").

2. Tell child how his behavior *tangibly* affects you. Did it cost you time, money, effort to do the job he should have done? (". . . and that meant that I had to put the puzzles away just before snack . . .")

3. Tell child how you felt (remember, do not accuse the child of causing your feeling) (". . . I felt annoyed that I had to do two jobs").

Things to avoid in constructing I-messages:

1. Avoid accusing and blaming child.
2. Do not induce guilt.
3. Avoid telling child that he caused your feeling.

USING LOGICAL CONSEQUENCES (chapter 3)

Purpose of the strategy: Safe consequences that would not have occurred naturally. Consequences are designed by adult.

Things to remember about logical consequences:

1. Child must understand exact nature of issue and how you feel.
2. Consequence should be *logically* related to the unsafe or inappropriate behavior.
3. Make consequence one that you can really accept and which the child will likely view as fair.
4. Time the consequence well.
5. Use a friendly, firm, nonthreatening tone of voice.

Steps in using logical consequences:

1. Respectfully restate expectations and tell child how to change things. Give child a choice; offer alternatives (e.g., "We are here for story. You can sit next to Sue and listen to the story without pushing her, or you can sit with Mrs. Doren and listen to the story. You choose.").
2. Allow child to make choice. You have designed safe, respectful choices, so you can accept any choice.
3. Tell child you accept her choice. Allow safe consequences to occur (e.g., if Janie continues to push Sue, "I see that you have chosen to sit next to Mrs. Doren for storytime"; if Janie stops pushing, "You chose to sit quietly next to Sue for storytime. I think she likes to have you next to her.").

RESOLVING CONFLICT THROUGH PROBLEM SOLVING (chapter 10)

Purpose of the strategy: Achieve a mutually agreeable solution to a problem without resorting to use of power. Support creative conflict resolution rather than punishing behavior accompanying conflict between children (e.g., teach children who are arguing how to resolve the conflict rather than punishing them for fighting).

Steps in using the "no-lose" method of conflict resolution:

1. Identify and define conflict in nonaccusatory way (e.g., "Vinnie and Rachael, you have a problem. You both want the green paint . . .").

2.   Invite children to participate in fixing problem ("Let's think of how to solve the problem").

3.   Generate possible solutions with children. Accept a variety of solutions. Avoid evaluating them (". . . Yes, you could *both* use the same paint cup . . . you could take turns . . .").

4.   Examine each idea for merits and drawbacks. With children, decide which to try. Thank children for thinking of solutions (". . . You want to *both* use the green paint at the same time . . .").

5.   Put plan into action ("You might have to take turns dipping your brushes into the paint . . . Try your idea").

6.   Follow up. Evaluate how well the solution worked (Teacher comes back in a few minutes, ". . . looks like your idea of how to solve your green paint problem really worked").

MANAGING STRONG EMOTIONS RESPONSIBLY (chapter 7 for specific strategies, chapter 3 for brief description)

Purpose of the strategy: To support children in recognizing and learning responsible ways to manage strong emotions like anger. To avoid simply punishing children for behavior resulting from strong emotions.

Steps in teaching responsible anger management:

1.   Model responsible anger management.

2.   Create a *safe* emotional climate. Allow and encourage children to acknowledge all feelings while firmly not permitting them to hurt anybody because of those feelings.

3.   Help children understand the things to which they react with anger.

4.   Help children understand their body's reaction to anger.

5.   Teach children how to deal with the stress of anger.

6.   State your expectations for responsible anger management.

7.   Help some children learn to use words to describe angry feelings, and help other children expand their *feelings* vocabulary.

8.   Use appropriate books and stories about anger management.

WITHDRAWING FROM CERTAIN SITUATIONS (*NOT* TIME-OUT) (chapter 3)

Goal: Solve a basic problem, not to punish.

Purpose of the strategy: To teach children how to take themselves out of situations when they lose control, are extremely angry, or endanger their own or someone else's safety; to teach children to avoid simply reacting to strong emotions, to get themselves under control so that they can deal with the cause of the strong emotion.

Steps in withdrawing from certain situations:

1. Identify and teach the child to recognize the behavior that is causing a problem.

2. Tell child when you will request that she withdraw.

3. Demonstrate, explain, and make sure a child understands the process. Have child help you pick a safe, calming, nonfrightening place for retreat *when her anger heats up. This is not punishment or time-out.*

4. Follow through. Help child recognize target behavior.

5. Be respectful and unobtrusive as you help child withdraw.

6. If appropriate, show child how to do relaxation exercises to regain control.

7. Teach and encourage more appropriate behavior when child returns to activity, or talk about the original problem that elicited such strong emotion.

HELPING CHILDREN PRESERVE THEIR DIGNITY AND SAVE FACE (chapter 3)

Purpose of the strategy: To treat children respectfully no matter what positive strategy is used. Recognize that, in spite of well-done positive discipline, children may feel embarrassed.

How can adults do this?

1. Rely on your abiding respect for children and your perspective-taking skills, and think about how you would want somebody to handle things if they had just told you to calm down or that you had done something wrong.

2. Once you are finished with the positive discipline strategy, let the episode become history and allow the child to get on with things. Do not keep preaching or explaining.

3. Do not pull out your power. Avoid saying "I told you so."

4. End the interaction quickly, simply, and gracefully. Quietly tell the child, especially if you've helped her calm down, "Let's go back and play now."

5. Help child deal with the root of the upset. Some children might be ready to talk about the emotion-arousing incident, but others need to wait before discussing it. Either way, schedule a time for talking about the original problem with the child. Do what is developmentally appropriate for this child at this time.

Name Index

Name Index

Name Index

Subject Index

Windows NT Backup & Restore